MEDICAL TOURISM

MEDICAL TOURISM

Mahesh Chandra Singh

CENTRUM PRESS
NEW DELHI-110002 (INDIA)

CENTRUM PRESS
H.O.: 4360/4, Ansari Road, Daryaganj,
New Delhi-110002 (India)
Tel: 23278000, 23261597, 23255577, 23286875
B.O.: No. 1015, Ist Main Road, BSK IIIrd Stage,
IIIrd Phase, IIIrd Block, Bangalore-560085 (INDIA)
Tel: 080-41723429
Email: centrumpress@gmail.com
Visit us at: www.centrumpress.com

Medical Tourism

First Edition, 2010

ISBN 978-93-80540-10-8

PRINTED IN INDIA

Printed at Mehra Offset Press, Delhi

Contents

Preface

Medical tourism (also called medical travel, health tourism or global healthcare) is a term initially coined by travel agencies and the mass media to describe the rapidly-growing practice of travelling across international borders to obtain health care. It also refers pejoratively to the practice of healthcare providers travelling internationally to deliver healthcare.

Services typically sought by travellers include elective procedures as well as complex specialized surgeries such as joint replacement (knee/hip), cardiac surgery, dental surgery, and cosmetic surgeries. However, virtually every type of health care, including psychiatry, alternative treatments, convalescent care and even burial services are available. As a practical matter, providers and customers commonly use informal channels of communication-connection-contract, and in such cases this tends to mean less regulatory or legal oversight to assure quality and less formal recourse to reimbursement or redress, if needed.

Over 50 countries have identified medical tourism as a national industry. However, accreditation and other measures of quality vary widely across the globe, and there are risks and ethical issues that make this method of accessing medical care controversial. Also, some destinations may become hazardous or even dangerous for medical tourists to contemplate.

In the context of global health, "medical tourism" is a pejorative because during such trips health care providers often practice outside of their areas of expertise or hold different (i.e., lower) standards of care. Greater numbers than ever before of student volunteers, health professions trainees, and researchers from resource-rich countries are working temporarily and anticipating future work in resource-starved areas. This emphasizes the importance of understanding this other definition.

The concept of medical tourism is not a new one. The first recorded instance of medical tourism dates back thousands of years to when Greek pilgrims travelled from all over the Mediterranean to the small territory in the Saronic Gulf called Epidauria. This territory was the sanctuary of the healing god Asklepios. Epidauria became the original travel destination for medical tourism.

Spa towns and sanitariums may be considered an early form of medical tourism. In eighteenth century England, for example, patients visited spas because they were places with supposedly health-giving mineral waters, treating diseases from gout to liver disorders and bronchitis.

Tourism has the potential to bring about social and cultural development. It is also essential to take advantage of information technology to develop tourism. A well thought out plan should be in place to harness the potential of various media of communication.

—*Mahesh Chandra Singh*

1

Introduction

Medical tourism (also called medical travel, health tourism or global healthcare) is a term initially coined by travel agencies and the mass media to describe the rapidly-growing practice of travelling across international borders to obtain health care. It also refers pejoratively to the practice of healthcare providers travelling internationally to deliver healthcare.

Services typically sought by travellers include elective procedures as well as complex specialized surgeries such as joint replacement (knee/hip), cardiac surgery, dental surgery, and cosmetic surgeries. However, virtually every type of health care, including psychiatry, alternative treatments, convalescent care and even burial services are available. As a practical matter, providers and customers commonly use informal channels of communication-connection-contract, and in such cases this tends to mean less regulatory or legal oversight to assure quality and less formal recourse to reimbursement or redress, if needed.

Over 50 countries have identified medical tourism as a national industry. However, accreditation and other measures of quality vary widely across the globe, and there are risks and ethical issues that make this method of accessing medical care controversial. Also, some destinations may become hazardous or even dangerous for medical tourists to contemplate.

In the context of global health, "medical tourism" is a pejorative because during such trips health care providers often practice outside of their areas of expertise or hold different standards of care. Greater numbers than ever before of student volunteers, health professions trainees, and researchers from resource-rich countries are working temporarily and anticipating future work in resource-starved areas. This emphasizes the importance of understanding this other definition.

History

The concept of medical tourism is not a new one. The first recorded instance of medical tourism dates back thousands of years to when Greek pilgrims travelled from all over the Mediterranean to the small territory in the Saronic Gulf called Epidauria. This territory was the sanctuary of the healing god Asklepios. Epidauria became the original travel destination for medical tourism.

Spa towns and sanitariums may be considered an early form of medical tourism. In eighteenth century England, for example, patients visited spas because they were places with supposedly health-giving mineral waters, treating diseases from gout to liver disorders and bronchitis.

Description

Factors that have led to the increasing popularity of medical travel include the high cost of health care, long wait times for certain procedures, the ease and affordability of international travel, and improvements in both technology and standards of care in many countries.

Medical tourists can come from anywhere in the First World, including Europe, the Middle East, Japan, the United States, and Canada. This is because of their large populations, comparatively high wealth, the high expense of health care or lack of health care options locally, and increasingly high expectations of their populations with respect to health care. An authority at the Harvard Business School recently stated that "medical tourism is promoted much more heavily in the United Kingdom than in the United States".

A forecast by Deloitte Consulting published in August 2008 projected that medical tourism originating in the US could jump by a factor of ten over the next decade. An estimated 750,000 Americans went abroad for health care in 2007, and the report estimated that a million and a half would seek health care outside the US in 2008. The growth in medical tourism has the potential to cost US health care providers billions of dollars in lost revenue.

A large draw to medical travel is convenience and speed. Countries that operate public healthcare systems are often so taxed that it can take considerable time to get non-urgent medical care. Using Canada as an example, an estimated 782,936 Canadians spent time on medical waiting lists in 2005, waiting an average of 9.4 weeks. Canada has set waiting-time benchmarks, e.g. 26 weeks for a hip replacement and 16 weeks for cataract surgery, for non-urgent medical procedures.

Additionally, patients are finding that insurance either does not cover orthopedic surgery (such as knee/hip replacement) or imposes unreasonable restrictions on the choice of the facility, surgeon, or prosthetics to be used. Medical tourism for knee/hip replacements has emerged as one of the more widely accepted procedures because of the lower cost and minimal difficulties associated with the travelling to/from the surgery. Colombia provides a knee replacement for about $5,000 USD, including all associated fees, such as FDA-approved prosthetics and hospital stay-over expenses. However, many clinics quote prices that are not all inclusive and include only the surgeon fees associated with the procedure.

According to an article by the University of Delaware publication, U Daily:

> *"The cost of surgery in India, Thailand or South Africa can be one-tenth of what it is in the United States or Western Europe, and sometimes even less. A heart-valve replacement that would cost $200,000 or more in the US, for example, goes for $10,000 in India—and that includes round-trip airfare and a brief vacation package. Similarly, a metal-free dental bridge worth $5,500 in the US costs $500 in India, a knee replacement in Thailand with six days of physical therapy costs about one-fifth of what it would in the States, and Lasik eye surgery worth $3,700 in the US is available in many other countries for only $730. Cosmetic surgery savings are even greater: A full facelift that would cost $20,000 in the US runs about $1,250 in South Africa.*

Popular medical travel worldwide destinations include: Argentina, Brunei, Cuba, Colombia, Costa Rica, Hong Kong, Hungary, India, Jordan, Lithuania, Malaysia, The Philippines, Singapore, South Africa, Thailand, and recently, Saudi Arabia, UAE, South Korea, Tunisia and New Zealand.

Popular cosmetic surgery travel destinations include· Argentina, Bolivia, Brazil, Colombia, Costa Rica, Cuba, Mexico and Turkey. In South America, countries such as Argentina, Bolivia, Brazil and Colombia lead on plastic surgery medical skills relying on their experienced plastic surgeons. In Bolivia and Colombia, plastic surgery has also become quite common. According to the "Sociedad Boliviana de Cirugia Plastica Reconstructiva", more than 70% of middle and upper class women in the country have had some form of plastic surgery. Colombia also provides advanced care in cardiovascular and transplant surgery.

In Europe Belgium, Poland and Slovakia are also breaking into the business. South Africa is taking the term "medical tourism" very literally by promoting their "medical safaris".

A specialized subset of medical tourism is reproductive tourism and reproductive outsourcing, which is the practice of travelling abroad to undergo in-vitro fertilization, surrogate pregnancy and other assisted reproductive technology treatments including freezing embryos for retro-production.

However, perceptions of medical tourism are not always positive. In places like the US, which has high standards of quality, medical tourism is viewed as risky. In some parts of the world, wider political issues can influence where medical tourists will choose to seek out health care.

Health tourism providers have developed as intermediaries to unite potential medical tourists with provider hospitals and other organisations. Companies are beginning to offer global health care options that will enable North American and European patients to access world health care at a fraction of the cost of domestic care. Companies that focus on medical value travel typically provide nurse case managers to assist patients with pre- and post-travel medical issues. They also help provide resources for follow-up care upon the patient's return.

Process

The typical process is as follows: the person seeking medical treatment abroad contacts a medical tourism provider. The provider usually requires the patient to provide a medical report, including the nature of ailment, local doctor's opinion, medical history, and diagnosis, and may request additional information. Certified medical doctors or consultants then advise on the medical treatment. The approximate expenditure, choice of hospitals and tourist destinations, and duration of stay, etc., is discussed.

After signing consent bonds and agreements, the patient is given recommendation letters for a medical visa, to be procured from the concerned embassy. The patient travels to the destination country, where the medical tourism provider assigns a case executive, who takes care of the patient's accommodation, treatment and any other form of care. Once the treatment is done, the patient can remain in the tourist destination or return home.

International Healthcare Accreditation

Because standards are important when it comes to health care, there are parallel issues around medical tourism, international healthcare accreditation, evidence-based medicine and quality assurance. In the United States, the best known accreditation group is the Joint Commission International (JCI). They have been inspecting and accrediting health care facilities and hospitals outside of the United States since 1999. Many international hospitals today see obtaining JCI accreditation as a way to attract American patients.

Joint Commission International is a relative of the Joint Commission in the United States. Both are independent private sector not-for-profit organizations that develop nationally and internationally recognized procedures and standards to help improve patient care and safety. They work with hospitals to help them meet Joint Commission standards for patient care and then accredit those hospitals meeting the standards. In the UK and Hong Kong, the Trent International Accreditation Scheme is a key player. The different international healthcare accreditation schemes vary in quality, size, cost, intent and the skill and intensity of their marketing. They also vary in terms of cost to hospitals and healthcare institutions making use of them. A forecast by Deloitte Consulting regarding medical tourism published in August 2008 noted the value of accreditation in ensuring quality of healthcare and specifically mentioned JCI, ISQUA and Trent.

Increasingly, some hospitals are looking towards dual international accreditation, perhaps having both JCI to cover potential US clientele and Trent for potential British and European clientele. As a result of competition between clinics for American medical tourists, there have been initiatives to rank hospitals based on patient-reported metrics. Other organizations providing contributions to quality practices include:

- The Society for International Healthcare Accreditation (SOFIHA), a free-to-join group providing a forum for discussion and for the sharing of ideas and good practice by providers of international healthcare accreditation and users of the same. The primary role of this organisation is to promote a safe hospital environment for patients.

- Healthcare Tourism International, the first US-based non-profit to accredit the non-clinical aspects of health tourism, such as language issues, business practices, and false or misleading advertising prevention. The group provides accreditation for all major groups involved in the health tourism industry including hotels, recovery facilities, and medical tourism booking agencies.
- The United Kingdom Accreditation Forum (UKAF) is an established network of accreditation organisations with the intention of sharing experience good practice and new ideas around the methodology for accreditation programmes, covering issues such as developing healthcare quality standards, implementation of standards within healthcare organisations, assessment by peer review and exploration of the peer review techniques to include the recruitment, training, monitoring and evaluation of peer reviewers and the mechanisms for awards of accredited status to organisations.
- The International Medical Travel Association, (IMTA, based in Singapore), is a non-profit association formed to help address quality standards, liability issues, continuity of care, and other issues.

Risks

Medical tourism carries some risks that locally-provided medical care does not. Some countries, such as India, Malaysia, or Thailand have very different infectious disease-related epidemiology to Europe and North America. Exposure to diseases without having built up natural immunity can be a hazard for weakened individuals, specifically with respect to gastrointestinal diseases (e.g. Hepatitis A, amoebic dysentery, paratyphoid) which could weaken progress, mosquito-transmitted diseases, influenza, and tuberculosis. However, because in poor tropical nations diseases run the gamut, doctors seem to be more open to the possibility of considering any infectious disease, including HIV, TB, and typhoid, while there are cases in the West where patients were consistently misdiagnosed for years because such diseases are perceived to be "rare" in the West.

The quality of post-operative care can also vary dramatically, depending on the hospital and country, and may be different from US or European standards. However, JCI and Trent fulfil the role of accreditation by assessing the standards in the healthcare in the countries like India, China and Thailand. Also, travelling long distances soon after surgery can increase the risk of complications. Long flights and decreased mobility in a cramped airline cabin are a known risk factor for developing blood clots in the legs such as venous thrombosis or pulmonary embolus economy class syndrome. Other vacation activities can be problematic as well — for example, scars may become darker and more noticeable if they sunburn while healing. To minimise these problems, medical tourism patients often combine their medical trips with vacation time set aside for rest and recovery in the destination country.

Also, health facilities treating medical tourists may lack an adequate complaints policy to deal appropriately and fairly with complaints made by dissatisfied patients.

Differences in healthcare provider standards around the world have been recognised by the World Health Organization, and in 2004 it launched the World Alliance for Patient Safety. This body assists hospitals and government around the world in setting patient safety policy and practices that can become particularly relevant when providing medical tourism services.

Legal Issues

Receiving medical care abroad may subject medical tourists to unfamiliar legal issues. The limited nature of litigation in various countries is one reason for the lower cost of care overseas. While some countries currently presenting themselves as attractive medical tourism destinations provide some form of legal remedies for medical malpractice, these legal avenues may be unappealing to the medical tourist. Should problems arise, patients might not be covered by adequate personal insurance or might be unable to seek compensation via malpractice lawsuits. Hospitals and/or doctors in some countries may be unable to pay the financial damages awarded by a court to a patient who has sued them, owing to the hospital and/or the doctor not possessing appropriate insurance cover and/or medical indemnity.

Ethical Issues

There can be major ethical issues around medical tourism. For example, the illegal purchase of organs and tissues for transplantation has been alleged in countries such as India and China prior to 2007.

Medical tourism may raise broader ethical issues for the countries in which it is promoted. For example in India, some argue that a "policy of 'medical tourism for the classes and health missions for the masses' will lead to a deepening of the inequities" already embedded in the health care system. In Thailand, in 2008 it was stated that, "Doctors in Thailand have become so busy with foreigners that Thai patients are having trouble getting care". Medical tourism centred on new technologies, such as stem cell treatments, is often criticized on grounds of fraud, blatant lack of scientific rationale and patient safety. However, when pioneering advanced technologies, such as providing 'unproven' therapies to patients outside of regular clinical trials, it is often challenging to differentiate between acceptable medical innovation and unacceptable patient exploitation.

Medical Tourism Poised for Growth in Middle East

The Middle East has a number of advantages that make it well positioned to emerge as a leader in the medical tourism sector, but it needs to do more to change perceptions about the quality of care that is offered in the region, according to an expert in the industry.

Unlike other tourism sectors, medical tourism has grown during the economic downturn as countries around the world have struggled to control health care costs and ensure medical procedures are available when needed, said Dr. Prem Jagyasi, a medical tourism consultant and CEO of ExHealth in Dubai Healthcare City.

'Healthcare in the developed world is in serious crisis, and each country has a different problem,' he noted. 'For example, in the US, there are 50 million people uninsured, 250 million underinsured, and 150 million without dental insurance. So if they need medical services they cannot go to the local hospital because of the high cost.' But cost is just one of just several factors driving growth in the industry. In countries such as Canada and the UK, a major complaint is not the price but the wait times for many elective procedures. 'In some cases you need to wait three-to-six months for a surgical procedure, and sometimes even a consultation takes two-to-three months,' he noted.

Another key driver is the availability of certain medical procedures, which is a problem in underdeveloped countries and some Middle East states.

These factors have helped boost the value of the medical tourism industry to about $50bn a year, with over 50 countries actively seeking a slice of the pie.

Growth Opportunity

The rise of medical tourism provides an opportunity for the Middle East, which so far has made few inroads in the sector. 'Until a few years ago, a top priority for medical providers around the world was to attract medical tourists from the Middle East,' Jagyasi told AME Info.com. 'Now the trend has reversed as the Middle East is seeking to attract medical tourists from places such as the US and Europe where the cost of health care and delays in getting treatment have risen sharply.'

Around 20% of people in the UAE used to visit the US prior to 9/11 for medical treatment, but now that has decreased to less than 5%, he noted. Instead, locals from the UAE and other countries in the region are going to Singapore, India, and Malaysia for medical procedures.

Many hospitals in these countries have received international accreditation, which gives tourists some assurance that these facilities are high quality. 'This is lacking in the Middle East,' he noted.

The lack of trust in the quality of care in the Gulf is evidenced by the fact that large numbers of locals travel outside the region for medical services, including simple check-ups.

Key Considerations

However, the Middle East still has a good opportunity to capture a larger slice of the international market, but to do so it needs to recognize the most critical factors that medical tourists consider in choosing a medical tourism destination, Jagyasi said. The first is the quality of care offered at the destination, and the Middle East is making headway in this area through its development of GCC-wide medical accreditation standards.

The second is the perception of the destination, including safety or quality of facilities and infrastructure. In this regard the GCC is also making strides through its investment in its medical facilities, while crime the region is perceived to be relatively low.

The final consideration is whether the destination offers leisure or cultural attractions, as medical tourists will often combine medical and leisure tourism. Again, the Middle East can compete in this category with its rich cultural heritage and high-quality resorts.

Looking ahead, the Middle East should initially focus on capturing medical tourists from within the region, which is a huge market and perhaps the easiest to attract because of the shared cultural beliefs, Jagyasi said.

The region also must establish legal protections and guidelines, which are lacking at present and could create problems down the road as more medical tourists arrive from places like the US and Europe where patients' rights are taken for granted.

With this in mind, another major priority must be to develop a board of key stakeholders from within and outside of the healthcare industry to establish common standards and promote the medical tourism industry in the region, Jagyasi added.

Employer-sponsored Health Care in the US

Some US employers have begun exploring medical travel programs as a way to cut employee health care costs. Such proposals have raised stormy debates between employers and trade unions representing workers, with one union stating that it deplored the "shocking new approach" of offering employees overseas treatment in return for a share of the company's savings. The unions also raise the issues of legal liability should something go wrong, and potential job losses in the US health care industry if treatment is outsourced.

Employers may offer incentives such as paying for air travel and waiving out-of-pocket expenses for care outside of the US. For example, in January 2008, Hannaford Bros., a supermarket chain based in Maine, began paying the entire medical bill for employees to travel to Singapore for hip and knee replacements, including travel for the patient and companion. Medical travel packages can integrate with all types of health insurance, including limited benefit plans, preferred provider organizations and high deductible health plans.

Insurers are beginning to establish partnerships with overseas health providers to treat their insureds as well. A 2008 article in *Fast Company* discusses the globalization of healthcare and describes how various players in the US healthcare market have begun to explore it.

Subfields

Dental involves individuals seeking dental care outside of their local healthcare systems.

Fertility

Fertility tourism is the practice of travelling to another country for fertility treatments. The main reasons for fertility tourism are legal regulation of the sought procedure in the home country, or lower price. In-vitro fertilization, donor insemination and surrogacy are major procedures involved.

Destinations in Africa and Middle East

Countries in this region involved in medical tourism include Saudi Arabia, South Africa, and Tunisia.

Israel

Israel is emerging as a popular destination for medical tourists. In 2006, 15,000 foreigners travelled to the country for medical procedures, bringing in $40 million of revenue. Medical tourists choose Israel for several reasons. Some come from European nations such as Romania where certain procedures are not available. Others come to Israel, perhaps most commonly from the US, because they can receive quality health care at a fraction of the cost it would be at home, for both surgeries and in-vitro fertilization treatments. Other medical tourists come to Israel to visit the Dead Sea, a world-famous therapeutic resort. The Israel Ministry of Tourism and several professional medical services providers have set out to generate awareness of Israel's medical capabilities.

Jordan

Jordan is an emerging medical tourism destination, with related revenues exceeding one billion dollars in 2007. More than 250,000 patients from other countries sought treatment in Jordan that year. This included an estimated 45,000 Iraqis and approximately 25,000 patients each from Palestine and Sudan. An estimated 1,800 US citizens, 1,200 UK citizens, and 400 Canadians also sought treatment in Jordan that year. Treatment costs can be as low as 25 percent of costs in the US. The kingdom was rated as number one in the region and fifth in the world as a medical tourism hub in a study by the World Bank.

UAE

Hospitals in Dubai and other emirates have expressed an intent to develop in medical tourism. Some have American-sourced international healthcare accreditation, while others are looking towards the UK, Australia and Canada for accreditation services.

The Americas

Countries in the Americas that are treating foreign patients include Argentina, Bolivia, Brazil, Colombia, Costa Rica, Cuba, Dominican Republic, Guatemala, Mexico, Panama, Peru and Uruguay.

Brazil

Brazil has long been known as a destination for cosmetic surgery. For non-cosmetic procedures, Brazil is only now entering the global market. However, Albert Einstein Jewish Hospital in Sao Paulo was the first JCI-accredited facility outside of the US, and more than a dozen Brazilian medical facilities have since been similarly accredited. Brazil requires visas for US citizens based on a reciprocal arrangement since Brazilians are required to obtain a visa to visit the US.

Canada

Canada has entered the medical tourism field. In comparison to US health costs, medical tourism patients can save 30 to 60 percent on health costs in Canada. Canada's quality of healthcare is cited by the World Health Organization as equal to if not better than that of the US in most categories.

Cuba

Cuba has been a popular medical tourism destination for more than 40 years. Thousands of patients travel to Cuba, particularly from Latin America and Europe, attracted by the "fine reputation of Cuban doctors, the low prices and nearby beaches on which to recuperate." In 2006, Cuba attracted nearly 20,000 health tourists. Medical treatments included joint replacement, cancer treatment, eye surgery, cosmetic surgery and addictions rehabilitation. Costs are about 60 to 80 percent less than US costs.

Cuba has hospitals for Cuban residents and others that focus on serving foreigners and diplomats. In the 2007 American documentary film, *Sicko*, which criticizes the US healthcare system, producer Michael Moore leads a group of uninsured American patients to Cuba to obtain more affordable medical treatment. *Sicko* has greatly increased foreigners' interest in Cuban healthcare. A recent Miami Herald story focused on the high quality of health care that Canadian and American medical tourism patients receive in Cuba.

The Cuban government has developed Cuban medical tourism to generate income for the country. Residents of Canada, the UK and most other countries can travel to Cuba without any difficulty a tourist visa is generally required. For Americans, however, because of the US trade policy towards Cuba, travellers must either obtain US government approval, or, more frequently, travel to Cuba from Canada, Mexico, the Bahamas, Jamaica or the Dominican Republic. Cuban immigration authorities do not stamp the passports of US visitors so that Americans can keep their travels a private matter. To date no Cuban facility has achieved JCI Accreditation.

Mexico

Americans, particularly those living near the Mexican border, now routinely cross to Mexico for medical care. Popular specialities include dentistry and plastic surgery. Mexican dentists often charge one-fifth to one-fourth of US prices, while other procedures typically cost a third what they would in the US.

This trend has alarmed American healthcare providers who, fearing a loss of business, warn patients away from Mexico. "The phenomenon has unsettled US-based dentists who tell horror stories of rampant infections, undetected cases of oral cancer and shoddy work south of the border", claims hotly disputed by Mexican dentists. "In Texas, legislators explored the possibility of allowing health maintenance organizations to operate on both sides of the border. However, physicians in south Texas lobbied against the changes, arguing that local doctors could not compete with the lower costs in Mexico". US doctors point out that the Mexican legal system makes it almost impossible to sue Mexican doctors for malpractice. However, many who travel to Mexico for care report that they are satisfied. According to a report commissioned by Families U.S.A., a Washington advocacy group for healthcare issues, "About 90 percent the care they had received in Mexico had been good or excellent. About 80 percent rated the care they had received in the United States as good or excellent".

Indeed "some U.S. dentists... have conceded to the competition and begun a 'reverse migration' opening offices in Mexico to take advantage of lower costs". More American insurers are providing coverage for travellers, as the out-of-pocket costs to them are much lower. "With healthcare costs in the United States continuing to rise, many employers in Southern California are turning to insurance plans that send their workers to Mexico for routine care, plans that are growing by nearly 3,000 people a year."

In addition to dental and plastic surgery, Mexican hospitals are popular for bariatric surgery for weight loss, considered an elective procedure that is not covered by some US insurers. A popular bariatric procedure, lap band surgery, which was approved by the FDA in the US in 2001, has been performed for longer by Mexican surgeons.

Panama

In Panama, health and medical tourism is growing rapidly. Factors drawing medical tourists include Panama's tourist appeal, position as a hub for international travel, and use of the American dollar as the official currency. Many of Panama's doctors are bilingual, board certified, and accustomed to working with the same medical equipment and technology used in the United States and Europe. On most procedures, Panama offers savings of more than 50% compared to the US and Europe. No Panamanian hospitals currently have international healthcare accreditation, whether through US, British, Australian or Canadian sources.

United States

Although much attention has been given to the growing trend of uninsured Americans travelling to foreign countries, a report from 2008 found that a plurality of an estimated 60,000 to 85,000 medical tourists were travelling to the United States for the purpose of receiving in-patient medical care. The availability of advanced medical technology and sophisticated training of physicians are cited as driving motivators for growth in foreigners travelling to the U.S. for medical care. Also, it has been noted that the decline in value of the U.S. dollar is offering additional incentive for foreign travel to the U.S. However, costs differences between the US and many locations in Asia far outweigh any currency fluctuations. Several major medical centres and teaching hospitals offer international patient centres that cater to patients from foreign countries who seek medical treatment in the U.S. Many of these organizations offer service coordinators to assist international patients with arrangements for medical care, accommodations, finances and transportation including air ambulance services. It should be noted that many locations in the US that offer medical care comparable in price to foreign medical facilities are not Joint Commission Accredited.

Uruguay

Uruguay recently entered the medical tourism market. A private medical tourism initiative, Uruhealth, has been created with support from the Ministries of Tourism and Public Health. The initiative involves the infrastructure, human resources and experience of two healthcare companies: MP Personalized Medicine (Montevideo) and SEMM-Mautone Hospital.

Asia/Pacific

Many Asian Pacific countries are medical tourism destinations.

China

China is fast emerging as a desirable destination for individuals seeking medical care in a wide range of medical specialities, including cardiology, neurology, orthopedics and others. A number of private and government hospitals in major cities have established international departments. Many leading hospitals provide treatments integrating Traditional Chinese Medicine with Western medical technology and techniques. China is home to leading stem cell research and treatment hospitals that offer Westerners who want to take advantage of stem cell treatments that are still considered experimental or have yet to be approved in their home country.

Hong Kong

As of 2006, Hong Kong had 12 private hospitals and 39 public hospitals, providing 3,124 and 27,755 beds respectively. A wide range of health care services are offered. All 12 of Hong Kong's private hospitals have been surveyed and accredited by the UK's Trent Accreditation Scheme since early 2001. This has been a major factor in the ascent of standards in Hong Kong's private hospitals. The Trent scheme works closely with the hospitals it assesses to generate standards appropriate to the locality (with respect to culture, geography, public health, primary care interfaces etc.), and always uses combinations of UK-sourced and Hong Kong-sourced surveyors. Some of Hong Kong's private hospitals have now gone on to obtain dual international accreditation, with both Trent and JCI (and have therefore attained a standard surpassing some of the best hospitals in Thailand and Singapore). Others are looking towards dual international accreditation with Trent and the Australian group. Hong Kong public hospitals have yet to commit to external accreditation.

India

India's medical tourism sector is expected to experience an annual growth rate of 30%, making it a Rs. 9,500-crore industry by 2015. Estimates of the value of medical tourism to India go as high as $2 billion a year by 2012. Advantages for medical tourists include reduced costs, the availability of latest medical technologies and a growing compliance on international quality standards, as well as the fact that foreigners are less likely to face a language barrier in India. The Indian government is taking steps to address infrastructure issues that hinder the country's growth in medical tourism.

Most estimates claim treatment costs in India start at around a tenth of the price of comparable treatment in America or Britain. The most popular treatments sought in India by medical tourists are alternative medicine, bone-marrow transplant, cardiac bypass surgery, eye surgery and orthopedic surgery. India is known in particular for heart surgery, hip resurfacing and other areas of advanced medicine.

Ministry of Tourism India (MoT) is planning to extend its Market Development Assistance (MDA) scheme to cover Joint Commission International (JCI) and National Accreditation Board of Hospitals (NABH) certified hospitals. A policy announcement of this effect is likely soon.

The south Indian city of Chennai has been declared India's Health Capital, as it nets in 45% of health tourists from abroad and 30-40% of domestic health tourists. Other major cities where medical tourists are catered to include New Delhi, Bangalore and Mumbai.

Korea, Republic of

Listed on CNN.com as one of the "hot destinations" for medical tourism, Korea is quickly establishing itself in the field of medical tourism. Korea is especially popular with Japanese cosmetic surgery patients due to the cheap costs and high standards of care practiced by Korean medical facilities. In 2008, Korea had 27,480 foreign-based patients and the Korean health ministry expects that number to increase to 140,000 by 2015. Due to legislation passed in May 2009, state-licensed clinics and hospitals are now allowed to directly seek out foreign patients through various promotional activities. Korean hospitals and clinics provide a variety of medical services for medical tourists including comprehensive health screening, cancer treatment, organ transplantation, joint/rheumatism care, spinal treatment, ophthalmology, dental care, infertility treatment, otorhinolaryngology, and Korean traditional medicine. Currently, the most popular treatments for medical tourists are cosmetic procedures such as eyelid surgery, nose jobs, face-lifts, and skin lightening. Over 30 Korean hospitals and clinics are member providers under the Council for Korea Medicine Overseas Promotion (CKMOP). Among these facilities are the "Big Four" – Seoul National University Hospital, Samsung Medical Centre, Asan Medical Centre, and Yonsei Severance Hospital. Severance Hospital is Korea's only JCI accredited hospital and with over 2,000 beds, is also the world's largest JCI accredited hospital.

Malaysia

Malaysia is well on its way to develop itself as a medical tourism hub. The country has excellent hospitals, English is widely spoken, and many staff have been trained to a high level in the UK or in the US. There is a highly active Association for Private Hospitals of Malaysia working to develop medical tourism. However, while Malaysia has a national accreditation healthcare scheme (MSQH) and many Malaysia's hospitals are currently firmly on the way to achieve international healthcare accreditation. Malaysian hospitals International Specialist Eye Centre, Penang Adventist Hospital and many others such as Gleneagles Hospital Kuala Lumpur have or are going to be JCI accredited. The Ministry of Health has launched a medical tourism page with medical tourism portals such as Wellness Visit.

New Zealand

New Zealand is a relatively new destination to medical travel. It has all the hallmarks of a very successful destination especially for North American based patients. This includes being a first world, developed economy with a sophisticated and comprehensive medical system. It is first and foremost English speaking with a rich heritage of producing world class doctors and medical research. Many of its private hospitals are internationally accredited, state of the art and offer an integrated package of care. The surgeons in New Zealand are trained both in New Zealand and abroad, usually spending years of their training in either North America or Western Europe. While New Zealand is aligned medically and culturally to North America, the cost of the surgical care is significantly cheaper. On average it is considered that New Zealand's surgical costs are around 15 to 20% the cost of the same surgical procedure in the USA. One patient who had his prosthetic hip replaced in New Zealand said the total cost including travel, lodging and the surgery at a private hospital was $20,000, as opposed to the $80,000-$140,000 he was told the operation would have cost at home. Added to this the personalized level of medical care, the world renown natural beauty and tranquillity, the fact that New Zealand is one of the safest places in the world and only 12 hours direct flight from the west coast of North America, then New Zealand as a medical travel destination looks set to develop.

Philippines

The Philippines has been growing as a destination for medical tourism. The US Medical Tourism Association magazine reported that this services sub-sector grew 8.0% in 2007. The Philippines is one of a few countries that sends qualified physicians and dentists to the US, a testament to its quality of medical education. Procedures can be performed at a fraction of the amount that a patient would spend on the same procedure in the US or Europe. Some medical centres are accredited by the American accreditation group Joint Commission International (JCI).

Singapore

Singapore has a dozen hospitals and health centres with JCI accreditation. In 1997, the World Health Organization ranked Singapore's health care system sixth best in the world and the highest ranked system in Asia. "Singapore Medicine" is a multi-agency government-industry partnership committed to strengthening Singapore's position as a medical hub and promoting Singapore as a destination for advanced patient care. Patients come from neighbouring countries, such as Indonesia and Malaysia, and patient numbers from Indochina, South Asia, the Middle East and Greater China are growing. Patients from developed countries such as the United States and the UK are also beginning to choose

Singapore as their medical travel destination for relatively affordable health care services in a clean cosmopolitan city.

Taiwan

The Taiwanese government has declared its determination for the country to become a medical tourism centre. It is estimated that the government will contribute NT$44.4 million to construct a platform for the collaboration of the government and the medical sector in promoting medical tourism. Costs for procedures remain comparatively low. Taiwan is known for liver transplants, joint replacement surgery, bone marrow transplants, and reconstructive and plastic surgery.

Thailand

Medical tourism has been a growing segment of Thailand's tourism and healthcare sectors. In 2005, one Bangkok hospital took in 150,000 treatment seekers from abroad. In 2006, medical tourism was projected to earn the country 36.4 billion baht. Treatments for medical tourists in Thailand range from cosmetic, organ transplants, cardiac, and orthopaedic treatments to dental and cardiac surgeries. Treatments also include spa, physical and mental therapies. One patient who had coronary artery bypass surgery at Bumrungrad International hospital in Bangkok said the operation cost him US$12,000 (8,200 euros), as opposed to the $100,000 (68,000 euros) he estimated the operation would have cost him at home. Bumrungrad treated approximately 55,000 American patients in 2005 alone, a 30% increase from the previous year.

Hospitals in Thailand are a popular destination for other Asians. Bangkok Hospital, which caters to medical tourists, has a Japanese wing, and Phyathai Hospitals Group has interpreters for over 22 languages, besides the English-speaking medical staff. When Nepal Prime Minister Girija Prasad Koirala needed medical care in 2006, he went to Bangkok.. Many Thai physicians hold US or UK professional certification. Bumrungrad International hospital states that many of its doctors and staff are trained in the UK, Europe and the US. Bumrungrad International was accredited most recently in 2005 by the Joint Commission. Some of the country's major hospitals have also achieved certification by the International Organization for Standardization's ISO 9001:2000. However, ISO 2000 is not an accreditation scheme.

The US consular information sheet gives the Thai health care system high marks for quality, particularly facilities in Bangkok.. The

World Health Organization's 2000 ranking put the Thai healthcare system at number 47, below the USA's ranking at 37 and the United Kingdom's ranking at 18. The UK's Foreign and Commonwealth Office web site states "There are excellent international hospitals in Bangkok but they can be expensive".

Serious political problems during late 2008, including mass demonstrations and the complete closure of major airports, have made travel to Thailand less appealing than in the past, and the US State Department has issued a travel alert for the country.

Europe

Countries in Europe that have active medical tourism sectors include Cyprus, Germany, Hungary, Lithuania, Malta, Poland, Portugal, Czech Republic, Slovakia, Spain, and Ukraine.

Czech Republic

Czech Republic has built its medical tourism on spas and medical care equalling the world standards.

Germany

Germany is a destination for patients seeking advanced medical technology, high standards, safety, and quick treatment. All German citizens have health coverage, resulting in a high hospital density, with twice as many hospitals per capita as the United States. The high hospital density results in shorter waitlists for treatment. Costs for medical treatment compete well with other developed European countries and are commonly 50% of those in the USA.

Germany is an attractive destination for patients from the Middle East since travelling to the USA has become more difficult for them since the September 11 attacks. US citizens sometimes travel to Germany to seek treatments such as artificial cervical disc replacement that are not US Food and Drug Administration (FDA) approved.

Poland

Since 2004, when Poland joined the European Union, it has become another locale for people seeking cheaper medical treatments. The quality of care in Poland must comply with EU standards. One well-known medical centre in Poland is "medical-poland.com" with The Clinical Hospital No. 10 and Polyclinic in Bydgoszcz.

Turkey

Turkey has since many years attracted medical tourists from Europe, the United States and the Middle East as the country combines quality healthcare, the newest medical technologies (Cyberknife) and low-cost. Many tourists come to Turkey for medical or cosmetic surgery but the country is also seeking to build on its geothermal resources for an expansion of therapeutic spas. The German Hospital in Istanbul operates the country's first ISO-certified IVF centre, while Memorial Hospital was the first private hospital to receive American JCI accreditation. Since then, over 34 hospitals and medical institutions have achieved Joint Commission International accreditation.

2

Trade of Health Tourism

The worldwide trends in trade of health-related services are looked at in detail in the fourth paper in The Lancet Series on Trade and Health, written by Professor Richard Smith, London School of Hygiene and Tropical Medicine, UK, and colleagues. In their analysis, the authors use the classification provided by the WTO for the General Agreement on Trade and Services (GATS): cross-border supply of health services, consumption of services abroad, foreign direct investment, and movement of health professionals.

Cross-border supply of health services does not receive much media attention, but many countries have invested heavily in this area. Teleradiology, for example, has benefited from the shift from hard copy to digital imaging. India, the Philippines, and Cuba are leaders in the exportation of medical-transcription services, telepathology, and telediagnostic services. The authors say: "Demand for cross-border e-health is related to cost and, to a lesser extent, timing. For instance, the yearly salary for US non-specialised radiologists is $300 000, but only $20 000 for their Indian counterpart." But e-health brings its share of concerns as well as benefits. Who is legally liable when there are problems? And concerns have been raised about care becoming fragmented and disintegrated when e-services are used in this way.

Private patients seeking healthcare abroad "health tourism" is becoming big business. Thailand is the leading exporter at over 1 million patients per year and revenues of $615 million, but India is predicted to have revenues of $2•2 billion, Singapore $1•6 billion, and Malaysia $590 million by 2012. The demand for services abroad is driven by domestic non-availability, often in specialised and niche or alternative treatment areas. Low labour costs combined with high-quality medical professionals (many of whom trained in the USA or UK) give many developing countries a huge cost advantage. And it is not, as often thought, just cosmetic procedures that are 'selling'. Heart-bypass surgery can be performed in Thailand for US$8,000, compared with $20,000 in the UK and $24,000 in the USA. The average cosmetic surgery comes in at around $3500 in Thailand, $10,000 in the UK and $20,000 in the USA. The potential for expansion of this trade is enormous. The authors say: "The main constraint on trade is the scarcity of insurance portability. Many national insurance schemes restrict patients seeking foreign service providers when that service is available domestically. In the European Union (EU), for example, although there is portability across member countries for emergency care, elective care needs previous approval from domestic health authorities."

Foreign direct investment (FDI – mode 3), typically in new hospitals or clinics, has grown rapidly. Between 1990 and 2000, FDI from developed to developing countries grew from US$36 billion to $155 billion (over three-times that of official development aid) and FDI in services accounted for more than half of all FDI.

However, FDI in health remains small compared with other sectors, because of the nature of the services (many health facilities are publicly owned) and the existence of regulatory barriers. Developing countries are increasingly looking towards FDI as a source of capital investment in their health sector, as well as the potential for general infrastructure development, and investment in and transfer of technology and skills. But concerns exist about foreign control of healthcare provision; increased privatisation of health (in mainly public systems); and associated concerns about the diversion of resources to curative and high-end procedures, domestic brain drain, and advantageous patient selection.

Migration has historically been the main pathway for health-services trade. Currently around 30% of UK doctors are of foreign origin, with India, Ireland, Pakistan, South Africa and Egypt providing the majority of these. In the USA, Canada and Australia around 20% of doctors are foreign; many of whom are from the UK. Loss of doctors from poorer countries has a disproportionate effect on the national stock of skills in those nations. For nurses, low- and middle-income countries provide the majority of foreign nurses working in the UK – in 2002, around half of the 25,602 work permits issued to foreign workers for nursing were to nurses from The Philippines or India. Job satisfaction, pay and career opportunities are among the reasons healthcare workers wish to migrate. The authors say: "However, the effect of migration on human capital stocks (so-called brain drain) is a cause of concern. The ultimate destination of workers to rich countries, and often the private sector within these countries, has knock-on effects down the chain to public sectors within wealthy nations, private and public sectors in low-income countries, and ultimately the rural areas within poorer countries."

The authors conclude: "Perhaps because health care is fundamentally about people-health professionals and patients-that modes 2 and 4 of service delivery are the most prevalent and arguably most important areas of trade in health services is unsurprising." "No universal policy recommendation can be made concerning a country's involvement with trade in health services. Instead, every country needs to assemble the relevant information to assess how such trade can affect its key areas of concern… The stewardship of a domestic health system in the context of the trade environment in the 21st century needs a sophisticated understanding of how trade in health services affects, and will affect, a country's health system and policy."

Healthy Trade in Health Tourism

As food and oil prices rocket all over the world, consumers are getting a crash course in economics: when demand increases, prices increase. Although food and oil dominate the headlines, life's other essentials also obey this cast-iron law, including healthcare, which is threatening to bust government budgets all over the world. As with food, part of the solution lies in opening up trade and competition.

The Organization of Economic Community and Development estimates that world average healthcare expenditure last year accounted for 9 percent of GDP, up from just over 5 percent in 1970. The US now spends more than US$2 trillion per year on healthcare, eight times the amount in 1980. US healthcare costs are currently increasing by twice general inflation, a general trend in rich countries.

As populations grow older and more demanding, these inflationary pressures will increase. Politicians are finding cashed-strapped voters increasingly unwilling to stump up the large amounts of tax needed to fund government health systems, forcing them to deny treatments to patients in a bid to constrain costs. In the US, healthcare costs have become a major issue in the presidential election.

The last decade, by contrast, has seen very low inflation for other goods, partly because of a massive increase in global trade. The arrival of China and India as major new exporters has meant that most countries have been able to import goods cheaply, keeping prices down.

While the role of free trade in driving down prices and driving up quality has long been accepted by economists (and, to an extent, politicians), healthcare has been one area in which there has been almost no international trade. It is time for this to change.

Communications technology makes it increasingly easy for hospitals to outsource services such as diagnostics to laboratories overseas, cutting costs and treatment time. Patients can get treatment overseas where costs are lower. Open-heart surgery in India costs only one-sixth of the price in the US, including travel, accommodation and medicines. If only 10 percent of US patients went abroad for 15 types of treatment, they and insurance firms could save US$1.5 billion a year, including travel.

Patients are already voting with their feet. In 2006 alone, Singapore treated 500,000 foreign patients, India treated 600,000 and Thailand around 1.2 million. Other favourite destinations include Malaysia, South Africa and Cuba. Taiwan's Council for Economic Planning and Development believes it could bring in NT$7 billion (US$230.4 million) a year.

While the benefits of free trade in health are clear for rich countries, developing countries also stand to gain. Most obviously, there are opportunities for much-needed investment of foreign capital. These financial opportunities would also give developing countries' medical staff a far greater incentive to remain at home, reducing the debilitating "brain drain." As more money came into the health sector, some of the burden on government healthcare would be removed.

Despite the significant benefits, only two developed countries have ratified a WTO agreement on trade in healthcare — Iceland and Norway. While developing countries such as Gambia, Jamaica, Malawi and South Africa are prepared to liberalize, wealthier countries seem bent on protectionism.

This reluctance is largely down to lobbying by interest groups in developed countries. Public sector unions seek to protect their members and industries from competition. Non-governmental organizations ideologically oppose trade in healthcare, claiming that only governments can ensure "equity" and "universal" treatment — even though public healthcare in most of the world fails patients miserably.

This is a massive wasted opportunity. Free trade in healthcare could help rich countries keep the lid on healthcare inflation while helping poorer countries attract investment and skills and retain valuable medical professionals.

For this to happen, developed countries must encourage insurers to cover overseas treatment and open up their medical sectors to international competition. Developing countries need to standardize their qualification and licensing requirements in order to attract customers and improve skills.

Healthcare doesn't have to go the same way as food prices. Rich and poor countries should ignore calls for protectionism and liberalize their healthcare for the good of patients everywhere. Health tourism can be healthy for everyone.

Ayurvedic Tourism

Ayurvedic medicine is a form of unconventional medicine in use mainly in the Indian subcontinent. The word "Ayurveda" means the "Science of Life". It deals with the therapies and treatments for the rejuvenation and renewal of mind, body and soul. Ayurveda is also one among the few conventional method of medicine involving surgery. Ayurveda is a knowledge of life so to know more about it, we must know what is life. Life according to Ayurveda is an amalgamation of senses, mind, body and soul. So it is clear from this description of life that Ayurveda is not only restricted to body or physical symptoms but also gives a wide-ranging knowledge about spiritual, mental and social health.

The Ayurvedic scaffold can be used to structure working models of the special state of each patient, and to project a vision or goal for a whole state of health, again unique to each case.

Ayurveda offers specific references to each individual on lifestyle, diet, exercise and yoga, herbal therapy, and even spiritual practices to renovate and maintain balance in body and mind. Ayurveda sees a strong link between the mind and the body, a huge quantity of information is accessible regarding this correlation.

History

Ayurveda is said to have been first conformed as a text by Agnivesha in the book Agnivesh tantra. Verses related Ayurveda are also mentioned in the Atharvaveda. In the earlier days of its formation, the structure of Ayurvedic medicine was orally transferred via the Gurukul system until a written script came into subsistence.

What is interesting is Ayurveda's utilization of herbs, foods, aromas, gems, colours, yoga, mantras, lifestyle and surgery. Consequently Ayurveda nurtured into an esteemed and widely used method of healing in India in ancient times. Ayurveda was marked out into eight definite branches of medicine. There were two main disciplines of Ayurveda at that time. Atreya (the school of physicians) and Dhanvantari (the school of surgeons). These two schools made Ayurveda a more systematically confirmable and classifiable medical structure.

Benefits

* eradicate toxins and toxic conditions from your body & mind
* refurbish your constitutional balance, refining health & wellness
* reinforce your immune system & become more defiant to illness
* repeal the negative effects of stress on your body & mind, thereby dawdling the aging process
* augment your self-reliance, strength, energy, potency & mental clarity
* Bring about deep respite & a sense of comfort.

Ayurveda provides both remedial and precautionary measures towards finest physical, mental and spiritual well-being. More than merely medicinal care, Ayurveda offers a viewpoint whereby one may avert unnecessary distress and live a long, healthy life. Ayurveda has undergone unremitting research, development and refinement over thousands of years.

Ayurvedic Medicare is based on natural and herbal procedures and appendages. Ayurveda does not consider antidotes and antigens, very seldom those techniques are used, Ayurveda works not to restrain the system of body, but to go to the origin and treat the basic disturbing element. In such treatments there are very small chances of side effect and the benefit of the body is everlasting. It gives you a absolute health treatment, which works on the full body system so it makes you feel healthier in your whole body.

Worldwide Popularity

In modern years, Ayurveda has achieved worldwide fame. People are looking for a medicinal system that allows lowest intake of chemicals, whose side effects and reactions are well identified. Thus, alternate health care systems are becoming more fashionable. Ayurveda, which is a total system including preservation of health, avoidance and curing diseases, can be the best exchange to today's medical sciences. A natural concord between Ayurvedic principles and the human structure is the main factor for its efficiency.

The present man-made lifestyle has led to many health hazards. The stress and tension of everyday life is a chief factor for many health problems. Lack of exercise, tainted environment and climatically inapt menu further sap away energy. Ayurveda rectifies these health issues through therapy and massage. Ayurveda can lessen the problems created by the hectic lifestyle we lead today. Hence Ayurveda is a science that is gaining wide recognition and international fame today. With its innate remedies Ayurveda has grown into an absolute healthcare system without any side effects.

What is Ayurveda?

The word Ayurveda is composed of two Sanskrit terms— Ayu meaning 'life' and Veda meaning 'knowledge'. Therefore Ayurveda means the knowledge of life or science of life. It is defined as the science, through which one can obtain knowledge about the useful and harmful ways of life, happy and miserable types of life, conditions that lead to the above types of life, as well as, the very nature of life.

Benefits of Ayurveda

* Ayurvedic and herbal medicines ensures physical and mental health without side effects. The natural ingredients of herbs help bring 'arogya' (health) to human body and mind.
* According to the original texts, the goal of Ayurveda is prevention as well as promotion of the body's own capacity for maintenance and balance.

* Ayurvedic treatment is non-invasive and non-toxic, so it can be used safely as an alternative therapy or alongside conventional therapies.
* Ayurvedic physicians claim that their methods can also help stress-related, metabolic, and chronic conditions.
* Ayurveda has been used to treat acne, allergies, asthma, anxiety, arthritis, chronic fatigue syndrome, colds, colitis, constipation, depression, diabetes, flu, heart disease, hypertension, immune problems, inflammation, insomnia, nervous disorders, obesity, skin problems, and ulcers.

Promoting Ayurveda-Health Tourism in India

Ayurveda has gained a lot of global attraction. Being one of the main features of tourist attraction down south, many Ayurvedic centres are on a rise today. India is emerging as a great destination for medical tourism because it has several pull factors like Excellent medical treatment at low cost, easy accessibility, picturesque locations for excellent holiday, etc. The medical tourism market in India is expected to grow to $2 billion a year by 2012-13. South India is the preferred location and is the health capital of the country. In their quest to attract foreign patients, hospitals are opening up a wide of facilities like foreign cell for each country among the others. Hopefully, by the next few years, India will be the preferred location worldwide for good medical facility.

India Major Player of Health Tourism

Marketing Ayurveda as part of the 'health tourism' has brought a new definition to vacationing in India itself. Medical treatment combined with leisure activities, fun and fitness. India has originated as one of the most important hubs for medical tourism.

Top-class medical expertise and facilities: India has lot of tourists from other countries coming for the rejuvenation promised by yoga and Ayurvedic massage. Add to it, a nice blend of top-class medical expertise at attractive prices which is helping more and more Indian corporate hospitals to lure foreign patients, including patients from the UK and the US, for high end surgeries like Cardiac ByPass Surgery or a Knee/ Hip Replacement. Indian corporate hospitals are well equipped, proficient and could measure up to or even outshine any hospital in the West, making the nation an attractive destination for health tourism.

Low medical costs compared to other countries: As the inflow of more patients from affluent nations with high medical costs look for effective options, are increasing, health care tourism in India is definitely on the cards for most of them and the fast growing Indian corporate health sector is fully geared to meet that need.

No waiting period: Not just cost savings or the high standard of medical care facility, but also the waiting time is much lower for any treatment in India than in any other country. Medical help is

often an emergency and situations can turn worse if the treatment is delayed. While you might have to wait for several months to get a surgical operation done in the US, in India things can be arranged within a week.

Ayurvedic Centres in Kerala

1. Nagarjuna Ayurvedic Centre: Nagarjuna Ayurvedic Centre is part of the Nagarjuna group and are the pioneers in the promotion and treatment of Aurveda in Kerala. The centre is located on the banks of the river Periyar and offers the best of Ayurvedic treatments.
2. Kottakkal Arya Vaidya Shala: The Arya Vaidya Shala is a complete encyclopedia of ayurvedic procedures, including cultivation of medicinal plants, manufacturing of herbal medicines, publishing books and seminar reports on ayurveda and related subjects, and beyond obvious, encouraging a Kathakali Academy. The treatment is based on Panchakarma Principles.
3. Amrita Ayurveda Medical Centre, Cochin: Amrutha Ayurveda centre is in the heart of Kochi engaged in the traditional Ayurvedic treatment to provide mental and physical health to the needy. Its aim is to increase the health status of human beings and to make them aware of the same.

Ayurvedic SPa Tourism to Kerala, India

Kerala is the only state in India where ayurveda is practised with full dedication and knowledge. The main reason for this is the climatic condition here is much suited for this Indian traditional system of medicine. Especially the cool monsoon season and the green forests enhances this treatment much. Though Ayurveda has been practised in India and Kerala for a huge number of years it is only a few years that it became a tourism promoting mean here. According to Ayurvedic specialists monsoon season is the best season for ayurvedic treatment as our atmosphere becomes dust free and cool. Many Spa resorts are available now in Kerala and they mainly aims tourists. Foreigners also now understood the positive effect of Ayurveda and are now coming here on a large scale for spa tourism and returns happily with freshness. Treatment plans ranges from Rs 2500 a day to Rs 65000 for 3 weeks are available and they are ready to pay what is asked. In the changed condition of life people are suffering from a lot of pressure stress and tension in their day today life. Ayurvedic spa tourism is a best way to refresh you mind and body and to refill your spirit with freshness and peace. Ayurvedic treatments such as yoga meditation steam bath and massage have been proved to be effective for stress relief and also for a sound body. Though you are not suffering from such problems still you can opt this because it will give more freshness and health and also pleasure. And you can make it fully useful your holidays to Kerala.

10 Types of Ayurvedic Treatments in Kerala

1. Abhyangam: This is a type of oil massage treatment which takes a fourtnight length. It is a good treatment for problems like obesity and is done for 45 minute everyday.
2. Lepanam: The herbs are grind and is applied on the body parts. Mostly for allergies and inflammatory problems.
3. Thalam: A treatment for diseases related to head such as head ache, memory loss, hair graying, Insomnia etc. In this medicated oil is applied on the top of the head and is a very important one. I takes upto 40 minutes length.
4. Dhanyamla Dhara: This is a very useful treatment helping in curing diseases related to spinal chord and nerval system. This is found to be effective for curing diseases like spondylosis, rheumatism, paralysis, disc problems, back pain, asthma and arthritis. This takes a length of 14 days and 1 hour/day.
5. Dhara: Very effective for diseases promoted by vatha dosha and also for many skin diseases. In a special order and way medicated milk buttermilk and herbal oils are poured on the body and it takes upto 3 weeks for the treatments having periods of length 45 minutes/day.

6. Kizhi: Kizhi is for curing swellings and injuries. Diseases related to bones such as arthritis ans sports injuries etc. can be cured in this way. In this treatment herbal leaves and powder immersed in warm oil is applied all over the body for 1 hour a day for 14 days.
7. Nasyam: For neurological diseases, skin diseases and also for diseases such as migrain nasyam is found to be much useful. In this the medical oil is applied through the nose fore one week.
8. Pizhichi: The treatment is used for problems like Paralysis sexual weakness and Nervous weakness. The method is applying luke worm oil all over the body in a special way by four skilled therapists.
9. Vasthi: Treatment for the curing of diseases such as Arthritis, *Hemiplegia*, Numbness and constant constipation. Herbal oils with other herbal medicines are applied through the rectum everyday. Treatment continues for periods upto 25 days.
10. Yoni Prakshalanam: In this herbal oils and other herbal extracts are applied through the vaginal route. It is very effective in curing gynecological disorders.

Ayurvedic SPA Resorts in Kerala

1. Coconut Lagoon, Kumarakom, At the shore of Vembanad Lake.
2. Marari Beach Resort, Mararikkulam.
3. Kairali Health Resorts, Palakkadu.
4. Somatheeram Beach Reasort, Kovalam.
5. Spice village, Periyar.
6. Taj Garden Retreat, Kumarakom.
7. Taj Garden Retreat, Thekkady.

Ayurvedic Tour

The Indian system of nature cure: Life is a combination of the body, the senses, the mind and the atma (spirit or the soul). They can't be separated from each other, and none can be neglected. From this combination ensues 'Ayus'- the span of life.

Ayurveda-the science of life is the knowledge of this association and of how to maintain it as long as possible. Ayurveda or the 'science of longevity' is the system of nature cure. It is known to promote positive health, natural beauty and long life. Although rooted in antiquity, Ayurveda is based on universal principles and is a living, growing body of knowledge-as useful today as it was in earlier centuries. It is said that Ayurveda is as old as the world itself. Its very basis is the spiritual knowledge of the ancient seers of India and the cosmic consciousness in which they lived. Into its ancient well profound healing wisdom, some of the greatest doctors and sages over time have poured their finest insights and discoveries, transforming it into one of the oldest systems with a consistent theoretical basis and practical clinical applications. Its strength lies in its broad, all encompassing view of all dynamic inter-relationship between organic philological processes, external factors including climate, life works and diet along with internal psychological and spiritual condition.

Very much like various other systems of cure based on naturopathy, Ayurveda believes that disease occurs not as an arbitrary phenomenon but for definite reasons which if correctly understood could help to cure and, more importantly, prevent recurrence of the disease. Ideally human being and nature should be in perfect harmony. Disease occurs when the equilibrium between these two is disrupted. Restoration of this fundamental balance, through the use of nature and its products, is main goal of this medical system. "The object of Ayurveda", said Susruta the famous physician some 2600 years ago, "is the restoration to health of those who are afflicted with diseases and preservation of sound health of those who are well".

Evidently Ayurveda believes in the treatment of not just the affected part, but also the individual as a whole. The stress is on prevention of bodily ailments and not just curing them. There are no distressing side effects and it has, today, become an internationally acclaimed form of healing, rejuvenation and healthy living.

Trends in Health Industry

In the rapidly changing health care industry, technological advances have made many new procedures and methods of diagnosis and treatment possible. Clinical developments, such as organ transplants, less invasive surgical techniques, skin grafts, and gene therapy for cancer treatment, continue to increase the longevity and improve the quality of life of many Americans. In addition, advances in information technology continue to improve patient care and worker efficiency with devices such as hand-held computers that record notes on each patient. Information on vital signs and orders for tests are transferred electronically to a main database; this process eliminates the need for paper and reduces recordkeeping errors.

Employment Outlook

Job opportunities should be excellent in all employment settings because of high job turnover, particularly from the large number of expected retirements and tougher immigration rules that are slowing the numbers of foreign health care workers entering the U.S. Wage and salary. Employment in the health care industry is projected to increase 27 percent through 2014, compared with 14 percent for all industries combined. Projected rates of employment growth for the various segments of the industry range from 13 percent in hospitals, the largest and slowest growing industry segment, to 69 percent in the much smaller home health care services.

About 545,000 establishments make up the health care industry; they vary greatly in terms of size, staffing patterns, and organizational structures. About 76 percent of health care establishments are offices of physicians, dentists, or other health practitioners. Although hospitals constitute only 2 percent of all health care establishments, they employ 40 percent of all workers.

Trends & Emerging Issues

Macro Trends

- The population of the United States is expected to grow 29.2% between 2000 and 2030, from 282,125,000 to 363,584,000.
- Rates of all cancers for men declined between 1990 and 2001 (almost 1% per year), while for women the rates increased (an average of 0.4% per year).
- The prevalence of overweightness and obesity among adults has dramatically increased.
- The number of persons covered by employer-based health insurance decreased steadily between 2000 and 2004, and during that period the total number of uninsured adults increased by 6 million.

Market Trends

- 8 out of 20 occupations projected to grow the fastest are in health care.
- More new wage and salary jobs — about 19 percent, or 3.6 million — created between 2004 and 2014 will be in health care than in any other industry.
- Most workers have jobs that require less than 4 years of college education, but health diagnosing and treating practitioners are among the most educated workers.

Forecasts

- Researchers have found that by electrically stimulating certain nerves they can influence human movement, and possibly create better prosthetics.
- A California biotech company expects to begin trials of a treatment for spinal cord injuries next year.
- New drugs that target the brain's nicotine receptors, without the addictiveness of cigarettes, might help memory impairment in Alzheimer's disease and schizophrenia.
- Researchers predict significant health and cost benefits from linking data from individual biomonitors, as well as community health monitoring, to encourage healthy behaviour changes.
- Accenture is developing a talking medicine cabinet to help the elderly manage their medications and keep track of their vitals.

Health Care Industry Trends

Health care industry trends manifest an upward growth but several areas need to be attended to for enhancing health care services for the common man.

Different countries like Indonesia, Russia, Mexico, Brazil, India, Turkey and China comprise approximately 1/5th of the worldwide health care sales. Health care industry trends also suggest that the medical related conditions in the developing countries which are chronic in nature, will be similar to the ones existing in the developed countries. In order to meet international standards, the existing health care industry is required to alter the mode of operation for generation of higher revenue and greater contribution to the Gross Domestic Product of the country.

Facts about the health care industry trends:

- The cost related to health care was seen to rise in the 90s. Americans not possessing any health care coverage or any kind of health insurance attained the 42 million mark.
- It has been anticipated that the elderly sick people will impose considerable stress on the health care sector of US.
- The total number of different health care programs and different health care insurance coverages are likely to increase in the coming years. There has been an escalation in the medical plans from 42.5 million in the year 2006. The health care industry trends also show that it is likely to attain 70.2 million in the year 2025.
- The health care industry trends also indicate that the expenses for preventive measures is negligible as compared to the amount spent on treating chronic diseases which accounts for 70% of the fund used for health care.
- Trends suggest that there are very less Americans (around 23%) who make an effort to prevent any lifestyle diseases by consuming the optimum level of vegetable and fruits.

Health care industry trends suggests changes in the following spheres:

- The companies manufacturing medicines provide health care plans
- More stress is to be laid on prevention than treatments
- Sufficient supply of the essential health care products should be made available to the consumers to meet the demand of the health care industry.

Health care industry trends manifest an upward growth but several areas need to be attended for enhancing health care services for the common man.

Introduction to the Health Care Industry

Health Expenditures and Services in the US

Health care costs continue to rise rapidly in the U.S. and throughout the developed world. Total U.S. health care expenditures are estimated to have grown from $2.39 trillion in 2008 to $2.50 trillion in 2009.

The health care market in the U.S. in 2009 was made up of hospital care (about $789.4 billion), physician and clinical services ($539.1 billion), prescription drugs ($244.8 billion), nursing home and home health ($213.6 billion), dental care ($101.9 billion) and other items totalling $611.2 billion. Registered hospitals totalled 5,708 properties in 2008, containing 945,199 beds serving 37 million admitted patients.

Net federal spending on Medicaid and Medicare accounted for about 22.3% of all federal government expenditures in fiscal 2009. Medicare, the U.S. federal government's health care program for Americans 65 years or older, provided coverage to 45.5 million seniors in 2009 (up from 44.8 million the previous year). Federal Medicare costs for fiscal 2009, net of premiums paid by beneficiaries, were projected to be $430.8 billion. By 2030, the number of people covered by Medicare will balloon to about 78.0 million due to the massive number of Baby Boomers entering retirement age.

Medicaid is the federal government's health care program for low-income and disabled persons (including children), as well as certain groups of seniors in nursing homes. The federal government incurred Medicaid expenditures totalling $180.6 billion in fiscal 2006, $190.6 billion in 2007 and $201.4 billion in 2008. This amount was projected to reach $262.4 billion in 2009, but the actual amount may be higher due to temporary spending. At one time or another during 2007, 61.9 million people (about 20% of all Americans) were enrolled in Medicaid, and average enrolment for the year was 49.1 million. State governments incur large expenses for Medicaid benefits as well. For example, in 2007 alone the states spent $149 billion on Medicaid, over and above the federal expenditure. The Great Recession devastated the budgets of most of the 50 states. Tax revenues plummeted while demand for many state services rose. For example, as of October 2009, unemployment remained at a very high rate in the United States, just below 10%. This pushed more people into poverty, which increased the number of people eligible for Medicaid by several million. Federal stimulus spending included a temporary, $87 billion increase in Federal support for state Medicaid spending for the period October 2008 through December 2010.

Health spending in the U.S., at about 17.6% of Gross Domestic Product (GDP) in 2009, is projected to grow to about 20.3% by 2018 unless drastic reforms take place. Health care spending in America accounts for a larger share of GDP than in any other major industrialized country. Despite the incredible investment America continues to make in health care, 15.4% of people in the U.S. (46.3 million people) lacked health care coverage for the entire year of 2008. For some, insurance was unavailable or unaffordable. In other cases, a lack of insurance was due to a personal decision not to pay for it. For example, a significant number of the uninsured, about 8.2 million, were in households with annual incomes above $75,000. A large number of the uninsured, approximately 8 million, are illegal immigrants. According to the Centre for Immigration Studies, about 64% of illegal immigrants were uninsured in 2006. The actual number may be much higher today. A Kaiser Family Foundation study, "Medicaid and the Uninsured," dated February 2007, estimated that one-fourth of the uninsured are eligible for public programs but are not enrolled. These are largely low-income children, and in some cases their parents.

Clearly, the large number of people with no coverage is a problem, but there is little-to-no agreement as to what to do about it, if anything. As of late 2009, a sweeping health care reform and expansion of coverage was being pushed by the White House, to the extent of universal health care for nearly all Americans. Agreement among members of Congress as to the advisability, method and funding of such care is far from certain. At the same time, large numbers of Americans are relatively well satisfied with their current payors and methods of coverage. Likewise, many Americans and their legislators are extremely reluctant to see government take a lager role in the health care system, fearing runaway costs, bloated bureaucracies and less competition in the marketplace. Some feel that it is not the role of government to penalize patients or employers who do not purchase coverage. Others are reluctant to see America follow in the footsteps of nationalized medicine in neighbouring Canada, where patients for many types of common treatments are on extremely long waiting lists or find it next to impossible to receive certain types of advanced therapies. Yet another concern is that expensive treatments or drugs may be made off limits under a national system in order to restrain costs.

As of October 2009, the Obama Administration was pushing an agenda of health reform based on federally-mandated universal coverage. If such a bill is passed by Congress, it will likely contain some or all of the following elements:

1) Roughly 25 million of the current 45 million will remain uninsured. This includes 8 to 10 million illegal immigrants who will not be covered. (A small number have already obtained health coverage independently.) Among citizens and residents who reside in America legally, many will remain uninsured because they cannot afford even subsidized insurance, they make a personal choice not to participate (and thus face potential tax penalties) or otherwise fall through the cracks.
2) To help pay for a large portion of the federal cost of universal care, the government will attempt once again to cut waste and fraud in Medicare and reduce Medicare expenses overall.
3) Private health insurance companies, makers of medical equipment and other health industry firms will face higher taxes or fees to help pay for the new system.
4) Individuals who receive particularly generous work-related health insurance plans, or the companies that provide these plans, may be charged an excise tax. High income individuals who incur large medical expenses may receive lower tax write-offs for health care costs.

Health Expenditures Globally and in OECD Developed Nations

A comprehensive study published by the OECD (Organization for Economic Cooperation & Development), covering 33 nations with the world's most developed economies, found stark contrasts between health costs in the United States and those of other modern nations. In 2006 (the latest data available), the average of 33 OECD nations, such as France, Germany, Mexico, South Korea, Australia, etc., including the U.S., spent 8.9% of GDP on health care. The highest figures were in the U.S. with 15.3% of GDP, Switzerland 11.3% and France 11.1%. Health expenditures per capita for these 33 nations in 2006, on a purchasing power-adjusted basis (PPP), averaged $2,824.

Globally, the total prescription drug market was in the $600 billion range in 2009. Total health care expenditures around the world are difficult to determine, but $5 trillion would be a fair estimate for 2009. That would place health care at about 8% of global GDP, with health care expenditures per capita at about $800. This $5 trillion figure breaks down to approximately $2.4 trillion in the U.S., $2.3 trillion in non-U.S. OECD nations, and $0.3 trillion elsewhere around the world. (Outside the U.S. and the rest of the OECD, that would allow $50 per capita per year in lesser-developed nations.) Clearly, there is vast disparity in the availability and cost of health care among nations, as there is with personal income and GDP.

Health Care Costs in the US

Particularly in the U.S., continuous increases in the cost of health care, growing at rates far exceeding the rate of inflation in general, are hammering health consumers and payors of all types. Insurance providers continue to struggle to contain costs. Meanwhile, employers are hit hard by vast increases in the cost of providing coverage to employees and retirees. In 2009, employer-provided health care insurance coverage for a typical family cost an average of $13,375 for the year (up from $12,680 in 2008), according to a study conducted by the Kaiser Family Foundation, and $4,824 for single coverage for the year (up from $4,704). Employees were required to pay $3,515 of that cost for families and $779 for single coverage in 2009, on average, with employers picking up the balance. According to Kaiser, premium costs for family coverage rose 131% from 1999 through 2009, while the employee contribution rose 128%.

Many major employers are utilizing unique new programs in efforts to reduce employee illness, and thereby reduce costs. For example, the use of preventive care programs is growing, as is the use of employee education aimed at better managing the effects of diseases such as diabetes.

Smart employers are showing their employees how to use the Internet to obtain better information about diseases and prevention. Insurance providers are jumping on the Internet bandwagon as well. Some employers are even hiring in-house physicians and nurses to provide primary and preventive care in the work place.

Patients and insurance companies are also dealing with sticker shock over the nation's prescription drug costs. Other factors edging costs upward include expensive new medical technologies and patients' demands for greater plan flexibility in choosing doctors and specialists at their will. At the same time, hospitals and health systems write off massive amounts of revenues to bad debt, which increases costs for bill-paying patients.

In the wake of the tremendous growth of all aspects of the health care industry from the end of World War II onward, efficiency, competition and productivity were, regretfully, largely overlooked. Much of this occurred because employers plus federal and state governments paid such a large portion of the health care bill.

Physicians are caught between the desire to provide quality care and the desire for cost control on the part of payors, including PPOs, Medicare and Medicaid. The cost versus care debate has spawned an energetic movement to improve the quality of health care in the U.S., much of it centred on patients' rights, disease management, preventive health care and patient education. Nonetheless, wellness programs, preventive medicine and health education remain woefully inadequate.

A study released by the Milliken Institute in 2007 found that during the year 2003 (the year on which the study focused), 109 million Americans suffered from one or more of the most common, chronic diseases, including cancer, diabetes, heart disease, pulmonary conditions, mental disorders, stroke or hypertension. This means that more than one-third of all Americans had these conditions to one degree or another. The study estimated one year's cost of treatment of these conditions at $277 billion, but estimated lost economic productivity to be vastly higher at $1 trillion. In other words, lost work and lost output due to these illnesses reduced the nation's GDP by about 10%. These burdens could be vastly reduced through better consumer health practices and better preventive medicine. For example, obesity, lack of exercise and cigarette smoking are immense contributors to these diseases. The Centres for Disease Control and Prevention reported that medical costs for obesity-related diseases rose as high as $147 billion in 2008, compared to $74 billion in 1998.

Meanwhile, technology marches ahead relentlessly. Be sure to read our descriptions of such innovations as HIFU, Proton Beam Radiation Therapy and the newest biotech developments later in this chapter.

The American health care industry faces more challenges than ever, due to a number of significant factors:

- While the advent of managed care appeared to tame health care cost inflation during the early and mid-1990s, costs have been rising very rapidly since then.
- The number of Americans who are underinsured or are without any type of insurance coverage at all remains staggering at more than 45 million.

- The U.S. population is aging rapidly. At the same time, the life expectancy of seniors is extending. Senior citizens will place a significant strain on the health care system in coming years. America's 76 million surviving Baby Boomers begin turning 65 in 2011.
- The future obligations of Medicare and Medicaid are enough to cause vast problems for the federal budget for decades to come. The number of seniors covered by Medicare will continue to grow at an exceedingly high rate, from 45.5 million people in 2009 to 78.0 million in 2030.
- Likewise, costs for Medicaid, which is administered at the state level, have grown so rapidly that they are decimating state budgets and causing cuts in education and other vital state-provided services.
- The pharmaceuticals industry faces continued financial challenges. Pharmaceutical costs have created a large backlash among health consumers and payors. Patents for money-making, blockbuster drugs are expiring at a rapid rate, increasing competition from makers of generic drugs. At the same time, the drug industry remains under intense public scrutiny and is facing continued calls for increased government regulation.
- We are now entering what will long be remembered as the beginning of the Biotech Era. Breakthroughs in research for drug therapies are occurring at a rapid pace, creating financial and ethical challenges along with opportunities. Personalized medicine is beginning to emerge, but it remains to be seen who will be the early beneficiaries and who will pay the costs.
- Due to rising health care costs, employers large and small are straining under the financial burden of health care coverage expenses for current employees and retirees.
- Physicians, other care providers, pharmaceutical manufacturers and insurers face daunting pressure from litigation and potential claims regarding malpractice and denial of care. Lawsuit reform legislation has recently been enacted in many states with very promising results.
- Few Americans focus on leading healthy lifestyles that would prevent disease and cut both the amount and the cost of

medical care. Obesity-related illnesses are adding an immense amount to the nation's health care costs. A 2005 study led by researchers at Michigan State University estimated that 76% of Americans do not smoke, but only 40.1% maintain a healthy weight and only 22.2% exercise for at least 30 minutes, five times per week. Likewise, only 23.3% were found to eat the recommended amount of daily fruit and vegetable servings.

- The three biggest causes of death in the U.S. are heart disease, cancer and stroke. Nearly one-fourth of America's annual health expenditures go for treatment of these three killers.
- While only a relatively modest amount of money is spent on preventive medicine and health education, about 70% of health care funds are spent on chronic disease.

Health Care Industry Trends and Issues

Summary of Findings

While intense debate continues to swirl nationally around fundamental issues of equity and cost in the U.S. health care system, there seems little serious room for debate around a more narrow issue; e.g., the importance of health care to the local New York City economy and labour market. This FPI labour market update shows that:

1. The health care industry employs approximately 375,000 people in New York City, making it the city's number one sector in terms of employment, as well as the number one sector in every borough except Manhattan. Further, the industry overall has exhibited a growth pattern that persists through the ups and down of the wider economy.
2. The health care industry involves an extraordinarily wide array of occupations, including both direct service and non-direct service occupations. Many of these occupations are open to people with associates degrees or less. For example, according to the 1998 occupational data analyzed in this update, some 66,000 people were working in New York City as nursing aides, home health aides, and licensed practical nurses. An additional 46,000 or so people were employed in one of several health-related clerical support occupations, while some 16,000 worked as janitors, housekeepers, or food service workers.

3. The health sector labour market is both highly regulated and highly unionized, making for relatively well-paid jobs. In addition, certification requirements and terms of collective bargaining agreements on the direct patient care side of the labour market tend to create unusually well-defined career ladders.
4. The New York City health sector labour market is heavily female, and heavily non-white. For example, Equal Employment Opportunity Commission data on operations with over 100 employees (mostly hospitals) shows black females as the single largest employment category (at 28% of the work force), followed by white females (at 25%).
5. While employment growth in health care overall has been relatively steady, the decade of the 1990's produced substantial shifts in the internal composition of the health care work force. Employment growth moved away from large hospitals and toward outpatient, home care, and long-term care settings. At the same time, employment growth moved away from the public sector and toward the private/voluntary sector.

Employment Shifts: Steady but Uneven Growth

The decade of the 1990's saw pronounced shifts in the structure of the health care industry both nationally and locally. Just a few of the most important health care "megatrends" included the overall health system's shift toward managed care, hospital consolidation, cost containment in the Medicaid and Medicare programs, and deep funding and personnel cutbacks for New York City public hospitals.

The overall results of these shifts. Stated simply, employment growth moved away from large hospitals and toward outpatient, home care, and long-term care settings, and at the same time away from the public sector and toward the private/voluntary sector. Among major subcategories of employment, public hospitals were hardest-hit with a 33% decline, while home health care services saw the greatest gains with a more than 75% increase.

Despite the uneven employment growth, however, the overall health care sector grew by 14.1% over the course of the decade (from some 329,000 workers to some 376,000 workers). In comparison, overall New York City employment (private & public) grew only 3.3% between 1990 and 2000. Moreover, total health care employment continued to grow even through the sharp regional recession of the early 1990's that saw the loss of hundreds of thousands of jobs citywide. Health care is particular important as a stable anchor for the economies of the four boroughs outside Manhattan, as Note that many additional home care workers are counted under the Standard Industrial Classification code for social services.

Fiscal Policy Institute

At the peak of the year 2000 boom, the business services industry briefly eclipsed the health care sector as New York City's single largest private sector employer. Recent downsizing in the business services sector, however, has vaulted health care back into its traditional leading position.

What's most unique about health care, however, is the importance of the sector to the economy of every borough. The health care industry is the top private sector employer in the Bronx, Brooklyn, Queens and Staten Island. The public health care sector by itself would be the third largest employer in the Bronx if it were incorporated into Compared to other industries, the health care sector is unusually regulated, monitored, and structured.

This is true in at least four general senses:

First, on the direct patient care side of the industry, employment ladders are defined by an extensive and legally binding system of professional certifications. This characteristic makes pathways for advancement more clear than in most other industries, and places an emphasis on the importance of educational institutions granting the certifications. The system also seems to have the general effect of both raising and buffering wage levels.

Second, the industry as a whole is highly unionized. Unionization tends to formalize employment and wage levels, and makes health care unions important institutional players in the labour market. Third, health care costs and reimbursements to providers are regulated. This is especially true of Medicare and Medicaid reimbursements. Finally, health care providers themselves must be licensed by the State's Department of Health.

The State provides operating certificates to (and also reviews any service provision or facility changes carried out by) the following entities:

diagnostic and treatment centres; certified home health care agencies; hospices; hospitals; residential care facilities (nursing homes); and long-term home health care programs. In addition, there are "licensed" home health care agencies, which are regulated by a separate branch of the Department of Health.

Fiscal Policy Institute

Labour market demographics: a heavily female and minority work force 1997 Equal Employment Opportunity Commission (EEOC) data shows that health care workers in New York City are majority female and majority non-white.

The specific ethnicity/sex breakdown of New York City private sector health care workers. Black females represent the single largest category, followed by white females. Note that since the EEOC data used for this table only covers entities over 100 employees, it may be best interpreted as a reflection of large institutions like hospitals.

Befitting its size, the health sector includes an unusually large array of distinct occupations. These occupations include both direct service and non-direct service work. They also include work that requires different kinds and levels of qualification and training – jobs from surgeon to stock clerk. All in all, the State Department of Labour lists exactly 300 separate occupations connected in some way to health care. More than 50 of these occupations involve 1,000 or more industry workers. The occupational matrix for the health care sector involves a lot more than doctors and nurses (though note that RN's are the single largest employment category and that substantial opportunities exist in this field given the current nursing shortage). For example, according to the OES data, some 66,000 people were working in New York City as nursing aides, home health aides, and licensed practical nurses in 1998. An additional 46,000 people were employed in one of the several clerical support occupations listed, while some 16,000 worked as janitors, housekeepers, or food service workers.

The list could go on, but the point remains that the health care labour market is highly diverse, and includes large numbers of low to moderate skill-level occupations.

Occupational Wage Scale: Many Middle-income Jobs

According to 1998 Occupational Employment Survey data, the vast majority of NYC health practitioners and technicians on the direct service side of the industry are earning at least $15 per hour. Some of the highest paid positions include physicians and surgeons ($48.58 per hour) and registered nurses ($28.95 per hour). Licensed practical nurses earn a median hourly wage of $16.25 in comparison. Pharmacy technicians are the lowest paid direct service health care workers, earning a median wage of $10.27.

Getting a bead on wage levels in the non-direct service side of the industry is somewhat more difficult, as the OES data lists median wages for individual occupations on an all-industry basis only. So, for example, while we know that the median hourly wage for food preparation workers citywide is $7.67, it is difficult to determine without further research whether health care food service workers get paid more or less. We can say as a generalization, however, that high unionization levels would tend to point to higher wages relative to the same occupation in non-unionized industries.

Occupational Projections

While a detailed discussion of occupational projections would be beyond the scope of this update, it's worth noting that the New York State Department of Labour projects significant growth in nearly all direct health service occupations. Such projections – always a tricky proposition – are perhaps more reliable in health care than for other more cyclical industries.

A particularly important issue, with quite substantial public health as well as economic implications, relates to growth in the number of registered nurses versus nurses aides. In our State of Working New York report, FPI has already pointed out a statewide trend toward substitution of nurses aides for higher paid and higher-skilled registered nurses. While the current "nursing shortage" may signal that this worrisome trend has for the time being played itself out, official employment projections show much faster expected growth rates for job classifications such as home health aides, nursing assistants, and medical assistants than for RN's.

Medical Market Overview & Industry Trends

Growing Population & Healthcare Spending

The worldwide healthcare market is influenced by a number of demographic trends, including the following:

- Growing and Aging Population: The U.S. Census Bureau predicts that the majority of the U.S. "baby boom" population (28% of the total U.S. population) will begin to turn 65 between 2010 and 2020.
- Consumer expectations for improved healthcare are increasing in both developed and developing countries.
- Reimbursement and coverage of medical expenses by insurances companies and employers are on the decline—customers/ patients have to contribute more money.
- Technology is giving rise to new clinical therapies, which in turn are addressing more and more medical ailments and aiding in earlier diagnosis and prevention of diseases.

As shown in Figure 1, healthcare spending per capita has gown significantly across the world. In the U.S., it has increased from $144 per capita in 1960 to almost $4,400 by 1999. The U.S. per capita spending is projected to grow to $7,500 by 2008. Equipment suppliers understand that in order to be successful in the medical market they have to be focused and successful in the U.S.

Figure 1. Growing World-Wide Healthcare Spending Per Capita

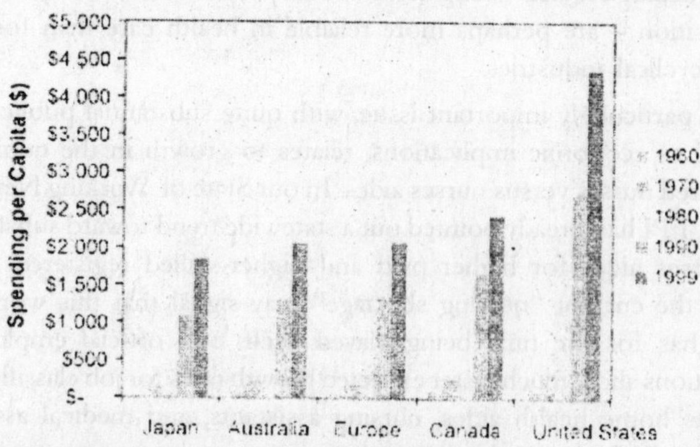

Technology Fuels Healthcare Productivity

In the next 10 years, the healthcare market will focus on early diagnosis, digitized patient information that can be accessed from numerous locations, and "total solution" selling that contributes to healthcare productivity gains.

Early diagnosis and prevention is enabled by emerging diagnostic technologies. For example, positron emission tomography (PET) is used to detect many kinds of cancer with great accuracy.

A "paperless" hospital is another emerging trend. Digital patient records enable doctors to access patients' records—wherever the doctor is. In a digitized hospital, healthcare providers do not have to wait days for an x-ray to "come back from the lab" because the x-ray machine is digital and the image is instantly available.

Hospitals are also moving away from purchasing point solutions and toward buying equipment from different vendors that is interoperable and that has a uniform user interface. Hospitals are developing internal networks that connect all diagnostic equipment that feeds all patient information (e.g., computed tomography (CT) scans, x-rays, positron emission tomography (PET) scans) over a network to data storage servers for instant access. This drives medical equipment vendors to develop interoperable equipment that has a uniform user interface. In effect, vendors are beginning to sell complete solutions that include not only the diagnostic equipment but also the data storage servers as well as the interface software.

All these trends lead to an increase in healthcare productivity—this means more patients can be put through the healthcare system by using better, faster diagnostic equipment, which leads to early ailment diagnosis and treatment. When the paperless hospital becomes a reality, productivity is further enhanced because of instant patient test results and records access.

Programmable Logic Advantage

Majority of medical products have some type of semiconductor in it. In fact, the semiconductor content continues to increase in these myriad of products. Programmable Logic Devices (PLDs) continue to see a much higher rate of adoption than other semiconductor types. PLDs offer a viable and powerful alternative to both ASICs and ASSPs in medical equipment development. PLDs eliminate the up-front non-recurring engineering (NRE) costs and minimum order quantities associated with ASICs, and the costly risks of multiple silicon iterations through the capability to be reprogrammed as needed during the design process. When compared to ASSPs, PLDs provide the design flexibility and board integration opportunities to differentiate against competing medical equipment manufacturers. Additionally, PLDs can be upgraded in the field as standards evolve or requirements change. Also, the ability to re-use a common hardware platform allows designers to create differentiated systems which support a variety of feature sets with one basic design, resulting in reduced manufacturing costs. Whether designing a CT machine or patient monitoring equipment, programmable logic is a flexible, low-risk path to successful system design—offering optimum cost efficiencies while providing value-added differentiating capabilities versus other medical equipment manufacturers.

Last but not the least, PLDs have a very long life cycle and protect customers against product obsolescence, which is very critical in the medical industry because of long product cycles.

Medical Applications for Programmable Logic

By using programmable logic, engineers can cost-effectively develop leading-edge equipment for many applications in the medical space, including:

- Diagnostic imaging: X-ray, ultrasound, CT, magnetic resonance imaging (MRI), and nuclear/PET.
- Electromedical: Patient monitoring, life support, and anesthesia equipment.
- Cardiac Rhythm Management (CRM): Pacing systems, implantable cardiac defibrillators (ICDs), and automatic external defibrillators (AEDs).
- Life Science & Hospital Equipment: Lab instrumentation, radiation equipment, and various hospital equipment.

The Altera Advantage

Altera gives medical electronics equipment manufacturers a competitive edge. Altera's solutions are currently found in various medical end-applications worldwide; they combine a wide range of PLDs with optimized intellectual property (IP) cores, hard and soft microprocessors, powerful design software, and a variety of development kits to create a complete, easy-to-use design platform.

Altera's PLDs, including the Stratix® II, Stratix GX, and Cyclone™ II FPGA families, which include a rich feature set of logic, memory, dedicated digital signal processing (DSP) blocks, and I/O standard support, which give medical equipment designers all the tools they need to win in this highly competitive market.

Altera® PLDs offer medical electronics equipment manufacturers a flexible, cost-effective, obsolescence-free path to successful system design. Some of the opportunities that Altera offers manufacturers are:

- Cost reduction by avoiding ASICs' extensive NREs and minimum ordering costs,
- Time-to-market advantage by avoiding the lengthy and risky ASIC development cycle,
- Cost reduction and differentiation by integrating multiple ASSP functions into FPGAs,
- Reprogrammability during the design process and after equipment is in the field,
- Reusability of one hardware platform for various systems with one basic design,
- Adaptability to multiple industry standards and protocols.

Intellectual Property

Off-the-shelf IP cores that have been optimized for Altera's products can reduce engineering costs and shorten time-to-market. Standard interfaces and IP cores are available from Altera or approved Altera Megafunction Partners Program (AMPP℠) partners. Prior to licensing, the OpenCore® evaluation feature allows users to evaluate Altera MegaCore® functions and AMPP megafunctions at no cost.

Altera designs, supports, and sells Altera MegaCore functions. All MegaCore functions have been rigorously tested and optimized for the highest performance and lowest cost in Altera PLDs.

Development Kits

Altera and its partners offer a variety of development kits to support the development and verification of system-on-a-programmable-chip (SOPC) designs.

Emerging Trends in Health Care Industry – Medical Tourism

It has often been said that "medical tourism 'is nothing new. This is true. It is also true that since man has been a nomad he, or she has always been looking for greener pastures and a better life, quality of life or services than they have presently available. So is it with medical care.

The "baby boomer" generation is ending. So is or has the birth rate in industrialized countries. Who will physically provide the service? Who will pay to it? Medical or home care is a labour and attention intensive service. In Italy now – once now for large families – people pay to "rent "grandparents. There certainly are no valued, privileged children, who in many societies are given the revered task and privilege of caring for aged parents. Never mind the money involved, in most of the wealth, industrialized countries there will not be the staff to care for the aged, or the ill. It is not as if an electronic chip or even robots can ever do these tasks. Each situation is different, each unique.

Hence it is no startling fact that medical tourism will grow and grow and will become a major growth industry. More and more baby boomers, many with means, some with benefits and lesser means. It is estimated that these numbers, within North America, – US and Canada, Europe, Australia and New Zealand will approximate 250 million people. The health care system – and overall budgets of these countries – whether they provide health care universally by the government purse – such as Canada or privately – as in the USA – will not be able to provide either the resources – labour or funds for quick, prompt, quality health care. What makes more sense than medical tourism – both from a cost and logistical standpoint where treatment and labour is available and at a reasonable cost?

The Issue: Emerging Outsourcing Trends in the Healthcare Industry

As the scope of potentially outsourced functions and processes in the healthcare industry continues to expand, EquaTerra anticipates market growth could be even faster than some project. Buyers across the healthcare industry are facing acute cost pressures that make business as usual impossible. Thus, they must accelerate efforts to gain greater process efficiency and effectiveness. These efforts are facilitated by improved and consolidated IT systems, greater automation and selfservice capabilities, and some amount of labour cost reduction. This involves changing the service delivery model for back-office functions as well as core healthcare administration and operational functions and processes.

Healthcare Provider and Payer Market Trends

Healthcare providers are hospitals, nursing homes, long-term care facilities, physician and other professional services groups, and specialized therapeutic enterprises. While outsourcing is occurring in this market segment, it is not doing so at the scale or scope seen in other segments of the market, given its more fragmented and decentralized nature. On the provider side, outsourcing is more likely to occur at the corporate level around back-office IT and business process functions and processes.

The healthcare payer segment of the market is becoming more aggressive in its pursuit of new service delivery models for core business processes. Healthcare payer organizations include commercial insurers, government insurer programs, not-for profit insurers and benefit management firms.

The commercial payer segment has recently experienced consolidation, primarily due to competition for bargaining leverage with providers, as well as a focus on the scale associated with consolidated operations. Additionally, the rapidly evolving nature and complexity of health plan product lines are changing in response to increases in healthcare service expenses, and support and customer satisfaction requirements. These and other factors have produced the following conditions:

Merger, acquisition and divestiture activity has increased demands on technical and support infrastructures, further driving the need for change.

- The costs and infrastructure to update and maintain these systems is driving the requirement for innovation and transformation. Many of the larger payers have remained with legacy hardware and proprietary or internally developed applications that no longer meets their needs. They are looking for ways to reduce costs and minimize expenses for all sales, general and administrative (SG&A) processes.
- The growing complexity of offerings, and government and regulatory changes, have increased delivery and support requirements.
- Governmental payers have moved much faster than commercial payers in sourcing their operational support requirements. This should encourage a "follow the leader" mentality.
- Confidentiality and privacy issues around personal health data has caused an increase in expenses associated with the delivery of services.

Overall, the healthcare industry is characterized by older systems that did the job a decade or so ago, but have not kept up with the times. Consequently, payer organizations have taken a "we will patch it now and fix it later" approach. But they are now starting to look at functions and processes that are less core to their business and are thus more viable candidates for outsourcing, like broader elements of policy maintenance and claims administration. Additionally, they are assessing speed-to-market and cost reduction in those areas that offer value and payback to the organization through an outsourcing lens.

The operating model of many large healthcare firms can complicate their back-office outsourcing management efforts. According to one EquaTerra advisor:

> *"Healthcare firms are very driven by cost reduction and capital avoidance, even though most say they want to make the back-office more strategic. It is all about the money." Said another EquaTerra advisor: "Cost structure in healthcare has shifted radically, and governmental regulations, the ability for consumers to become and remain informed, the Internet, new health plan creation and execution, price controls and real-time adjudication are all putting pressure on margins."*

Get to What Matters. How are Healthcare Buyers Responding?

The healthcare industry is now facing a wake-up call in terms of slumping stock prices, additional competition, regulatory pressure and an informed consumer that is demanding the best service at the lowest possible cost. For these reasons, payers must become more competitive and cost effective. Given their experience in forging and managing complex business partner relationships, they should view outsourcing as another example of this type of partnership-oriented relationship. The healthcare industry faces unique outsourcing challenges, however, because of application and system integration challenges exacerbated by the highly regulated nature of the market. First, firms typically have older systems and applications in place. Second, there is overstaffing in back-office functions. Third, the industry has gone through change, and many of the firms have not adapted to the evolving business climate. Fourth, healthcare buyers are facing more financial challenges and need to continue to innovate and transform. Outsourcing is a catalyst for changing behaviour and reducing "the fat."

EquaTerra recently polled the top outsourcing service providers in the U.S. healthcare payer space and, coupled with its own direct market experiences, mapped the level of buyer demand across functions and processes specific to the healthcare payer space. The demand level ranking is based on a one-to-10 scale, with one equating to low buyer demand and 10 indicating high demand levels. Process areas that exhibited the greatest level of buyer demand included claims and enrolment data entry and claims adjudication. Further, there was growing demand in a variety of other functional and process areas including emerging knowledge services, such as reporting, planning and related analytics.

EquaTerra and the outsourcing service providers also assessed the market maturity of providers delivering services into these areas. Characteristics of market maturity on the supply side include the size of the installed client base, the depth, sophistication and standardization of the service offerings, and the degree to which the offerings are formalized as opposed to assembled and delivered on an ad-hoc basis. Figure 1 illustrates these maturity levels, as well as the gap between buyer demand and supplier maturity.

Overall, we see that buyer demand is outpacing supplier maturity, which is characteristic of an outsourcing market in more of a demand-pull than a supplier-push mode. This is due to the recent increase in buyer demand levels, coupled with a supplier lag in developing and expanding service offerings as a result of historically weak demand for outsourcing services in this market sector.

EquaTerra also polled healthcare outsourcing service providers on the leading drivers for growth in outsourcing, particularly around emerging BPO areas. Not surprisingly, cost reduction was the leading driver. However, citation levels in healthcare were even higher than those usually found in other industries, scoring 90 percent among service providers polled. This reflects the cost pressures facing U.S. healthcare payers today. Process improvement as a driver ranked second. Interestingly, cost avoidance scored near the bottom, as did access to new technologies. The low scoring for accessing technologies is in part a function of assessing BPO versus ITO drivers. While achieving cost reductions is obviously critical to U.S. healthcare payer organizations, they should not lose sight of ancillary and complementary opportunities to improve process performance, or overstates on pursuing levels of cost reduction that compromise the integrity of the business processes involved.

How are Outsourcing Service Providers Responding?

Leading outsourcing service providers that target the healthcare industry are generally in sync with EquaTerra relative to outsourcing trends. These providers focus on how to enable broad, global outsourcing efforts and place strong emphasis on moving beyond traditional "lift and shift" efforts to those that embed transformation and process improvement into the initiative.

Healthcare outsourcing service providers that have traditionally targeted the ITO and back-office BPO market segments have, in many cases, been slow to expand offerings into emerging BPO and KPO areas. Or, their efforts in these areas have not been leveraged or made repeatable across their client portfolio. Recently, however, legacy multi-national outsourcing service providers have become more proactive in targeting these areas, and the leading Indian service providers that focus on the healthcare payer space have also been aggressive in pursuing these newer areas.

EquaTerra polled healthcare outsourcing service providers on what they believed to be the key attributes required to effectively compete in the emerging healthcare payer BPO space. As expected, industry knowledge was cited as the key attribute to compete in this market. EquaTerra also appreciates and supports the citings of the importance of cultural fit between the buyer and service provider and the need to take a collaborative approach to the BPO effort. Highlighting the increasing global nature of the healthcare services market, the requirement for offshore and global service delivery capabilities also ranked high.

While past positive client experiences ranked lower, EquaTerra attributes this to the fact that, for deals in emerging BPO areas involving multi-national service providers, buyers have typically worked with these same providers in prior ITO engagements. Most Indian service providers in this market segment also have previously performed ITO work for the buyers. In both cases, buyers have a positive track record with the outsourcing service provider used in the new areas. EquaTerra feels this past experience is an important aspect to account for when entering into emerging and more complex BPO efforts. Overall, outsourcing service providers in the healthcare and healthcare payer markets are more aggressively investing in and expanding their outsourcing – especially their BPO and KPO – offerings. They must, however, remain sensitive to some of the specific challenges healthcare buyers face. Missteps in outsourcing deals are always problematic, but can become even more so when healthcare services and patient care and information are involved.

The Advisor Perspective – critical Points to Consider

Healthcare organizations that have not recently done so should update and reassess their strategy and action plan for use of alternative service delivery models for both back-office and core operating functions and processes. Emerging areas of BPO, if successfully executed, can play a positive and growing role in helping healthcare organizations address the serious challenges they are facing today. While buyers should use caution when exploring and assessing emerging BPO areas, the market is expanding and rapidly maturing, and what was premature in the past could be ready for primetime today. Healthcare buyers should also view the increased use of emerging BPO and KPO services as part of a service continuum. Some of this work will always be performed internally. Some activities are or will become more suitable for a shared services or offshore captive environment, and others are best suited for outsourcing. Buyers need to have a flexible global sourcing delivery model and framework that continually assesses the best delivery model for different services. For further insights, follow this link to access the EquaTerra Perspective "How to Design and Optimize Global Services Delivery Models." Operationally, buyers must focus on the critical, but often misunderstood or under-supported, areas of outsourcing transition and governance. As the number of outsourcing efforts and relationships grow, buyers must adequately invest in their outsourcing governance capabilities and strive to take a portfolio approach to managing these efforts. Outsourcing service providers must also become more sensitive to the governance needs of their clients, and better support relationships that can span multiple service providers.

Conclusion

The healthcare industry around the world, and especially in the United States, is under extreme pressure to reduce costs while also expanding services and maintaining high service levels. Addressing inefficiencies in delivering both back-office as well as core operational services can play a key role in addressing these challenges. While the healthcare industry has historically lagged other industries in its uptake of alternative service delivery models, this has begun to change. Healthcare payers, in particular, are more aggressively pursuing a broader outsourcing agenda that includes emerging and strategic business and knowledge process outsourcing services. Outsourcing service providers targeting the healthcare space – both legacy multinational service providers and India-based firms moving beyond IT into business services – are starting to develop more targeted and compelling outsourcing offerings. While there are alternatives to outsourcing, as well as many complexities to consummating it successfully, healthcare buyers are heeded to carefully reexamine their outsourcing strategy and plans in light of prevailing industry conditions.

3

Assessing the Impacts of Wellness Tourism

Introduction

Tourism is the fastest growing industry internationally with destinations not only in industrialised countries, but also in less developed countries in East Africa, Central America and South East Asia. Developing countries which were previously seen as less likely destinations or were closed to tourism altogether are now considering the marketing of their natural and/or cultural attractions to receive a share of this global industry. Adventure tourism, and cultural tourism take advantage of this development. Each year more exotic places are offered on the tourism market for those who have seen everything else, or prefer destinations 'off the beaten track'. The close contact with locals in isolated areas and their customs seems to be one of the main attractions of developing countries, and this is used extensively in marketing strategies.

At the same time, the scientific study of tourism has developed such that tertiary education institutions worldwide offer degree courses in tourism studies. The perspectives and approaches one can adopt to study the topic are as diverse as tourism itself. Jafari (1990) presented an overview of disciplines and approaches in the study of tourism. The disciplines offered are of considerable diversity but 'health' does not rate a mention in this model of approaches.

Tourism and Health

Literature dealing with the combination of tourism and health abundantly covers health aspects of travellers to particular locations, health education, medical aspects of travel preparation, health problems in travellers or in returning tourists, and economic or administrative consequences of tourists' ill health. In short, 'Tourism and Health' usually focuses on the travellers' wellbeing. However, despite this necessary and applaudable development in protecting travellers from health problems, one needs to consider that there are people on the other end of the journey who may be subjected to a change in their health status as well, due to visiting fellow humans. 'Tourism and Health' rarely includes the hosts in its consideration. Tourism's potential impact on the health of the local host communities can be direct or indirect. One example of direct impact is the possible transmission of diseases from travellers to locals. Nowadays, the emergence of new infectious diseases or the reemergence of diseases thought to be eradicated are causing great concern, and travel is a major contributor to their spread. Lea (1988) rightly pointed out that tourism has the dual effect of promoting the provision of improved health care in Third World destinations but, in addition, acts as a vehicle to spread some forms of disease.

Other possible direct health impacts are chronic diseases or disabilities, and accidents causing injuries or deaths of local tourist guides in the course of their employment in tourism. Indirect impacts can be attributed to the social, cultural, environmental and economic impacts which are the usual focus of accounts on tourism impact.

Methodology

Aim of the Study

The aim of this study was to ascertain the current knowledge on health impacts of tourism in developing countries, to provide information on gaps in this knowledge as a baseline for future research, to identify research topics which could be investigated by researchers from health, tourism and other disciplines, and to propose elements of a framework for the assessment of health impacts of tourism.

Design of the Study

First, a literature review was conducted. Publications related to the topic were identified in the fields of health and tourism. A few sources were located through networking with people working in disciplines pertinent to the subject. The key areas for the search were: travellers' health; tourism and health; tourism in developing countries; economic, environmental, sociocultural impacts of tourism; public health; and tropical medicine. The literature was reviewed to identify any references made in relation to the topic under study to recognise unresearched issues and, if possible, to obtain ideas for an innovative approach of investigation. Only publications in English, German and Spanish were sought and utilised.

Second, a field trip was undertaken to test the findings from the literature analysis against fieldwork in Easter Island/Chile and Peru. First, a range of tourism destinations (including some very popular and others only visited by few individual travellers) were examined with the aim of detecting evidence of positive or negative impacts of tourism on the health of the local population. The emphasis here was on potential environmental impacts; potential health hazards due to running a tourism destination, e.g., construction, equipment, transport; and possible transmission of diseases. Second, semi-structured interviews were conducted with health practitioners, tour operators and conservationists to elicit their assessment of tourism's health impacts. Discussions centred around medical aspects, such as changes in disease pat terns, introduction of previously nonendemic infectious diseases, and work place health and safety aspects; tour operators' recollection of possible anecdotal evidence of health impacts; and conservationists' views on tourism in environmentally fragile destinations.

Tourism's Health Impact-a Review of the Literature

The Impact of Travel on the Health of the Hosts: An Historical Overview

Travel is inseparably linked with human existence. Historical accounts of travel and migrations as the main source of epidemics are numerous. The Roman Empire was struck by the bubonic plague, spread along the trade routes of the time, leading eventually to the dramatic and largest epidemic of the 'Black Death' in the 14th century. It had started in the Gobi desert in 1320 and reached Europe 30 years later, where it is estimated to have killed one-third to half of the population in some European countries.

Venetian authorities who observed outbreaks after the arrival of ships from the East assumed that travel may have to do with the spread of the plague. The first regulations governing the arrival of ships were introduced in Venice and Rhodos in 1377, detaining ship, passengers, crew and cargo at a distance for 40 days ('quaranta giorni' became quarantine) before being allowed into the harbour.

The conquest of the 'New World' is probably the best known event in history which has been linked to the spread of fatal diseases to non-immune peoples. It was clear from the first written accounts of the Spanish invasion of the Americas in the 15th century that the native peoples were not only killed in battle and through hard labour or physical punishment but also succumbed to a great extent to introduced infectious diseases to which they lacked immunity. In some parts of the New World, infections such as smallpox and influenza reduced the native population dramatically. When this lead to an acute shortage in the work force, the ensuing slave trade from West Africa lead to an even greater range of diseases. The arriving ships, for example, not only brought the yellow fever virus but also its vector *Aedes aegypti*.

Similar transmissions occurred in the Pacific region some hundred years later. It is not clear from historic travel logs if early explorers were aware of their potential role in the transmission of diseases. Beaglehole (1934) in his account of the exploration of the Pacific clearly focused on the exploratory aspect of journeys into the area with only one mention of "the visits of European ships destroyed utterly and horribly its primitive freedom from pestilence".

Captain James Cook seems to have been the first to actively at tempt the prevent ion of a transmission of infectious diseases from crew to native populations by confining any person found to be diseased to the ship while the rest of the crew was permitted to go ashore. Apart from syphil is, other often deadly diseases such as measles and dysentery were transmitted from Europeans to native people.

Uncertainty about the transmission of diseases did not seem to exist 100 years later when it was purposefully employed as the following excerpt illustrates. In 1860, three captains arrived at Port Resolution on Tanna (Vanuatu) to occupy the island. Alexander (1895) cited Rev. John Paton reporting: Our watchword is, "Sweep these creatures away and let white men occupy the soil". They then invited a chief by the name of Kapuku on board one of their vessels, promising him a present, and confined him for twenty-four hours without food in the hold among natives ill with measles, and finally sent him ashore without a present to spread the disease. The measles thus introduced spread fearfully, and decimated the *population of the island.* Epidemics occurring in isolated 'virgin' populations, i.e., populations without immunity to a certain disease, are not confined to the Middle Ages. Forty years ago on Easter Island, Heyerdahl (1958) observed the influenza epidemic which accompanied the arrival of the yearly supply ship from the Chilean mainland:

> *The conongo was the natives' great terror-the annual influenza epidemic which always accompanied contact with the mainland. It came and went with the regularity of clockwork. After the ship's visit it always raged through the village for a month or two. It got into chests, heads, and stomachs: everyone was ill, and there was always a toll of human lives before the conongo passed and left the people in peace for the rest of the year.*

A mumps epidemic in 1957 on St. Lawrence Island (Alaska) was started by a boy returning from the mainland after undergoing surgery. Similar outbreaks on other 'virgin' island populations in Alaska occurred in 1965 and 1967-68. Although it is generally argued that it is unlikely that there are any 'virgin' populations left due to the contacts of people around the world, partial or selective immunity still allows the transmission of diseases by people on the move. Today, business and leisure travel is claimed to be the driving force in the spread of disease and the (re)emergence of infectious diseases.

Potential Indirect Impacts of Tourism on the Health of the Host Community

The impacts of tourism are a popular topic in the literature, usually covering the economic, environmental and social aspects. However, few discourses are based on research evidence. Cater (1987) attributed this to the difficulty of studying impacts due to their complexity. An additional problem is that social and cultural dimensions are difficult to quantify and, therefore, out of reach of most researchers employing conventional methods. Using the tourism literature as a baseline, one can develop the arguments further and identify ways in which these impacts can affect health in positive or negative ways.

Economic impacts affecting health Economic benefits are certainly the primary cause for the promotion of tourism in developing countries. The benefits are mainly seen in the gain of (often desperately needed) term problem is water pollution. The following examples are taken from a compilation by Maurer (1992). Frequently, tourism developments in developing countries do not have an appropriate system for sewage and waste management and they use rivers and the sea for disposal. This can pose two problems. First, fish and molluscs eaten by the local population as a source of protein may be unsuitable for consumption due to pollutants deposited in these animals. Second, swimming in polluted water can lead to ear, eye, skin and gastrointestinal infections in even epidemic proportions. Herbicides used on golf courses have been shown to pollute the freshwater supply and impact on health directly or through food obtained from the water. The pollution of waterholes in deserts through the tourists' use of soap and shampoo poses another problem.

Redirection and overuse of freshwater for hotels, swimming pools and landscaping purposes in tourism facilities can lead to the local population having less or no clean drinking water which in turn puts them at risk of contracting diseases. Lack of water also impacts on the local agriculture leading to poor crops and a scarcity of food.

There is a need to substantiate examples such as those mentioned above. Very little research evidence supports numerous anecdotal accounts of environmental problems caused, at least partially, by tourism. More specific investigations into pollution and redirect ion of drinking water need to be carried out. Also, resulting health problems need to be documented carefully to support strategies for improvement.

Garbage generated by tourists poses another public health hazard for host communities as, apart from its unaesthetic appearance, it creates breeding tourist areas in Argentina, 96.3% of respondents to a survey claimed that tourism was to blame for increasing costs, but the results have to be treated cautiously as the study had only a return rate of 23%. There seems to be a paucity of research supporting anecdotal accounts of economic impacts of tourism. Research needs to be conducted into changes of living costs and their effect on locals. For example, D'Sousa (1985) reported from Goa that, in addition to a lack of improved health, local tax payers paid for tourists' free medical care.

A different type of negative economic impact on health was reported by Loval and Feuerstein (1992): "There is said to be a drain of trained nurses away from the health sector in some Pacific areas as they seek jobs in tourism". No other reference could be found supporting this claim. Considering the expenses of training health personnel, it is important to know if this is a common trend in developing countries where salaries of health professionals are known to be very low. The problem of locals leaving their traditional activities of fishing or farming for seemingly more lucrative work in the tourism industry has been presented in the literature.

Environmental Impacts Affecting Health

Unfortunately, tourism seems to be the culprit for a number of environmental problems that pose health hazards to local communities. A serious longforeign exchange and the creation of employment. Archer (1986) claimed that "tourism generates a considerable secondary economic activity in a destination country" with income percolating to the public sector, business and private households. Consequently, locals' possession of foreign or local currency earned in the tourism industry enables them to purchase more or better food leading to a better health status (although more money may also mean more junk food). It also allows them access to better health facilities if earnings from tourism have been used to improve the services. Hundt (1996) presented Jamaica as an example where tourism development has lead to prosperity and improved health of the population.

However, the same author admitted that "more important is the realisation that the profits of tourism generally are not used to improve the health status of the poor, marginalised natives in host countries". The following example from Peru may illustrate this statement. In 1995, the country received almost half a million tourists. The area around Cusco is certainly one of the main attractions of the country and the majority of foreign tourists include a visit in their itinerary. Tourism generated income, however, does not seem to percolate to everybody in the general population in the area if the nutritional status of children in the Cusco Health District (as investigated by Wolff, Pérez, Gibson, Lopez, Peniston and Wolff, 1985) is taken as one outcome criterion. Tourism development may eventually lead to increasing living costs. In two sites for disease-carrying arthropods and rodents. Harrington (1993) reports the pollution of the Amazon through tourists. In 1980, the South American Explorers Club collected approximately 400 kg of unburnable garbage on the Inka trail in Peru. An aspect not yet located in the literature is the possible danger of injuries (cuts, lacerations) caused by garbage. This may be of particular concern if people contract infections but are unable to access or pay for the treatment required.

Clearing for tourism developments or sports facilities causes serious ecological changes and can lead to flooding or landslides destroying crops, homes and lives. Apart from that, mosquitos which are potential vectors for diseases tend to move into cleared areas. When people (locals and tourists) move in to utilise the cleared land, they are at risk of contracting serious diseases such as malaria or yellow fever if the mosquitos are infected. The cutting of firewood along the world's trekking routes adds to the deterioration of forest already damaged due to cutting of wood for domestic purposes as can easily be seen in Nepal or Peru. At present, no statistics could be found indicating the exact extent of destruction of forest or bushland for tourism purposes.

On the other hand, tourism can have positive environmental effects, when generated income is used for environmental planning and education, or for the construct ion of appropriate sewage systems. Investing in the conservation of natural areas and safe tourist facilities in these areas ultimately benefits the physical and mental well-being of locals and visitors alike. Hellen (1995) argued that research into tourism in the developing world "opens up the prospect that global tourism may itself become a vehicle for investment in environmental health programs and securing improved health for all". So far, there is a striking paucity of examples supporting this vision.

Sociocultural Impacts Affecting Health

This third major category of impacts is similarly widely discussed in the literature. Generally, it is stated that tourist-host encounters may lead to better understanding between cultures, remove prejudices and promote cultural pride eventually leading to the preservation or a renaissance of the local art/craft. Despite these positive arguments, it seems that tourism's impact on society and culture in developing countries is mainly perceived as negative. It is acknowledged that social and cultural change is a phenomenon attributed to modernisation in general but it seems that the frequent and fast exchange of encounters of people from different backgrounds accelerates this change at a rate not always favourable for the host communities. Obvious health problems accompanying these changes originate in the appearance or increase of prostitution, alcoholism, drug use and violence.

Also, lifestyle and food preferences of visitors seem to be imitated often leading to higher body weight, greater percentage of body fat, and high blood pressure, conditions previously unknown in these communities. Farrell (1982) named Hawaii and other areas in the Pacific as an example of areas where these changes occurred. Little additional research evidence on unhealthy lifestyles due to the influence of tourism could be located.

Mental health problems are less frequently discussed. Changes in the traditional lifestyle or loss of identity through changes in social and cultural values can put a considerable mental strain on people. Negative implications through changes in social and cultural values include potential mental health problems. Currently, it is unclear how many confirmed diagnoses of mental alterations could be attributed to long-term impacts of tourism.

Physical and mental health problems caused by the forceful removal of peoples to make way for tourism are equally neglected in the literature. Examples of this practice can be found around the globe. A more recent case was reported from Botswana where Kalahari Bushmen appealed to the UN to save them from being evicted from their ancestral lands which were to be used for tourism purposes. Forced relocations of indigenous people in the Peruvian Amazon area are a common method to make space for tourist lodges. Research into changes of locals' health status is very scarce. Numerous questions arise when evaluating anecdotal evidence on sociocultural impacts. An important issue that needs investigation is if changes to lifestyle, the adoption of unhealthy food preferences, increase in prostitution, alcohol and drug use, and violence can clearly be attributed to tourism, or if they are symptoms of 'development' and modernisation. It is also of interest to ascertain if tourists engage in activities contradicting local rules and taboos, and of what type and frequency these actions are. Additionally, there has to be a closer investigation into the occurrence of people's forceful removal from their home and land for tourism purposes.

Potential Direct Impacts of Tourism on the Health of the Host Community

Health conditions which can affect local people directly and not as secondary implications of other impacts of tourism, are diseases, accidents, and conditions related to employment in tourism. The potential direct health impacts of tourism are mainly those occurring through the spread of infections by travelling individuals. These infections can be imported from the tourists' country of origin, or they could be contracted while travelling. The main infection risks for travellers in developing countries as compiled by Warren and Mahmoud. All of those can be transmitted to local individuals. There are diseases that are easily spread and are common, others require a range of factors and circumstances to be transmitted and are less common. Some diseases may have a minor impact on the individual and/or can be treated easily, others are difficult to treat and/or have serious impacts on the individual. The ease of spread of a range of diseases which can be transmitted from travellers to hosts and their level of impact on the host individual. The mode of transmission of some conditions is common knowledge and well researched, the spread of others has not been discussed in the light of tourist-host transmission, possibly because some diseases are less common. Nevertheless, sometimes only one case of infection may be enough to introduce a virulent agent to people without the necessary immunity and lead to a major epidemic. This potential risk warrants the consideration of all possibilities of disease transmission. An additional factor needs to be addressed when discussing the potential spread to people in developing countries, and here particularly indigenous communi ties. Poor hygiene, unfavourable economic conditions, inadequate housing and nutrition predispose people already to a range of diseases such as tuberculosis, parasitic infections or hepatitis, with individuals often having several acute and chronic conditions at the same time. It is obvious that an additional load of pathogenic agents, especially when the immune system is compromised, can only aggravate health problems.

Field Studies on Tourism's Health Impact

One objective of this study was to test if the findings of the analysis of published material applied to real situations in developing countries.

Health Problems Linked to Tourism in Easter Island and Peru

On Easter Island it was found that the (only) campground on the island at Anakena Beach had no fresh water supply, and the sanitary facilities provided, according to the locals, had been locked for a long time. On weekends, hundreds of locals and tourists gather at the beach usually staying the whole day. This was discussed with staff at the hospital who reported a relatively high prevalence of diarrhoea on the island but had attributed this to vegetables imported from the Chilean mainland. After discussing the lack of sanitary facilities which becomes even more obvious with the added tourists, they agreed that it was worthwhile to investigate this potential health hazard. Staff, however, saw the main problem regarding tourism and health as the transmission of Sexually Transmitted Infections (STIs) from tourists to locals.

This anecdotal evidence has not yet been systematically investigated. The issue of the availability of health facilities came up during conversations with locals in the market. It could be concluded that tourism on Easter Island has not improved the locals' health facilities. This may have to do with the fact that tourists generally stay only a short time, either because of the limited facilities on the island or because they are only having a brief stopover on the connection Tahiti-Santiago de Chile. If seriously ill, the people joked, they had "only two options, Santiago [some 3700 km away] or the cemetery".

Health professionals in Peru also maintained that cases of STIs were increasing and tourism was seen as a major contributing factor to this development, but they were unable to substantiate these claims. Toonen *et al.* (1996) conducted a health baseline study in the Camisea area in the Amazonian jungle where the Shell Company is prospecting. The potential risk of the native population to contract STIs was seen as very high because of people coming from outside (here mainly oil workers). The study does not clarify if locals also spoke of tourists, the term 'visitadores' in the study refers to prostitutes. Other diseases repeatedly named as being spread by people moving around were malaria and leishmaniasis. The important aspect of tourist-host encounters die each year in the Andes including mountain guides. The health of tourism workers, however, can also be in danger in the developed world. More than 50 climbers and guides died within a few weeks in the European Alps in the summer of 1997. Another form of 'occupational health hazard' has been observed on the Argentinian side of the Iguazu Falls where, at a certain point, locals drive tourists in an open boat equipped with a small engine close to the edge of the falls. The engine barely is able to get the boat out of the current and back to shore. A thin rope along the edge clearly is not sufficient to withstand a boat should the engine fail.

Increasingly, developing countries with access to spectacular reefs market their underwater attractions to encourage diving holidays. When the income of a diving guide depends on the number of dives, the minimum surface interval that is required for health reasons may not always be observed, putting them under considerable health risks. A lack of decompression chambers in developing countries, partly due to the failure of enforcing their installation, as Rudkin and Hall (1996) reported from Pacific islands, is of concern not only to the visiting diver but also to the local guide.

In many areas in the developing world, customs prevent people's exposure to physical danger by placing a taboo over a certain area. If such an area happens to become of interest to tourism, the reluctance of locals to go to such places may be overcome by the need to earn money. Two guides together with one tourist died in January 1995 at Mt. Yasur on Tanna/Vanuatu, killed by falling rocks ejected from the volcano. This author has witnessed local guides refusing to accompany visitors to the summit of this volcano.

In tribal areas in the jungle could not be examined during this field trip but needs urgent attention. This is so because some villages now seem to contact tour operators suggesting cooperation, and operators sensitive to potential problems need to be provided with information to facilitate their decision making. Environmental impacts of tourism in trekking areas with problems due to unregulated garbage disposal and the lack of sanitary facilities were suggested in the literature and could be observed in reality. The problem applies to areas with opportunities for short hikes as well as to trails representing major tourist attractions such as routes in the Cordillera Blanca/Huaraz or the Inka Trail near Cusco. The need for urgent action has been recognised in both areas and plans are already under way to implement solutions to the problems. A program is currently being designed to install sanitary facilities along well-used trails. This is of particular importance when the areas represent the main water supply for a large region.

Implications for Local Tourism Employees' Health

The neglect of local tourism workers' health in the literature is obvious. The importance of the consideration of this topic became apparent during the field trip. It seems that many tourism workers in Peru (and other developing countries) earn their living as tourist guides, often in destinations with little tourism infrastructure such as nature based adventure tours. Tourists are given advice about the dangers they may encounter on these trips. But tourists are only exposed to those hazards for a very short time compared to the guides. Their health risks increase through the frequency of exposure due to their job as well as the terrain they are working in.

Adventure tours to the Amazonian jungle are very popular. Like tourists, guides are exposed to health hazards such as snake and other animals' bites, diseases such as malaria or leishmaniasis, and car or boat accidents. Several cases of snake bites and accidents with boats and trucks were named by a tour operator in Cusco.

Probably the highest health risk exists for mountain guides who risk altitude sickness, injury or death in their attempt to lead tourists to spectacular summits. Peak season means a higher income but also a higher health risk. Shlim (1996) reported that in just one storm in the Nepal Himalayas on 10-11 November 1995, 22 foreigners and more than 45 Nepalese guides and porters died in different regions due to heavy snowfall, avalanches and mudslides. It was claimed that up to 30 people and porters should be assessed and monitored. The identification of potential occupational health problems and a documentation of the spread of diseases contracted during employment in tourism to family and community, would assist in strategies to minimise health hazards.

Towards a Framework for Understanding Tourism's Health Impacts

Anecdotal Versus Research Evidence

This study suggests that, at the moment, there is very little research based evidence on the impact of tourism on locals' health in developing countries. Sources that can be found related to the topic are mainly anecdotal, underline the need for further research. Diseases which had been reported as transmittable through people's movement, were found again in the field. Also, the health problems of local tourism workers proved to be a reality, and research into this area appears to be overdue. Although their numbers may be small compared to the entire population who may be at risk of infectious diseases, the concern over their work safety warrants further investigations. A retrospective and ongoing documentation of illness/death of local tour guides classified into areas of expertise, such as mountain, scuba diving, jungle and so on, should be established and a data bank created with links to neighbouring countries which have similar problems. Also, the health status of guides Health hazards for white water rafting guides have been described in the literature.

Sisson, Nichols and Hopkins (1983) reported schistosomiasis (blood flukes) infections among US rafting guides on the Omo River/Ethiopia. A year later, Istre, Fontaine, Tarr, and Hopkins (1984) described an outbreak of acute schistosomiasis among rafters on the same river, pointing out that commercial organisations were about to start business. This means that local guides, although partially immune, are exposed to repeated infections. A different potential health problem was identified in porters. For example, on the Inka Trail (with the highest altitude above 4000m.) one can find children carrying backpacks considered too heavy for well nourished healthy adult tourists. This may cause problems in later life such as bone deformation and chronic backpain which can prevent the individual from pursuing regular work.

The examples mentioned give a little insight into this complex area. Unfortunately, no research on this topic could be found. This may be because accidents or other health problems affect individual people, not groups or whole communities, cases are dealt with individually but not linked with other similar events. Because of the absence of data on frequency/occurrence, it is also difficult to make a risk assessment based on assumptions alone. Considering the fact that in developing countries there is rarely any organised support for such workers, health insurance or compensation for themselves or their families, this matter needs urgent attention if tourism is not to be seen as yet another type of exploitation.

On the other hand, however, it is to be expected that some local guides can indeed make a living without putting themselves at risk and, subsequently, even lead a much healthier life than before. The findings of the field work e.g., Pryor's (1980) account of residents' attitudes in Rarotonga, Cook Islands, or the many accusations about the role of (Western) tourists as transmitters of STIs and AIDS. Although there is no doubt that tourism contributes to the spread of diseases, facts are hard to obtain. Using Doxey's (1975) index of tourist irritation as a framework, one has to assume that anecdotal negative evidence on health impacts may have a lot to do with locals' antagonism toward tourists for whatever reason.

Comments, therefore, should be (or should have been) examined from this perspective to allow for a more realistic interpretation. Antagonism may even lead to the perception of transmission of diseases with entirely different aetiology. In this connection, one also needs to consider the well known conflict between national park management and the needs of the locals living within a park or in close proximity. For example, the conservation of flagship species such as the tiger or rhinoceros has to be weighed against the loss of lives of locals caused by those animals. Likewise, loss of livestock and crop destruction have impacts on the population's health status. In the context of this report, it is necessary to identify what events occur within the framework of conservation and which ones can clearly be attributed to tourism.

Numerous gaps have been identified in the current body of knowledge on the impact of tourism on the health of the local population in developing countries and topics for research have been suggested. It has been established that research into potential indirect health impacts has to go beyond the economic, environmental and sociocultural impacts already widely discussed in the literature, and focus specifically on their health implications. Research into potential direct health impacts should concentrate on epidemiological studies into the transmission of diseases through travellers and on investigations into the work place health and safety aspects in relation to local tourism employees.

In addition, a wide range of general issues is the focus for basic and applied research providing additional information to achieve a more complete picture of health impacts. Examples are offered here to illustrate the variety of study topics available to researchers from different disciplines. Historians could explore how visitors in the past (invaders, explorers, missionaries) changed the local health status. At present, it seems information on this topic can only be found by chance when studying old documents or travel diaries.

Addressing present day concerns, social scientists should establish if there is indeed an association between locals' negative attitudes towards tourism and anecdotal evidence of negative impacts (and then test those claims through epidemiological research). Another focus of interest is an examination of national and regional tourism strategies in developing countries with respect to the consideration of the local public health and specific strategic activities to prevent a deterioration of the health status. Public health interests could lie in: the comparison of the impact of different levels of low, moderate, and high degrees of tourism in small/isolated communities; the investigation of advice given to tourists in their home country or at the destination regarding their impact on local health; an assessment of tourists' knowledge of their potential role as transmitters of diseases; the identification of services offered for tourists' health care and the examination of their utilisation and availability for locals; the documentation of tourists using local health care facilities; or a comparison of the distribution of health care professionals and health services in touristic and non-touristic areas within one country. Finally, tourism education should be included in research on the topic and curricula in tourism degree courses examined regarding their inclusion of health aspects. These study topics can be researched not only in individual projects focusing on a particular geographic area but allow for comparison between areas with the aim of collaborative efforts in dealing with identified health problems linked to tourism. The addition and consideration of country specific research needs which may be proposed by local health authorities will be of particular importance when deciding on a specific topic for research.

The Need for Research as a Basis for Tourism Planning

The goal of tourism planning is usually said to be economic, sociological, biological and cultural sustainability. Ethical concerns have been raised in connection with tourism development in the 'Third World'. The four goals in tourism development:

(1) enhanced visitor satisfaction,
(2) improved economy and business success,
(3) protected resource assets, and
(4) community and area integration clearly include participation of and approval by the local population. Any development that does not protect local people and environment could be classified as unethical.

It becomes clear when examining available tourism strategies and plans that tourism planning is an immensely complex activity. Publications on two areas visited during the field trip have been reviewed with respect to their coverage of issues which may directly or indirectly affect the health of local populations.

Aguilar, Hinojosa and Milla (1992) suggested a wide range of strategies and actions to develop tourism in the 'Inka Region', an area extending over the Departments of Cusco, Madre de Dios and Apurímac, but no reference relating to health could be found. The 'Plan for Touristic and Recreation Use of the Huascaran National Park' applies to the national park in the Cordillera Blanca/Huaraz which predicted 104,000 conventional tourists and 4,000 adventure tourists (mountain climbers) for the year 1996, and 320,000 conventional tourists and 12,000 adventure tourists for the year 2005. As this plan relates to a national park, it comes as no surprise that considerable emphasis is placed on the environmental impact of tourism (garbage, lack of toilets, water and sewage system). It also recommends that conditions are to be established "for the rural population to participate in tourism in a manner which permits sustainable development". Both aspects influence the local health status but health as such is not mentioned explicitly. The plan also suggests that local guides be registered in order to monitor uncontrolled activities in the park. Such a register, i f implemented, could be an excellent opportunity to monitor their health status.

Research is the basis to appropriate tourism planning. It is obvious that the lack of research into health issues has prevented their inclusion in tourism strategic plans.

Methodological Considerations

The benefit of studying a little investigated area is that there are few conceptual restrictions for the researcher but a great opportunity for creativity and innovative approaches when defining research topics. Research in some of the areas suggested, clearly poses enormous methodological challenges for the investigator, not least because of the transient character of tourism. Here again creativity is needed in employing a range of different research approaches, going beyond the conventional. Two will be mentioned here. For example, for some of these topics an action research approach based on Critical Social Theory could be adopted. The philosophy behind Critical Social Theory is that empowering people helps them to change their situation, to help themselves. A classic text is Paolo Freire's (1972) *Pedagogy of the Oppressed* on the empowerment through education. In a similar way, communities affected by negative health impacts from tourism could work at overcoming these by adopting the problem solving approach based on empowerment. The core of action research is the employment of a problem solving approach whereby the researcher guides the representatives of a group/community (who also become part of the research team) through the process of change until a satisfactory outcome is achieved.

The usefulness of a Geographical Information System (GIS) for epidemiological purposes is now widely accepted. The inherent geographical element of tourism and the aspect of movement represent factors very suitable for the employment of GIS for research purposes on this topic. Furthermore, its use would allow the combination of epidemiological and tourism variables. At this stage, it could not be established if GIS has ever been used in this form. However, the combination of medicine and geography is not new. Hellen (1995) discussed the use of applied medical geography in, for example, disease hazard mapping, and emphasised the need for a "multidisciplinary approach to safeguarding the health of individuals and ensuring the sustainability of tourism to potentially hazardous areas", albeit from the perspective of travellers' health. It is quite clear that the range of research questions suggested in this paper indicates that a lot of these need to be approached in a multidisciplinary fashion. This would also provide a unique opportunity to cooperate with local professionals and to train locals as research assistants to enable them to continue research and monitoring on a long-term basis.

Towards a Framework for Understanding Tourism's Health Impacts

The purpose of research is to generate and test theories. Applied research emphasises its practical applicability to the field of study. Consequently, research undertaken on this hitherto under-investigated topic will contribute to a body of knowledge which may eventually be expressed in a more abstract form as theories and represented as models for easier understanding. The theories, in turn, will have to be tested and refined.

Bushell and Lea (1996) quite rightly pointed out that there is more to 'tourism and health' than traveller illness and suggest a reorientation towards 'traveller and host wellness'. They then continue to present a tourism health model linked to the concept o f eco logical public health as a framework for research. It defines 'tourism and health' as the interface between (1) tourists, (2) hosts and (3) the natural environment.

The model takes into account arguments by Brown (1985) supporting an epidemiology of health in contrast to the traditional epidemiology of diseases. Based on these arguments, the authors also propose a forced field approach considering the perspectives of promoting/preventing wellness/illness as a guideline for investigations, and request that a new public health framework be integrated in the existing field of 'tourism and health'. Without doubt, this is one possible avenue. However, it can be argued that this model is rather one-sided as it focuses on health with little evidence of including tourism aspects (apart from the tourists). The model may represent the broad field of tourism and health but it does not depict enough detail to accommodate attributing factors which are mentioned by Bushell and Lea, such as typology of tourists or destination categories. It does not seem refined enough to offer directions for further research incorporating both fields (tourism and health) sufficiently. A framework can be seen as a system where all components are interdependent and interlinked in a way that variations in one component affect the rest of the system. Based on the results of this study, a framework for understanding tourism's health impacts in developing countries will most likely consist at least of the following major components: tourists, type of tourism, operators/developers, local population, local authorities, the environment, the level of tourism, and the country's current economic status.

Tourists (As Individuals/as Groups)

Tourists are probably the most active part in this framework as they are the ones actually moving around and coming into contact with places and people. A range of factors need to be considered as attributes of this constant visit or host encounter: tourist typology; tourists' health status and educational status; knowledge required for a particular trip; advice given; activities sought and their implications; speed of travel; size and numbers of groups; mode of transport chosen; accommodation (e.g., enclave vs homestay); travel patterns; travel corridors; travel seasons; and the degree of contact with the local population. Some of these factors are deliberately chosen by the individual, others occur unintentionally or have been decided for the tourist.

Type of Tourism

A further component is the type of tourism occurring in a particular location, from individual adventure travel to mass tourism. This has an effect on the degree of contact tourists have with locals as well as the potential of introducing diseases or causing other negative impacts, for example, on the environment. Although mass travel implies that large numbers of people travel, the accumulation of large numbers usually only occurs at very popular destinations, and these visitors may not come in contact with locals at all or rarely. The impact of mass tourism on health is likely to be indirect, i.e. through economic, environmental or sociocultural affects. Adventure tourism is pursued by travelling individuals, alone or in very small groups, but their destinations are usually in more remote and isolated areas where they are also much more likely to come in c loser contact with local communities. These interactions most likely prepare the ground for potential direct impacts such as the transmission of diseases. Tourist activities are another dimension impacting on local destinations. Pearce and Moscardo (1989) developed a tool to investigate the Structure of Tourism Activities for Regions (STAR). A list of attributes allows the classification of activities. Some of those at tributes are based on interactions between tourists and the environment (and hence important in relation to possible impacts), but no attribute is allocated to a possible interaction with the local population. As this interaction obviously does occur, on a continuum from very little to very close, not only should this dimension be added to the STAR (Structure of Tourism Activities for Regions) instrument, but it is an important factor in the assessment of health impacts of tourism. It may be useful to design a modified STAR tool that allows the creation of profiles of activities and their impact on host communities' health. The dimensions of such a tool would be factors such as impact on the environment, degree of contact with locals, or potential risks to local employees.

Operators/developers A further important component are those individuals or companies/organisations who develop tourism destinations and provide services and facilities from travel agencies to transport companies and the accommodation industry. Clearly, the primary purpose of those businesses is to make a profit out of the tourism they promote. Ideally, operators should be mediators between tourists and hosts, if only to ensure sustainability of the operations. In reality, however, it seems that the links with the tourists are much closer, tourists and operator s are involved in a business transaction with one supplying what the other demands. Operators have a great responsibility when it comes to planning, developing and running tourism products as these rarely occur without impacts on the local populations. Very often, operators decide on activities offered, destinations visited, accommodation constructed and mode of transport provided. They, therefore, do represent a very important element in the health impact framework due to their intermediate position between visitors and hosts.

Local Population

Here, we are looking at the more passive, receiving end of the activity 'travel'. The following aspects are of importance: the geographical location; immunity and health status; level of education; previous contact with visitors; dependence on tourism; degree of contact with tourists; attitudes towards tourism; the difference between the cultural and social values of visitor and host; locals' involvement in tourism planning.

Brown (1985) strongly emphasised that a suitable approach to an epidemiology of health "must take account of complexity, open-endedness, multiple interactions, value choices, social rules and types of personality...". Nothing less should be applied to the local host population.

Local authorities (health tourism) So far, little attention has been paid to the role of local health and tourism authorities in the protection of the health of the local population. It is important to recognise the role of these authorities. Although the aims of both authorities may not seem to have much common ground, with one developing and promoting tourism and the principles of business in mind, and the other in charge of the public health status, if they are to achieve sustainable tourism which benefits all parties involved, a close cooperation between both is necessary. This applies particularly to activities such as monitoring the local health status in tourism destinations and implementing strategies of improvement if necessary; investigating health impacts (in cooperation with other agencies, such as conservation groups); approving of tourism destinations only after a positive outcome of a health impact assessment; or terminating an operation when its impact is detrimental. In this respect, local authorities play a central role in the monitoring of tourists, locals, and operators as well as environmental issues.

Environment

The environment represents an essential resource for tourism. Budowski (1976) proposed three possible relationships between tourism and nature, *conflict, coexistence* and *symbiosis,* claiming that the majority of relationships are those of coexistence moving toward conflict. It seems not much has changed 20 years later. Changes in the environment affect humans' health as a short-or long-term consequence. It is, therefore, important that every effort is made to closely observe the environment for changes attributable to tourism to allow for timely act ion in order to reduce the health risks to locals and tourists.

Economic Status

In order to achieve the required monitoring discussed above, not only is a substantial budget necessary but also professional expertise in fields such as health, tourism, and conservation. The same requirements apply i f research is to be conducted into topics suggested throughout this paper. A lesser developed country may well recognise negative impacts of tourism on the health of its people but may be in no position to do anything about it, not least because it is desperately dependent on tourism and foreign currency. Therefore, ways will have to be designed that allow countries with little expertise and economic abilities to still have strategies at hand to minimise a decrease in the local health status attributable to tourism.

These components and their relationships with each other can be seen as starting points for investigations A growth of research based knowledge on tourism's health impacts (as well as putting this area on priority lists of funding bodies) will allow the generation of theoretical frameworks in a reasonably near future. Such frameworks are necessary for applying this knowledge to practice, particularly for assessing health impacts. The ultimate goal will be to conduct such an assessment for prospective or current tourism developments in the same way as is already done for economic, environmental or, to a lesser extent, sociocultural impacts as, literally, prevention is better than cure.

Lacking such an assessment framework at the moment, other solutions have to be employed. Short-term solutions may centre around creating an awareness in tourists, locals and operators. In the longer term, other interventions may be necessary. Simmons' (1996) advice was meant for the protection of the environment but is equally applicable to health when he suggests the provision of 'honeypots' to draw people away from vulnerable spots. In practice, this could mean, rather than searching for isolated tribes in a rainforest, providing tourists with high quality interpretation centres.

The increase in tourism worldwide is likely to continue and the positive aspects of tourism in developing countries are acknowledged. However, it seems that health is being ignored in the process of tourism development, both "in terms of the local people and in the potential impact of travellers on the already scarce health resources" as Rudkin and Hall reported from the South Pacific. If visitor-host encounters lead to a decreasing health status of the hosts, action needs to be taken in order to promote people's well-being and, consequently, the sustainability of tourism destinations for the benefit of the visitor *and* the host. Otherwise, the World Tourism Organization's objective" to accelerate and enlarge the contribution of tourism (international and domestic) to peace, understanding, *health,* and prosperity throughout the world" cannot be met

Medical Tourism and its Negative Impact on the Rural Primary Health Care to the Poor Families in Rural India

Medical tourism refers to the practice of people travelling abroad to obtain medical care and services. In the past medical tourism has mainly consisted of wealthy people travelling to countries such as the United States and paying for the use of advanced medical facilities. Nowadays, there is an increasing trend whereby patients are travelling to middle and low-income countries to obtain low-cost health services with short waiting times. Medical and surgical procedures can cost between five to ten times less in India than the United States.

Some destination countries such as India have actively promoted medical tourism. This is because it can bring about benefits including increases in revenue, foreign exchange reserves and tourism. It is estimated that medical tourism generates over US$60 billion in business. In addition, it has led to the creation of high-tech private medical facilities in India.

Questions remain about whether local populations actually benefit from these facilities and national health systems from the revenues that they generate. Experience from India suggests that private hospitals attract health professionals away from the public health sector and rural areas in India. This internal brain drain creates shortages of trained health workers, thus reducing access to healthcare for local populations in rural India and exacerbating inequalities.

In India some private hospitals agreed to provide services to poor people for no costs and in turn received government subsidies in the form of land, tax breaks and medical equipment. However, the facilities oriented towards medical tourism (technology intensive tertiary services) do not meet the health needs of the average poor rural Indian and evidence suggests that few poor people have benefited from such care. It is important that the government does not overlook the negative impacts that health tourism can have on local populations, in particular on access to services and availability of public health professionals. They should also find ways of ensuring that the revenues accrued from health tourists are channelled into the public sector through national laws and regulations The article describes a trend, where large numbers of patients from wealthy countries, such as America, are travelling abroad to diverse countries including India, in search of less expensive health care. The article uses examples of India and Thailand to examine the implications of medical tourism in these countries. It shows that in both countries medical tourism has caused private hospitals to emphasise treatment over prevention, and promote technology-intensive tertiary services at the expense of primary health care. This has created distortions in the allocation of resources and spending that doesn't match the needs of local people.

UK conference discusses 'disastrous' impact of the myth of 'HIV health tourism' HIV health tourism is one of the Government's main justifications for "a harmful, costly and inhumane charging policy." The UK Government's policy of charging so-called 'health tourists' for HIV treatment and care is a "public health disaster" based on myth not fact, Yusef Azad, Director of Policy and Campaigns for the National AIDS Trust (NAT) told last week's British HIV Association (BHIVA) Autumn Conference during a session on treating migrant populations and their eligibility for care.

HIV health tourism is one of the Government's main justifications for "a harmful, costly and inhumane charging policy," according to a new NAT report, *The myth of HIV health tourism*. The results of that policy were highlighted at the conference by a panel consisting of an HIV clinician, a human rights lawyer, a GP who has cared for many asylum seekers with HIV, an HIV-positive migrant advocate, and Mr. Azad.

Since April 2004, overseas visitors, refused asylum seekers, undocumented migrants and visa overstayers have no longer been entitled to HIV treatment and care from the National Health Service (NHS) in England, although treatment for all other infectious diseases and sexually transmitted infections continues to be free to everyone on public health grounds irrespective of residency status. (The NHS in Scotland and Wales have different policies.)

Earlier this year, a High Court ruling resulted in HIV-positive refused asylum seekers being entitled to free HIV treatment and care for as long as they remained in the UK. But the judge refused a claim that there was a human right to NHS treatment, saying that any discrimination in the rules was justifiable so as to discourage 'health tourism'.

Yet a new NAT report that "separates facts and evidence around migration from fears and misinformation", argues that there is no evidence to demonstrate that HIV health tourism to the UK exists. Allegations of 'HIV health tourism', says the report, "make a serious charge against the integrity and truthfulness of many HIV-positive migrants to the UK, effectively alleging that stated reasons for migration to the UK are at best a pretext and at worst totally untrue. Given the discrimination and marginalisation experienced by many migrants we must question very carefully any claim which might add to social hostility".

The report also notes, "the claim of health tourism has been central to the Government's policy of charging refused asylum seekers and other migrants without lawful residency status for healthcare. The Government argues that free NHS care for those without what they deem to be a legitimate reason to migrate to the UK acts as a 'pull factor', encouraging illegal immigration and discouraging refused asylum seekers from leaving. Charges for NHS care for certain categories of migrant were introduced to end the 'pull' of free NHS care and address the so-called problem of 'health tourism'.

"Is there really evidence of HIV health tourism which would justify on grounds of immigration policy the singling out of HIV for NHS charges alone amongst all serious or sexually transmitted infections?"

asks NAT. Over the course of twelve pages, the paper robustly argues that there is no evidence to demonstrate that 'HIV health tourism' is "a significant or real motivation for migration to the UK" and considerable evidence to demonstrate otherwise, "in particular the lower rates of HIV prevalence compared with country of origin, the long average delays [an average of five years] between arrival in the UK and accessing HIV testing and care, and the evidence available on the actual motivations of migrants coming to the UK".

Dr. Le Feuvre, a Kent GP, told the conference that NAT's conclusions match his own experience. "We had tens of thousands of [refugees and asylum seekers] coming through East Kent in the last ten years. I only personally remember one person amongst those tens of thousands who seemed to be coming here for medical treatment and the majority of people diagnosed with HIV, and who left the, left with it being diagnosed after their arrival and not before." One of the paper's recommendations is that "since the provision of free HIV treatment has no bearing on migration trends, the basis for the Government's policy of charging for HIV treatment is wholly undermined. It has been demonstrated elsewhere that the policy actually increases costs to the NHS and endangers public health. The Government must review its policy on NHS charging so as to exempt HIV treatment from charges."

The impact of this policy was brought into sharp focus at the BHIVA conference by Professor Jane Anderson of Homerton University Hospital, east London, who provided a case study to illustrate the desperation faced by HIV-positive undocumented migrants in England. She told the conference about a 35 year-old East African woman who was refused a prescription by a medical team outside of London when she had only three days supply of antiretrovirals left and no means to return to her country of origin. "We gave her an immediate prescription for antiretroviral drugs...and gave her a travelcard from our charitable fund so she could get food and support from other charitable sources," she said.

She argued that HIV care in the UK should be for everyone. She noted that the new UK HIV testing guidelines, which include a list of 'indicator diseases' prompting the offer of opt-out testing "is only ethically acceptable if positive individuals are immediately linked into appropriate HIV treatment and care. Yet," she asked, "we are meant to send them to a place where they're going to get a big bill. Is this appropriate practice?" Adam Hundt, a human rights lawyer provided an overview of the complex rules and regulations governing access to secondary NHS treatment and care, which he described as "a bit of a minefield". He noted that there are situations, people, and diseases exempted from the charging regulations including treatment given at an emergency department, 34 infectious diseases (including TB and viral hepatitis) and all sexually transmitted infections apart from HIV which he said, "is a policy decision".

There is also an exemption for continuing a course of treatment, including treatment for HIV, as long as someone has lawfully entered the UK. "Unhelpfully," he noted, "there's no definition of what 'a course of treatment' is." The Government recently clarified that 'treatment' does not necessarily mean antiretroviral therapy, but in fact, can mean continued monitoring of immune and clinical status due to an HIV diagnosis.

He noted that there is also much confusion amongst clinicians over what constitutes 'immediately necessary treatment' which should be provided to anyone regardless of their ability to pay. "It basically specifies that if someone requires treatment because their condition is life threatening, or because if treatment is not given immediately it will become life threatening, or because permanent and serious damage would be caused by any delay then they must be given treatment regardless of whether they can pay or not and then be charged for it later," he said.

Dr. Ian Williams, BHIVA's Chair, recently wrote to the Department of Health to argue that HIV care should be considered immediately necessary in the same way as maternity care. "I think the most important thing to remember," noted Mr. Hundt, "is that it's a matter of clinical judgment which should not be second-guessed by administrative staff."

In the discussion that followed, Prof. Anderson pointed out the paradox of one Government department, the Department for International Development, supporting universal access to HIV treatment and care overseas, but another two Government departments, the Department of Health and the Home Office "denying that care free here and also sending people back through various legislation and legal decisions to places where there's no care. Why can't we have domestic policies that are the same as foreign policy?" she asked.

Environmental Impacts of Medical Tourism

Although medical tourism is a boon for people who cannot afford expensive treatments in their own country, there are certain disadvantages to it. One of the biggest disadvantages is the environmental impacts of medical tourism, which is always negative.

Most people going for medical treatment abroad tend to combine travel and tourism along with the medical procedure. This means that the country where you go for the treatment has to build more hotels to accommodate the ever growing number of patients cum tourists. The government resorts to deforestation to build more hotels and provide better civil amenities because medical tourism is a way of earning revenue and foreign exchange. In addition, medical tourism is also responsible for contributing to increased air emissions, noise, solid waste and littering, releases of sewage, oil and chemicals, even architectural/visual pollution; all which has negative impact on the environment.

Medical tourism creates great pressure on local resources like energy, food and other raw material, which could be already in short supply in that country. Even natural resources like water, especially fresh water, is affected as medical tourism like any other tourism generally tends to overuse water resources for hotels, swimming pools, and personal use of water by the tourists. This results in shortage of water and degradation of water supplies as well as generating large volumes of waste water. From fiscal aspect, medical tourism is good for a country but the environmental impacts of medical tourism are always negative.

Social Impacts of Medical Tourism

While people from America use medical tourism to get low cost medical care, people from Canada and Britain, where public healthcare systems are present, take advantage of medical tourism to avoid long waiting lists in their own countries.

Health insurance companies are now trying to understand how they can offer medical tourism to people and one of the plans they have in mind is to introduce lower premiums for certain services if the people go abroad for them. This will have a great impact on healthcare insurance premiums as well as hospital profitability.

However, the social impacts of medical tourism are in countries where people go for medical treatments. These countries are poor and developing countries where citizens cannot afford medical treatment, food, shelter or clothing. If medical tourism can bring about a change in their lives, it would be the perfect scenario. Hospitals specializing in medial tourism should use their earnings to provide free and adequate health services for the poor.

The other social impact of medical tourism is positive. Medical tourism is instrumental in creating jobs for people. This means as the developing country grows to accommodate increasing number of medical tourists, it creates more jobs for the locals. In addition, the medical tourism healthcare providers keep upgrading their capabilities and facilities which can be used to treat the domestic patients too at a reasonable price.

Impacts

Health Impacts

During the haze period, quite a number of people experienced respiratory related problems; asthma attacks, bronchitis. Many too suffered from coughing/wheezing, runny noses and sore throats. People complained of eye irritation and reddening of eyes.? Those with respiratory problems, heart conditions, skin conditions (Eczema) and the young and old would be severely affected by the haze. Professor Euston Quah, head of economics department of Nanyang Technological University, mentioned that there was even a possibility of stunted growth for children's lungs if the children were repeatedly exposed to haze for a long time.

From our interview with Doctor Chris Huang, he felt that this statement is not true. Haze is not likely to stunt the growth for children's lungs, except for babies because their lungs are not fully developed yet. Hence, when they are exposed to particulate matter from the haze and their lungs are irritated, the result might be the scarring of their lungs. Furthermore, it might lead to other serious health conditions such as pneumonia, which could cause permanent damage to lungs. Nonetheless, this does not stunt the lung growth of the babies.

The haze pollutants contain particles such as ozone and sulphur dioxide (also greenhouse gases) may cause damage to the heart and lungs. Particulate matter 10 (PM10), the more commonly-found particle in the smoke haze, happens to be the most dangerous threat to lungs. When breathed in, PM10 might cause lungs to function at a decreased rate, causing shortness of breath! During a serious haze situation, civilians would be advised by the government to stay indoors and limit outdoor activities so that the people are less exposed to unhealthy, polluted air. Nonetheless, PM10 is still able to enter buildings through fresh air vents.

In the First week of October 2006, when the haze was at its worst in Singapore, approximately 15 000 citizens complained of illnesses associated with the heart and lungs.

Haze has been linked to premature death recently according to HazeOnline website. If a person is exposed to too much pollutants from the haze, that could lead to premature death. The two main causes of this premature death are the two gases sulphur dioxide and nitrogen oxide which are part of the haze.

Environmental Impacts

The haze situation in Southeast Asia mainly resulted from the burning of the trees in Indonesian forests. The gases that evolved from the combustion are sulphur dioxide, ozone, nitrogen dioxide and carbon monoxide. These are greenhouse gases and hence contributed to global warming and affected the atmosphere tremendously. This in turn speeds up global warming, causing shifting climate changes and unpredictability of the weather. There is loss of biodiversity due to the forest fires. Flora and fauna are burnt and lost in the fires. We might have endangered even more species of animals and also destroyed rare species of organisms. This will cause a disruption in the ecosystem.

The haze pollutants cause a negative change in air quality in the neighbouring countries. This would also affect the human's respiratory system. Humans need fresh air, but if the air quality is not good, the human's health will be affected detrimentally. Therefore, there would be a rise in patients with respiratory and eye problems caused by the inhalation of haze pollutants.

PM 2.5 mostly causes reduction in visibility. Reduction in visibility might also cause trade transport to travel with lots of difficulty. Trading ships may crash accidentally into objects if sailors are not alert and careful about their course, especially when it is so difficult to see ahead during the haze. As for airplanes, the haze would hinder the sight of the pilot, making it difficult to manoeuvres the aircraft, hence compromising the safety of the passengers.

Impact on Tourism

When haze hit Thailand on 12th of March 2007, flights were disrupted (13 cancelled) and had to be delayed. Tourists normally tend to shun countries with images of smoke and civilians wearing surgical masks, hence resulting in the decline of the tourism rate in the countries affected by the haze. Due to the fact that flights were cancelled, many tourists were left stranded at the airport since they had already checked out of their hotels while locals could still return back to their homes.

Though immediate cancellations were less observed, this showed that people planning for trips may reconsider their holiday destinations. Fewer tourists have visited Thailand, posing a problem towards Thailand's tourism, and the root of the problem is haze. Should the haze problem be solved, then Thailand's tourism would not be affected negatively.

An interviewed tourist was very annoyed with the haze situation because there was no sight of the sun after 9 days when he had come to Singapore to enjoy the sun.

In 1997, 13 flights from Singapore were cancelled due to the poor visibility from the haze. In that same year, airports in Malaysia such as West Kalimantan were closed. Also, 9 out of 11 Indonesian airports closed due to the haze. Visibility had worsened to 300 meters. There was even an Indonesian plane crashed which involved the lives of 234 people. The cancelling of flights and closing of airports prevented tourists from coming in to Singapore, causing a fall in tourism.

Economical Impacts

There would be a surge in medical costs since there would be many people going to the doctors for treatment of cough, and other haze-related illnesses. As a result, less people would turn up for work, reducing the efficiency of the different industries during that period.

People would flock to pharmacies to purchase eye drops to sooth their irritated eyes; face masks to filter the air they inhale, facial masks to prevent their faces from getting too dry and air purifiers to purify the air inside air-conditioned buildings. Retailers and businesses may be affected due to the fact that most people try to stay indoors (definition: at home). However, there are some people who would rather stay indoors (definition: shopping centres) and spend their day there doing shopping, having meals, watching movies, et cetera. However, retailers in neighbourhood or places which are not air-conditioned will be affected adversely. During the haze period, theme parks, sports facilities and coaches, alfresco dining restaurants and sightseeing tours had losses between 10 to 50 percent.

Singapore lost an estimated S$425 million during the 1997 haze period which lasted 3 months. US$210 million tourism; US$95 thousand recreation; US$5 million health; US$41 million visibility-airplanes and ships cannot navigate properly. The highest PSI was 226.

Should the haze last for a month, economic losses for Singapore would be maximum of $70 million, according to Professor Quah. Imagine, if a worse haze were to last for more than a month, what would be the consequences be like to the country?

Hospitality Services

The concept of Hospitality Exchange, also known as "accommodation sharing", "hospitality services" (short "hospex"), and "home stay networks", refers to centrally organized social networks of individuals, generally travellers, who offer or seek accommodation without monetary exchange. Generally, these services connect users via the internet.

History

In 1949, Bob Luitweiler founded the first hospitality service called Servas Open Doors as a cross national, non-profit, volunteer run organization advocating interracial and international peace. In 1965, John Wilcock set up the Traveller's Directory as a listing of his friends willing to host each other when travelling. In 1988, Joy Lily rescued the organization from imminent shutdown, forming Hospitality Exchange. In 2000, Veit Kuhne founded Hospitality Club, the first Internet-based service. In 2004, Casey Fenton started CouchSurfing, now the largest hospitality exchange organization.

How they work

Generally, after registering, members have the option of providing very detailed information and pictures of themselves and of the sleeping accommodation being offered, if any. The more information provided by a member improves the chances that someone will find the member trustworthy enough to be their host or guest. Names and addresses may be verified by volunteers. Members looking for accommodation can search for hosts using several parameters such as age, location, sex, and activity level. Home stays are entirely consensual between the host and guest, and the duration, nature, and terms of the guest's stay are generally worked out in advance to the convenience of both parties. No monetary exchange takes place except under certain circumstances. After using the service, members can leave a noticeable reference about their host or guest.

Instead of or in addition to accommodation, members also offer to provide guide services or travel-related advice. The websites of the networks also provide editable travel guides and forums where members may seek travel partners or advice. Many such organizations are also focused on "social networking" and members organize activities such as camping trips, bar crawls, meetings, and sporting events.

Some networks cater to specific niche markets such as students, activists, religious pilgrims, and even occupational groups like police officers.

Benefits

Monetary savings: As these networks provide accommodation at no charge, monetary savings can be significant.

Local contact

Hospitality exchange gives travellers the chance to experience what life is like for people living in other places. In addition, making interpersonal connections and fostering understanding of different cultures may in the long run also be important to international relations. During hospitality exchanges, hosts may show off their local knowledge and exciting places "off the tourist map". Not only may travellers get a distinct experience, but they will also get a feel for the everyday lives of local residents.

Reciprocity

These systems foster richer and more convenient travel experiences not so much on the premise of altruism, but on the basis of social exchange theory. Implicit in the agreement to host travellers is the ability to ask to be hosted by them in the future. If one enjoys having interesting guests in their home, this works out well for both parties. It works comparatively better if you are visited by travellers from a locale you find particularly attractive. Thus, hosting someone from New York City in Gainesville, Florida seems to be an unbelievable opportunity.

Moreover, if you are a Westerner visiting someone in a developing country, your stay might be the only way that this individual or family could afford a trip to a rich nation. This may mean more than just a relaxing vacation for such disadvantaged parties.

Ecological Sustainability

Accommodation sharing reduces the demand for hotels, which, depending on the location can be detrimental for the environment.

Drawbacks

Lack of guarantee: There is no contractual agreement between users in these systems. Reservations are made, but if they are for some reason broken, there is no higher authority to which one could plead for a refund or other compensation. The only repercussion will be the poor rating you give that user and your only consolation will be that your warning will deter others from visiting or hosting them. For those who feel insecure unless their travel arrangements are written in stone before departure, this system will not be comforting.

Potential Interpersonal Conflict or Awkwardness

There is a chance that guest and host will not get along. Perhaps there will be scheduling or ideological conflicts. Maybe you will find that hosts or visitors have misrepresented themselves. Perhaps the experience will not live up to your expectations. Intense interpersonal communications in advance and a flexibility once you have arrived is your best bet. These experiences require additional planning and courtesy towards the demands of your host. Thus, your living conditions, length of stay, and overall experience will be circumscribed by the living conditions you enter into.

Digital Divide and Demographic Segregation

As use of these services generally requires access to the internet and knowledge of the English language, the sample population found in searches of these databases is really much less diverse than a geographical representation of worldwide users might suggest.

4

Health Tourism and Public Health

Health Tourism

General Information

Israel is fortunate to have a number of very attractive resorts frequented by tourists concerned about their health. Its widespread hot springs, sophisticated spa hotels and sunny climate make Israel a country that can offer its visitors a vacation focusing on their health, or a one-day visit to a health resort as part of the tour. The Dead Sea tops the list of therapeutic resorts, and is famous for its high concentration of salts and minerals.

A health problem is only one reason to visit one of the spa resorts. Normally, all these resorts satisfy the desire for a break from everyday life, whether you visit them for one day or for a longer vacation.

The main therapeutic resorts are located in the vicinity of Lake Kineret and the Dead Sea. But there are other therapeutic resorts throughout the country. Most of the natural therapeutic resorts, as well as, of course, the spa resorts, offer the possibility of combining your visit with a range of holistic treatments. In recent years, the field of alternative medicine has developed rapidly in Israel. Among the treatments offered are water therapy (hydrotherapy), ayurvedic medicine (Indian medicine), and conventional massages. Next to most of the therapeutic resorts are hotels offering special vacation packages that include treatments and pampering, as well as board and lodging.

Southern Part of Israel and the Dead Sea

The Dead Sea is one of the world's best-known and most unique therapeutic resorts. The region is characterized by an unusual combination of natural resources and climatic conditions – the saltiest sea in the world that is also mineral-rich; thermo-mineral waters; medicinal black mud; filtered sunrays; dry air rich in minerals; a pleasant temperature most of the year; a relatively high concentration of oxygen; air that is almost completely free of allergens and other air pollutants. Both a briefly bathing at one of the beaches or a stay for a pampering vacation at one of the hotels and guest rooms scattered along its shores are recommended. A thirty-minute ride from the Dead Sea is the city of Arad, whose cold, dry, clean air makes it a haven for people suffering from asthma, allergies and respiratory problems.

Mineral Beach

In Mineral Beach, on a well-tended shore of the Dead Sea, are two little pools: a fresh-water pool for small children, and a sulphur-water pool with a fixed temperature of 39 °C whose water arrives from an adjacent spring. On the shore there are open-sided, chill-out style, shelter pavilions from around the world, and plastic chairs. Right on the shoreline is natural mud – when spread on your body, it stimulates blood circulation, strengthens hair roots, and renews skin cells. On the site are cloakrooms, showers, a treatment room, a cafeteria, and a small shop where you can buy Dead Sea products and plastic sandals for entering the sea. A treatment room also awaits visitors, offering various types of treatments and massages by prior arrangement.

Ein Gedi Spa

The Ein Gedi Spa, a well-established site on the shores of the Dead Sea, has six indoor thermo-mineral pools – two for women, two for men, and two for mixed bathing. There is also an indoor resting area facing the primordial panorama of the Dead Sea. The pools are refreshed by a constant flow of salt and mineral rich water, and have a steady temperature of about 38 °C. Outside the building is a large bath containing rich, heavy black mud, which is great for ridding the body of poisons. An all-terrain-vehicle-type train, waiting outside the indoor baths, takes vacationers to the ever-receding seashore, for bathing. There is also a natural freshwater pool outside, which operates in the summer, as well as a spa treatment centre. Visitors can enjoy various treatments and massages in the private treatment rooms. It's worth while to book your treatment in advance, and to inquire about the pampering packages, which include a visit to the facilities on the site, a treatment of your choice, and a packet of cosmetics manufactured from the Dead Sea water.

Neve Midbar

Neve Midbar has baths extending over an area of 8,000 square meters. In the centre is a splendid building, inside and around which are stylish pools full of thermo-mineral water drawn from a depth of some 900 meters. The temperature of the water fluctuates between 40– 46 °C, and is rich in minerals, sulphur and magnesium. There are also saunas and treatment rooms, lawns and a cafeteria at the site. Next to them is Kibbutz Mash'abei Sade, which has guest units.

Khamam Tse'elim

After using the thermo-mineral water for agricultural irrigation for years, the members of Kibbutz Tse'elim discovered its healing powers, and turned the natural resource into a therapeutic site. The small site on the grounds of Kibbutz Tse'elim comprises a little whirlpool, whose water temperature is 40 °C, a dry sauna, a treatment complex, as well as a regular swimming pool. The kibbutz operates as a tourist centre, organizes trips in the vicinity and offers the experience of authentic Bedouin tent hospitality. Nearby are the kibbutz vacation apartments.

Ein Bokek

A resort and a therapeutic site at the estuary of Nakhal Bokek, on the western shore of the Dead Sea. The site has some ten hotels, therapeutic baths, two beaches, and a few restaurants. Next to Ein Bokek are several sites, including Nakhal Bokek, Metsad Bokek and Ma'ale Bokek. At Ein Bokek is also located Solarium-400, a site for the natural treatment of skin and arthritic diseases, and psoriasis. The Solarium offers treatments combined with bathing in the Dead Sea and exposure to sun rays used for the healing and treatment of skin and arthritic diseases. The site is located in an enclosure, and has separate sunning courts for men and for women. The main building has four professional clinics that specialize in skin diseases, a workout gym, cafeteria, pub and shops. The site also offers table games and social games, while the workout gym also holds physical activities focusing on joint problems, proper breathing, and the like.

Sea of Galilee Area

The north of Israel has an attractive concentration of spots for excursions and recreation. However, only two of them have authentic therapeutic baths. Besides these, a range of therapeutic hotels offer various spa services and health programs, as well as healers who use diverse methods.

Khamat Gader

The days of splendour of the Khamat Gader baths, located in the southern Golan Heights, started back in the Roman period when it served as a pleasure palace for the empire's entourage in Israel. The site's waters come from five thermo-mineral springs. The temperature of the mineral-rich water fluctuates between 25 °C and 51 °C, and bathing in it helps accelerate metabolism, renew skin cells, and relieve rheumatism and problems connected with the urinary and digestive systems, among other things. The site is one of Israel's most popular recreational and pampering sites. Next to the baths are spacious, shady lawns, beds and chairs, a whirlpool, water cannons, a cascade to relax in, treatment rooms, and more. There is a separate children's swimming pool, with a water slide and amusement devices, as well as special spa treatments. Children can enjoy the crocodile farm at the site. Next to the baths is the Spa Village hotel, enabling visitors to visit the site for more than one consecutive day, if they desire.

Khamei Tveriya ("Tiberias Hot Springs")

Since the days of the emperor Titus Flavius Vespasianus, who dropped by to bathe in the site's warm water on his way to conquer Gamla, and up until now, Khamei Tveriya has served as a popular therapeutic and recreational resort. The site is fed by 17 different springs that flow from the vicinity of Khamat Tveriya National Park, across the road. The water, rich with some 100 different natural minerals, bursts out from a depth of some 2,000 meters to the various pools, whose heat reaches 39 °C. Today, the site is divided into the old location, with separate bathing areas for men and women, and the spa site – Khamei Tveriya ha-Tse'ira ("Young Tiberias Springs"), with personal therapeutic pools, cosmetic mud pools, a sauna, a workout gym, a whirlpool, and treatment rooms. There is also a toddlers' pool at the site, as well as a lawn, and a private beach on the banks of the Sea of Galilee.

Central Area

The central area does not have many therapeutic sites. But, Tel Aviv and the vicinity have a selection of spa centres, offering a selection of treatments and pampering packages. Some are located in hotels, and others in private villas or facing the sea.

Khamei Ga'ash

At an approximate 20-minute ride from Tel Aviv are the main therapeutic springs in the centre of Israel, Khamei Ga'ash. The thermo-mineral springs were discovered in the 1980s while prospecting for oil. The site has two pools with thermo-mineral water: One is small and very hot, with a temperature of 40 °C, while the temperature of the other, bigger pool is 36 °C. In addition, there are special showers with therapeutic water, saunas, a treatment centre, and a regular swimming pool which is open in the summer season. Next to the baths are Kibbutz Ga'ash's guest rooms, which can rented for the day or for overnight stays. Next to the kibbutz is Ga'ash beach, where you can drop by after visiting the baths.

Khamei Yo'av

Khamei Yo'av, located south of the coastal plane, has hot sulphur pools whose temperature ranges between 37 – 39 °C. At the site are 11 sitting and standing pools whose temperature ranges between 37 – 39 °C, a whirlpool, cascades, a water massage hall, and a treatment centre.

Health Tourism"

Last summer, the European Commission put forward a proposal for a Directive on the application of patient's rights in cross-border healthcare as part of the Renewed Social Agenda. The proposal aims to help patients exercise their rights to crossborder health care in order to codify the case law of the EU Court of Justice and seeks to promote cooperation between the national health systems.

The ECJ has been ruling that patients have the right, under the EC Treaty, to seek healthcare within the EU and be reimbursed of healthcare costs received abroad that they would have been entitled to receive at the Member State of affiliation meaning where the patient is an insured person. According to the ECJ the requirement of prior authorisation for reimbursement of a patient's costs for treatment received in another Member State represents a barrier to the freedom to provide services.

The Commission has pointed out that "the uncertainty about the general application of rights to reimbursement for healthcare provided in other Member States is creating obstacles to the free movement of patients and of health services more generally in practice." Consequently, the Commission has addressed the issue of reimbursement of the cost of healthcare provided in other Member States in its draft proposal.

The EU Member States are widely divided on the need for such legislative proposal and on how this area should be regulated. Several Member states fear loss of national sovereignty over healthcare, that such proposal could have a negative impact on their ability to organise their respective national health systems or on the safety and security of patients. The Commission proposal might put the NHS financial stability at risk.

Member States have stressed that they should be able to make the use of cross-border healthcare subject to prior authorization. The main outstanding issues concern the definition of 'hospital' and 'non-hospital' care and 'specialised' care, as well as the principle of prior authorisation for care reimbursement and the management of incoming patient flows from outside their jurisdiction.

On 23 April, the European Parliament adopted a first-reading report on patients' rights in cross-border health care. The European Parliament underlined that the prior authorisation requirement must not create an obstacle to the freedom of movement of patients.

The Commission proposal would allow patients to seek healthcare in another Member State which would have been provided at home and be reimbursed up to the amount that would have been paid if they have had that treatment at home. Under Article 6 of the draft proposal the Member States of affiliation would be required to ensure that their patients seeking to receive healthcare provided in another Member State would not be prevented from receiving it.

However, it is not clear what it would be the scope of such duty of the home state or whether it is enforceable. According to the European Scrutiny Committee "(...) it is not apparent that the duty is limited to events within the home State, or that the home State has any power to require healthcare providers in another State to treat a patient." The ESC has doubts concerning home State ability to ensure that the patient is not prevented from receiving the treatment in question.

The Commission has stressed that a prior authorisation requirement on cross-border non-hospital care represents an obstacle to the free movement of health services which is not justified. The Commission has pointed out that the absence of a prior authorisation requirement will not undermine the financial equilibrium of social security systems or the organisation, planning and delivery of health services if the reimbursement of cross-border non-hospital care is within the limits of the cover guaranteed by the sickness insurance scheme of the Member State of affiliation.

Under the Commission draft proposal patients would be allowed to seek non-hospital care in another Member State and Member States would no longer be able to require prior authorization. A Member State would not be obliged to reimburse treatment provided in another Member State which is not offered by its own national health system.

The European Parliament agreed with the rule that patients are to be reimbursed up to the level they would have received in their home country. Whereas the Commission has proposed that the member state of affiliation would be obliged to reimburse only "the actual cost of treatment,", the MEPs added that "Member States may decide to cover other related costs, such as therapeutic treatment and accommodation and travel costs."

On the question of patients paying in advance and get reimbursed latter the European Parliament included a new provision under which Member States would be allowed to offer their patients a system of voluntary prior notification. Hence, citizens travelling abroad for treatment would obtain approval from their health authority in advance. In return, for such notification, reimbursement would be made directly by the Member State of affiliation to the hospital of treatment.

The European Parliament proposes therefore the creation of a system where the social security system of the member state of afiliation will make a direct payment to the hospital of treatment, either through a central clearing house or through a "bilateral voucher system" for the patient to take to the hospital and guaranteeing payment to the hospital by the member state of affiliation.

The European Parliament called on the Commission to carry out a study on the viability of establishing a clearing house to facilitate the reimbursement of costs under the draft Directive across borders, within two years of the directive's entry into force and, if necessary, to present a legislative proposal.

The Meps support the Commission proposal under which patients will have the right to seek healthcare abroad but Member States may nevertheless introduce a system requiring prior authorisation for the reimbursement of hospital costs if their social security system financial balance could be seriously undermined.

In what concerns hospital care Member States would be allowed to introduce a prior authorisation scheme for reimbursement. However, Member States must provide evidence that due to the directive implementation the outflow of patients is likely or seriously undermines the financial balance of the social security system or the planning of hospital capacity. Nevertheless, if a Member State has established a system of prior authorisation for assumption of costs of hospital care provided in another Member State, the costs of such care should also be reimbursed by the home Member State up to the level of costs that would have been taken had the same treatment been provided at home.

Meps agreed upon the possibility of introducing a system of prior authorization for the reimbursement of the costs of hospital care, but they voted for the definition for hospital care to come from the member states and not from the Commission, as was initially proposed.

The Commission believes that the absence of a common definition of what constitutes hospital care throughout the different health systems in the EU represents an obstacle to the freedom for patients to obtain healthcare services. Hence, unsurprisingly, the Commission has introduced a Community definition of hospital care which is "treatment that requires at least one night of stay in a hospital or clinic" and treatment that requires the use of highly specialised and cost-intensive medical infrastructure or medical equipment. The Commission will, through the comitology procedure, define a regularly updated technical list of such treatments. In fact, under the drat proposal a lot of room is left to comitology which will diminish Member States control over the content of such measures. It is clear that the Draft Directive would make more difficult for the member states to require prior authorisation for reimbursement of hospital treatment provided in another Member State.

The European Parliament also voted to introduce special rules for patients with rare diseases and disabilities who may need special treatment. These patients would have the right to access healthcare in another Member State not subject to prior authorisation and to reimbursement "even if the treatment in question is not among the benefits provided for by the legislation of the Member State of affiliation." The MEPs have excluded long-term care and organ transplants from the directive scope.

Under the draft proposal the home state is allowed to impose on a patient seeking healthcare provided in another Member State its general requirements, criteria for eligibility and administrative formalities for receipt of healthcare and reimbursement of healthcare costs, as it would impose if the same treatment was provided at home providing that such conditions are necessary, proportionate and are not discretionary and discriminatory.

Member States would be required to establish national contact points for cross-border healthcare to provide patients information on their right to seek care within the EU. The European Parliament also proposes the creation of a European Patients Ombudsman to take care of patients' complaints regarding prior authorisation, reimbursement of costs or harm. According to the European Scrutiny Committee any "European" Ombudsman should solely have the power to investigate the actions of the European Institutions but not the actions of national or regional governments. The ESC is concerned that the European Ombudsman could be a "court of appeal against the findings and conclusions of the national ombudsmen for health services."

The draft directive creates further bureaucratic and administrative burdens for health systems. According to Euractiv a member state representative has said "It is justifiable to ask how big the administrative burden will be compared to the number of people actually crossing borders to seek care and to calculate how much tax payers' money is spent on maintaining an administration to serve those few."

The draft directive will be discussed by ministers at the Employment, Social Affairs, Health and Consumer Affairs Council in June 2009. It remains to be seen what will come out from the negotiations but it should be noticed that the UK cannot veto the proposal as QMV is required at the Council. Long and fierce discussions at the Council and with the European Parliament are foreseen.

Public Health

Public health is "the science and art of preventing disease, prolonging life and promoting health through the organized efforts and informed choices of society, organizations, public and private, communities and individuals." (1920, C.E.A. Winslow) It is concerned with threats to the overall health of a community based on population health analysis. The population in question can be as small as a handful of people or as large as all the inhabitants of several continents (for instance, in the case of a pandemic). Public health is typically divided into epidemiology, biostatistics and health services. Environmental, social, behavioural, and occupational health are also important subfields.

There are 2 distinct characteristics of public health:

1. It deals with preventive rather than curative aspects of health,
2. It deals with population-level, rather than individual-level health issues,

The focus of public health intervention is to prevent rather than treat a disease through surveillance of cases and the promotion of healthy behaviours. In addition to these activities, in many cases treating a disease may be vital to preventing it in others, such as during an outbreak of an infectious disease. Hand washing, vaccination programs and distribution of condoms are examples of public health measures.

The goal of public health is to improve lives through the prevention and treatment of disease. The United Nations' World Health Organization defines health as "a state of complete physical, mental and social well-being and not merely the absence of disease or infirmity."

Objectives

The focus of a public health intervention is to prevent rather than treat a disease through surveillance of cases and the promotion of healthy behaviours. In addition to these activities, in many cases treating a disease can be vital to preventing its spread to others, such as during an outbreak of infectious disease or contamination of food or water supplies. Vaccination programs and distribution of condoms are examples of public health measures.

Most countries have their own government public health agencies, sometimes known as ministries of health, to respond to domestic health issues. In the United States, the front line of public health initiatives are state and local health departments. The United States Public Health Service (PHS), led by the Surgeon General of the United States, and the Centres for Disease Control and Prevention, headquartered in Atlanta, are involved with several international health activities, in addition to their national duties.

There is a vast discrepancy in access to health care and public health initiatives between developed nations and developing nations. In the developing world, public health infrastructures are still forming. There may not be enough trained health workers or monetary resources to provide even a basic level of medical care and disease prevention. As a result, a large majority of disease and mortality in the developing world results from and contributes to extreme poverty. For example, many African governments spend less than USD$10 per person per year on health care, while, in the United States, the federal government spent approximately USD$4,500 per capita in 2000.

Many diseases are preventable through simple, non-medical methods. For example, research has shown that the simple act of hand washing can prevent many contagious diseases. Public health plays an important role in disease prevention efforts in both the developing world and in developed countries, through local health systems and through international non-governmental organizations.

The two major postgraduate professional degrees related to this field are the Master of Public Health (MPH) or the (much rarer) Doctor of Public Health (Dr. PH). Many public health researchers hold PhDs in their fields of speciality, while some public health programs confer the equivalent Doctor of Science degree instead.

History of Public Health

In some ways, public health is a modern concept, although it has roots in antiquity. From the beginnings of human civilization, it was recognized that polluted water and lack of proper waste disposal spread communicable diseases (theory of miasma). Early religions attempted to regulate behaviour that specifically related to health, from types of food eaten, to regulating certain indulgent behaviours, such as drinking alcohol or sexual relations. The establishment of governments placed responsibility on leaders to develop public health policies and programs in order to gain some understanding of the causes of disease and thus ensure social stability prosperity, and maintain order.

Early Public Health Interventions

By Roman times, it was well understood that proper diversion of human waste was a necessary tenet of public health in urban areas. The Chinese developed the practice of variolation following a smallpox epidemic around 1000 BC. An individual without the disease could gain some measure of immunity against it by inhaling the dried crusts that formed around lesions of infected individuals. Also, children were protected by inoculating a scratch on their forearms with the pus from a lesion. This practice was not documented in the West until the early-1700s, and was used on a very limited basis. The practice of vaccination did not become prevalent until the 1820s, following the work of Edward Jenner to treat smallpox.

During the 14th century Black Death in Europe, it was believed that removing bodies of the dead would further prevent the spread of the bacterial infection. This did little to stem the plague, however, which was most likely spread by rodent-borne fleas. Burning parts of cities resulted in much greater benefit, since it destroyed the rodent infestations. The development of quarantine in the medieval period helped mitigate the effects of other infectious diseases. However, according to Michel Foucault, the plague model of governmentality was later controverted by the cholera model. A Cholera pandemic devastated Europe between 1829 and 1851, and was first fought by the use of what Foucault called "social medicine", which focused on flux, circulation of air, location of cemeteries, etc. All those concerns, born of the miasma theory of disease, were mixed with urbanistic concerns for the management of populations, which Foucault designated as the concept of "biopower". The German conceptualized this in the *Polizeiwissenschaft.*

The science of epidemiology was founded by John Snow's identification of a polluted public water well as the source of an 1854 cholera outbreak in London. Dr. Snow believed in the germ theory of disease as opposed to the prevailing miasma theory. Although miasma theory correctly teaches that disease is a result of poor sanitation, it was based upon the prevailing theory of spontaneous generation. Germ theory developed slowly: despite Anton van Leeuwenhoek's observations of Microorganisms, (which are now known to cause many of the most common infectious diseases) in the year 1680, the modern era of public health did not begin until the 1880s, with Louis Pasteur's germ theory and production of artificial vaccines.

Other public health interventions include latrinization, the building of sewers, the regular collection of garbage followed by incineration or disposal in a landfill, providing clean water and draining standing water to prevent the breeding of mosquitos.

Modern Public Health

As the prevalence of infectious diseases in the developed world decreased through the 20th century, public health began to put more focus on chronic diseases such as cancer and heart disease. An emphasis on physical exercise was reintroduced. In America, public health worker Dr. Sara Josephine Baker lowered the infant mortality rate using preventative methods. She established many programs to help the poor in New York City keep their infants healthy. Dr. Baker led teams of nurses into the crowded neighbourhood of Hell's Kitchen and taught mothers how to dress, feed, and bathe their babies. After World War I many states and countries followed her example in order to lower infant mortality rates.

During the 20th century, the dramatic increase in average life span is widely credited to public health achievements, such as vaccination programs and control of infectious diseases, effective safety policies such as motor-vehicle and occupational safety, improved family planning, fluoridation of drinking water, anti-smoking measures, and programs designed to decrease chronic disease.

Meanwhile, the developing world remained plagued by largely preventable infectious diseases, exacerbated by malnutrition and poverty. Front-page headlines continue to present society with public health issues on a daily basis: emerging infectious diseases such as SARS, making its way from China to Canada and the United States; prescription drug benefits under public programs such as Medicare; the increase of HIV-AIDS among young heterosexual women and its spread in South Africa; the increase of childhood obesity and the concomitant increase in type II diabetes among children; the impact of adolescent pregnancy; and the ongoing social, economic and health disasters related to the 2004 Tsunami and Hurricane Katrina in 2005. These are all ongoing public health challenges.

Since the 1980s, the growing field of population health has broadened the focus of public health from individual behaviours and risk factors to population-level issues such as inequality, poverty, and education. Modern public health is often concerned with addressing determinants of health across a population, rather than advocating for individual behaviour change. There is a recognition that our health is affected by many factors including where we live, genetics, our income, our educational status and our social relationships-these are known as "social determinants of health." A social gradient in health runs through society, with those that are poorest generally suffering the worst health. However even those in the *middle classes* will generally have worse health outcomes than those of a higher social stratum. The *new* public health seeks to address these health inequalities by advocating for population-based policies that improve health in an equitable manner.

Schools of Public Health

The Welch-Rose Report of 1915 has been viewed as the basis for the critical movement in the history of the institutional schism between public health and medicine because it led to the establishment of schools of public health supported by the Rockefeller Foundation. The report was authored by William Welch, founding dean of the Johns Hopkins Bloomberg School of Public Health, and Wycliffe Rose of the Rockfeller Foundation. The report focused more on research than practical education. Some have blamed the Rockfeller Foundation's 1916 decision to support the establishment of schools of public health for creating the schism between public health and medicine and legitimizing the rift between medicine's laboratory investigation of the mechanisms of disease and public health's nonclinical concern with environmental and social influences on health and wellness.

A year following the report, the Johns Hopkins School of Hygiene and Public Health was founded in 1916. By 1922, schools of public health were established in Columbia, Harvard and Yale universities. By 1999 there were twenty nine schools of public health enrolling around fifteen thousand students.

Over the years, the types of students and training provided have also changed. In the beginning, students who enrolled in public health schools had already obtained a medical degree. However, in 1978, 69% of students enrolled in public health schools had only a bachelors degree. Public health school training had evolved from a second degree for medical professionals to a primary public health degree with a focus on the six core disciplines of biostatistics, epidemiology, health services administration, health education, behavioural science and environmental science.

Education and Training

Schools of public health offer a variety of degrees which generally fall into two categories: professional or academic.

Professional degrees are oriented towards practice in public health settings. The Master of Public Health (M.P.H.), Doctor of Public Health (Dr.PH.) and the Master of Health Care Administration (M.H.A.) are examples of degrees which are geared towards people who want careers as practitioners of public health in health departments, managed care and community-based organizations, hospitals and consulting firms among others. Master of Public Health (MPH) degrees broadly fall into two categories, those that put more emphasis on an understanding of epidemiology and statistics as the scientific basis of public health practice and those that include a more eclectic range of methodologies.

Academic degrees are more oriented towards those with interests in the scientific basis of public health and preventive medicine who wish to pursue careers in research, university teaching in graduate programs, policy analysis and development, and other high-level public health positions. Examples of academic degrees are the Master of Science (M.S.), Doctor of Philosophy (Ph.D.), and Doctor of Science (Sc.D.). The doctoral programs are distinct from the M.P.H. and other professional programs by the addition of advanced coursework and the nature and scope of a dissertation research project. The Association of Schools of Public Health represents Council on Education for Public Health (CEPH) accredited schools of public health in the United States, Puerto Rico, and Mexico.

Delta Omega is the honorary society for graduate studies in public health. The society was founded in 1924 at the Johns Hopkins School of Hygiene and Public Health. Currently, there are approximately 50 chapters throughout the United States and Puerto Rico.

Public Health Programs

Today, most governments recognize the importance of public health programs in reducing the incidence of disease, disability, and the effects of aging, although public health generally receives significantly less government funding compared with medicine. In recent years, public health programs providing vaccinations have made incredible strides in promoting health, including the eradication of smallpox, a disease that plagued humanity for thousands of years.

An important public health issue facing the world currently is HIV/AIDS. Antibiotic resistance is another major concern, leading to the reemergence of diseases such as Tuberculosis.

Another major public health concern is diabetes. In 2006, according to the World Health Organization, at least 171 million people worldwide suffered from diabetes. Its incidence is increasing rapidly, and it is estimated that by the year 2030, this number will double.

A controversial aspect of public health is the control of smoking. Many nations have implemented major initiatives to cut smoking, such as increased taxation and bans on smoking in some or all public places. Proponents argue by presenting evidence that smoking is one of the major killers in all developed countries, and that therefore governments have a duty to reduce the death rate, both through limiting passive (second-hand) smoking and by providing fewer opportunities for smokers to smoke.

Opponents say that this undermines individual freedom and personal responsibility (often using the phrase nanny state in the UK), and worry that the state may be emboldened to remove more and more choice in the name of better population health overall. However, proponents counter that inflicting disease on other people via passive smoking is not a human right, and in fact smokers are still free to smoke in their own homes. There is also a link between public health and veterinary public health which deals with zoonotic diseases, that can be transmitted from animals to humans.

Definition of Public Health

Public health: The approach to medicine that is concerned with the health of the community as a whole. Public health is community health. It has been said that: "Health care is vital to all of us some of the time, but public health is vital to all of us all of the time."

The mission of public health is to "fulfil society's interest in assuring conditions in which people can be healthy." The three core public health functions are:

* The assessment and monitoring of the health of communities and populations at risk to identify health problems and priorities;

* The formulation of public policies designed to solve identified local and national health problems and priorities;
* To assure that all populations have access to appropriate and cost-effective care, including health promotion and disease prevention services, and evaluation of the effectiveness of that care.

There are many distinctions that can be made between public health and the clinical health professions. While public health is comprised of many professional disciplines such as medicine, dentistry, nursing, optometry, nutrition, social work, environmental sciences, health education, health services administration, and the behavioural sciences, its activities focus on entire populations rather than on individual patients.

Doctors usually treat individual patients one-on-one for a specific disease or injury. Public health professionals monitor and diagnose the health concerns of entire communities and promote healthy practices and behaviours to assure our populations stay healthy.

One way to illustrate some of the breadth of public health is to look at some of the notable public health achievements in the 20th century. The following were selected as the "Ten Great Public Health Achievements — United States, 1900-1999" by the U.S. Centres for Disease Control and Prevention (CDC).

Vaccination has resulted in the eradication of smallpox; elimination of poliomyelitis in the Americas; and control of measles, rubella, tetanus, diphtheria, Haemophilus influenzae type b, and other infectious diseases in the United States and other parts of the world.

Motor-vehicle safety Improvements in motor-vehicle safety have resulted from engineering efforts to make both vehicles and highways safer and from successful efforts to change personal behaviour (e.g., increased use of safety belts, child safety seats, and motorcycle helmets and decreased drinking and driving). These efforts have contributed to large reductions in motor-vehicle-related deaths.

Safer workplaces Work-related health problems, such as coal workers' pneumoconiosis (black lung), and silicosis — common at the beginning of the century — have come under better control. Severe injuries and deaths related to mining, manufacturing, construction, and transportation also have decreased; since 1980, safer workplaces have resulted in a reduction of approximately 40% in the rate of fatal occupational injuries.

Control of infectious diseases Control of infectious diseases has resulted from clean water and improved sanitation. Infections such as typhoid and cholera transmitted by contaminated water, a major cause of illness and death early in the 20th century, have been reduced dramatically by improved sanitation. In addition, the discovery of antimicrobial therapy has been critical to successful public health efforts to control infections such as tuberculosis and sexually transmitted diseases (STDs).

Decline in deaths from coronary heart disease and stroke Decline in deaths from coronary heart disease and stroke have resulted from risk-factor modification, such as smoking cessation and blood pressure control coupled with improved access to early detection and better treatment. Since 1972, death rates for coronary heart disease have decreased 51%.

Safer and healthier foods Since 1900, safer and healthier foods have resulted from decreases in microbial contamination and increases in nutritional content. Identifying essential micronutrients and establishing food-fortification programs have almost eliminated major nutritional deficiency diseases such as rickets, goiter, and pellagra in the United States.

Healthier mothers and babies Healthier mothers and babies have resulted from better hygiene and nutrition, availability of antibiotics, greater access to health care, and technologic advances in maternal and neonatal medicine. Since 1900, infant mortality has decreased 90%, and maternal mortality has decreased 99%.

Family planning Access to family planning and contraceptive services has altered social and economic roles of women. Family planning has provided health benefits such as smaller family size and longer interval between the birth of children; increased opportunities for preconceptional counselling and screening; fewer infant, child, and maternal deaths; and the use of barrier contraceptives to prevent pregnancy and transmission of human immunodeficiency virus and other STDs.

Fluoridation of drinking water Fluoridation of drinking water began in 1945 and in 1999 reaches an estimated 144 million persons in the United States. Fluoridation safely and inexpensively benefits both children and adults by effectively preventing tooth decay, regardless of socioeconomic status or access to care. Fluoridation has played an important role in the reductions in tooth decay (40%-70% in children) and of tooth loss in adults (40%-60%).

Recognition of tobacco use as a health hazard Recognition of tobacco use as a health hazard and subsequent public health anti-smoking campaigns have resulted in changes in social norms to prevent initiation of tobacco use, promote cessation of use, and reduce exposure to environmental tobacco smoke. Since the 1964 Surgeon General's report on the health risks of smoking, the prevalence of smoking among adults has decreased, and millions of smoking-related deaths have been prevented.

The World Health Report 2007

A Safer Future: Global Public Health Security in the 21st Century

Every day, millions of tons of cargo are shipped around the world by air, land and sea. Every day, the constant movement of people and products carries with it the potential to spread highly infectious diseases and other hazards more rapidly than at any time in history. A sudden health crisis in one region of the world is now only a few hours away from becoming a public health emergency in another. In the last five years, WHO has verified more than 1100 epidemic events. Among them was a deadly new disease, SARS – Severe Acute Respiratory Syndrome – which sparked an international alert in 2003. Today, there is a real and continuing threat of a human influenza pandemic that could have much more serious human and economic consequences.

The *World Health Report 2007* discusses these and other current challenges to global health security and asks: How can a safer future be achieved? It looks at the potential of new tools for collective defence, particularly the revised *International Health Regulations (2005)* which came into force this year. They are designed to achieve maximum security against the international spread of diseases, and have been expanded to include any emergency with international repercussions for health, including natural disasters and chemical or radionuclear events, whether accidental or deliberate.

For while acute health risks can and do spread quickly, nothing travels faster today than information. Increasingly armed with the latest communications, and supported by international networks, technology, expertise and legal obligation, countries can act promptly and collectively to health emergencies at their source and prevent their spread. The prospect of a safer future is within reach. It is both a collective aspiration and a mutual responsibility. As the causes and consequences of health emergencies expand, so does the range of players with a stake in the security agenda. *The World Health Report 2007* is directed towards all of them, and all who value public health.

Conclusions and Recommendations of the Report The report concludes with recommendations intended to provide guidance and inspiration towards cooperation and transparency in the effort to secure the highest level of global public health security.

1. Full implementation of *International Health Regulations (2005)* by all countries. The protection of national and global public health must be transparent in government affairs, be seen as a cross-cutting issue and as a crucial element integrated into economic and social policies and systems.
2. Global cooperation in surveillance and outbreak alert and response between governments, United Nations Agencies, private sector industries and organizations, professional associations, academia, media agencies and civil society, building particularly on the eradication of polio to create an effective and comprehensive surveillance and response infrastructure.
3. Open sharing of knowledge, technologies and materials, including viruses and other laboratory samples, necessary to optimize secure global pubic health. The struggle for global public health security will be lost if vaccines, treatment regimens, and facilities and diagnostics are available only to the wealthy.
4. Global responsibility for capacity building within the public health infrastructure of all countries. National systems must be strengthened to anticipate and predict hazards effectively both at the international and national levels and to allow for effective preparedness strategies.
5. Cross-sector collaboration within governments. The protection of global public health security is dependent on trust and collaboration between sectors such as health, agriculture, trade and tourism. It is for this reason that the capacity to understand

and act in the best interests of the intricate relationship between public health security and these sectors must be fostered.

6. Increased global and national resources for the training of public health personnel, the advancement of surveillance, the building and enhancing of laboratory capacity, the support of response networks, and the continuation and progression of prevention campaigns.

Asia's Health Tourism Hub

Thailand's increasing popularity as a destination for medical treatment isn't a phenomenon that's arisen by accident or overnight, but is part of a long-term government strategy in cooperation with private hospitals to establish the country as the 'health tourism hub of Asia'. Launched in 2004, this five-year strategy is jointly spearheaded by the Ministries of Public Health and Commerce, and extends beyond medical treatment, aiming to also establish the country as a world leader in the supply of health care services, such as spas, traditional Thai massage, and therapeutic and healing Thai herbal products.

So far, in respect of medical tourism, the aggressive marketing drive seems to be paying dividends. Once upon a time, the efficiency and professionalism of Thailand's medical services were secrets confined mostly to the country's contingent of foreign expatriates and employees of international organisations or companies. Nowadays things have changed markedly, with the number of tourists who travel here specifically to take advantage of the country's superior medical services rocketing year-on-year. In 2004, 600,000 foreign patients-expatriates and 'visiting patients'-had medical treatment here, generating just shy of 20 billion baht of revenue for the country. According to a Ministry of Public Health forecast, this figure is expected to grow by 66% in 2006 with around one million foreign patients generating around 27 billion baht of revenue. And by 2008, revenue from medical tourism alone is expected to reach a staggering 40 billion baht.

One area of concern, voiced by some in Thailand, is that such rampant growth in the health tourism sector may be at the expense of the quality of health care services available for Thais. However, the Ministry of Public Health has made it clear that the drive on medical tourism focuses purely on converting excess capacity in the private hospital sector into national assets, and will not divert resources away from the general population. However, and despite criticism, it seems the government and private hospitals will stop at nothing to win business from all corners of the globe. Health tourism in Thailand, with its first-world medical care at third-world prices, is here to stay.

Medical Tourism in Thailand

Thailand is leading Asia as a medical tourism destination. Medical tourism in Thailand is booming; bumping other nations down the list. The number of medical tourists that come in Thailand has been steadily growing since the early 2000's, putting the country on the top of the global medical tourism market. Major reasons that enabled Thailand to dominate this growing market are the low cost of medical treatments, the quality of treatments provided by hospitals and private clinics, and the highly developed tourism industry.

Thailand Healthcare System

There are approximately 400 hospitals in Thailand which offer advance healthcare services. The country takes pride in having the largest private hospital in Asia, as well as having the first Asian hospital to receive the ISO 9001 certification and JCI accreditation.

To date, 7 hospitals in Thailand have been accredited by the JCI: Bumrungrad International, Bangkok Hospital, Bangkok Hospital Phuket, BNH Hospital, Samitivej Srinakarin, Samitivej Sriracha, and Samitivej Sukhumvit Hospitals.

Thailand Medical tourism industry is largely driven by private hospitals. Leading the list are the Bumrungrad International Hospital, Bangkok Hospital Group, and Samitivej Hospitals. These hospitals are widely becoming renowned globally. They are known to cater mostly to foreign patients and have been actively seeking medical tourists in since 2004 or earlier. 40-50% of these hospitals patients are foreigners, being that they find these hospitals costs are cheaper than that of their home countries to a great extent, while most Thai locals still find these prices too costly.

Top Hospitals for Medical Tourism in Thailand

Bangkok Hospital Group: The Bangkok Hospital Group is a leading group of hospitals with specialized services for overseas patients. It is a network of 15 hospitals scattered all over Thailand. The Bangkok International Hospital in Bangkok tops the list. It has an International

Medical Centre which caters specially for medical tourists, completely employed with multilingual interpreters. It even has a Japanese Medical Centre with Japanese speaking physicians and nurses. Bangkok Phuket Hospital is another part of the group. It is the leading hospital in the city of Phuket, a pride of Thailand for its beautiful beaches. Phuket is a destination for medical tourists who seek sex reassignment surgeries, and Bangkok Phuket offers this service. The hospital is also recognized for having an extensive array of health check facilities.

Samitivej Hospitals: The Samitivej Hospitals is a well known chain in Thailand. The group has expanded and developed world class healthcare facilities, and has become recognized by medical tourists from all over the world. It has been collecting many prestigious awards in the recent years, including 3 JCI accredited hospitals. Samitivej Hospitals are equipped with state of the art medical equipment that compares to the leading hospitals in the North America and Europe.

Bumrungrad International: Bumrungrad International is known to have excellent facilities for medical tourists. The hospital has treated over 420,000 international patients in 2008, (including expatriates and medical tourists) from 190 countries worldwide. It gets more foreign patients than any other hospital in the world. More than half of the hospital's doctors have international training and/or board certification, including 200 who are US board certified.

Common Procedures Done by Medical Tourists in Thailand

Healthcare services and treatments offered by the hospitals and clinics in Thailand cover an extensive list. The procedures medical tourists come for varies diversely as well, but the top include the following:

Cosmetic plastic surgeries: Every aesthetic procedure in Thailand costs only a small fraction as compared to what patients in US and UK would be paying back home. Yet, the standard of service and treatment is usually high.

Dental procedures: From routine checkups to the most complicated dental surgeries, many Thailand dental clinics and hospitals are well equipped and employed to execute a complete range of dental treatments. The costs are also comparatively low and the standards are international.

Medical check-up programs: Medical check-up programs are a growing trend in the global medical tourism market. The programs are recommended for everyone, at intervals that would depend on the patient's age and condition. They are highly urged for patients in their 40's or 50's. Every major hospital in Thailand has inclusive check-up packages.

Cardiac procedures : Many hospitals in Thailand, including the Bangkok Heart Hospital, have cardiac surgery centres. Procedures carried out in Thailand include heart bypass, angioplasty, and heart valve replacement, among others.

Orthopedic surgery : Foreign patients fly Thailand to get different kinds of orthopedic procedures. Many orthopedic surgeons in Thailand have been trained overseas and equipment used for the procedures are assured to be modern and up to date, including the Computer Assisted Surgery (CAS) Micro Invasive Surgery (MAS). Commonly done orthopedic surgeries in Thailand are hip and knee replacement, as well as spine surgeries.

Price levels of common treatments in Thailand

Major surgeries

Procedure	***US***	***Thailand***
Heart bypass	130,000	11,000
Heart valve replacement	160,000	10,000
Angioplasty	57,000	13,000
Hip replacement	43,000	12,000
Knee replacement	40,000	10,000
Hysterectomy	20,000	4,500
Spinal fusion	62,000	7,000

Cost comparison of major surgeries between US and Thailand (in US$).

Stem cell therapy : A few hospitals and institutes in Thailand have pioneered the use of stem cells in different areas of medical surgeries. Among the recent developments is the application of stem cell therapy in cardiac surgeries. Stem cell therapy for Thalassemia is also being currently developed.

Sex reassignment surgeries: Sex change surgery is a long tradition in Thailand, starting in the 1970s. Patients can save up to 70%.

Cosmetic and plastic procedures

Cosmetic/plastic procedure	*US*	*Thailand*
Breast augmentation	3,500-4,000	2,600-3,200
Breast lift	4,000-4,500	2,600
Breast reduction	4,000-4,500	2,900
Buttock implant	4,000-5,000	4,000
Buttock lift	4,000-5,000	2,400
Cheek implant	2,000-2,500	1,200
Chin augmentation	1,700-2,000	700
Blepharoplasty	2,500-3,000	540
Facelift	4,500-5,000	2,400
Forehead lift	2,500-3,000	1,400
Nose reshaping	3,500-4,000	1,200
Liposuction	2,500-3,000	1,200
Tummy tuck	4,500-5,500	3,000
Vaginal rejuvenation	2,000-2,500	350-1,200
Hair transplant	4,000-4,500	1,000-2,000

Cost comparison of cosmetic and plastic procedures between US and Thailand (in US$).

Dental procedures

Dental procedure	*US*	*Thailand*
Cleaning	100-300	25-50
Tooth whitening	800-1,200	100
Tooth bleaching	350-500	150
Single implant	3,500	2,000
Amalgam filling	200-500	20
Porcelain crown	600-1,000	300-470
Ceramic crown	5,500	470-500
Root canal treatment	500-2,000	150

Cost comparison of dental procedures between US and Thailand (in US$).

Pros

There are many reasons why multitudes of foreigners seek medical treatments in Thailand.

Low cost of medical treatments: The treatment costs in Thailand amount to only a fraction that of their counterparts in most Western countries. The treatment prices are usually between 20-50% of an equivalent treatment in the west. This low cost leaves the medical tourist a budget for recuperation and even recreation.

High quality healthcare services: In the recent years, Thailand private sector has established a growing number of medical facilities that can be compared side by side with leading hospitals worldwide. The country has over 30 hospitals that cater to medical tourists, as well as numerous dental and cosmetic clinics and other medical and alternative medicine centres. 5 Hospitals in Thailand have the JCI accreditation, and all hospitals in Thailand are licensed by the country's Ministry of Public Health. Physicians in Thailand are also highly educated and trained. Many of them hold professional certifications obtained in the US and/ or Europe. In Bumrungrad for example, approximately 200 doctors in are US board certified and 400 were trained in Western hospitals.

Highly developed tourism infrastructure: Thailand is among the top holiday destinations in the world, being a paradise of inviting beaches and nature's best scenes and adorns. The country has a rich culture with a splendid cuisine, and people are friendly and accommodating to the foreigners. But if it were not for the integration of these tourism strengths to the medical service sector, the status of Thailand's medical tourism would not be this developed. Being a major tourist destination, service is one of the top factors that contributed to the industry's success. Thai people strive to give their best in rendering services to their country's visitors, and the foreigners are glad to receive the same quality of service be it in the hotel or in the hospital.

Cons

Lack of primary healthcare system: Despite many doctors in Thailand having had studies and training in the US or UK, most of them are specialists. Unfortunately, the healthcare system of Thailand relies heavily on specialized medicine. This means that common minor ailments or several medical problems on top of another are hard for a specialist to pinpoint. If underlying symptom is unknown, general medicine or internists would be the best bet.

Some doctors are employed part time: There are doctors in Thailand, including physicians and surgeons in different specialities, who work under various hospitals. They tend to juggle schedules between different hospitals all over Thailand, sometimes even having their own private clinical services somewhere. When choosing a doctor or surgeon, make sure you know their schedule in advance, and demand to get the attention you need before paying the money. Comparatively though, doctors and medical staff in Thailand are much more attentive than doctors in the West.

Lack of emergency transport facilities: While most hospitals have ambulatory services, there is still lack of transport in case of emergencies calling for immediate attention. This specifically points to air transport, as alternative to land transport in cases of heavy traffic or immediacy of need.

Statistics of Medical Tourists in Thailand

Medical tourism in Thailand has increased dramatically in the recent years. The official figures only state the number of international patients, but we estimate that 50% of those are medical tourists.

Year	*Number of internationalpatients*	*Number of medicaltourists*
2008	1,500,000	750,000
2007	1,400,000	700,000
2006	1,000,000	500,000

5

Development of Health Tourism in India

Opportunities and Challenges of Health Tourism in India

Medical Tourism is the concept of travelling to a particular destination to avail the opportunity of the world-class Healthcare services offered by the best experienced Healthcare professionals at the technologically most advanced medical facilities in complete privacy and for affordable costs. The Healthcare procedure is usually combined with a family vacation. The concept of Medical Tourism is not a new one. The first recorded instance of medical tourism dates back thousands of years to when Greek pilgrims travelled from all over the Mediterranean to the small territory in the Saronic Gulf called Epidauria. This territory was the sanctuary of the healing god Asklepios.

Epidauria became the original travel destination for medical tourism. In the recent past patients from underdeveloped countries used to travel to the advanced industrialized developed countries to take the benefit of advanced medical health care in the hospitals, recently the trend is reversing. As far back as 3,000 BC, people with eye problems made pilgrimage to Tell Brak, Syria, where healing deities were said to perform miracles. Ancient Roman spas that were believed to cure an endless list of ailments still offer hope and relief to bathers today. The World Tourism Organization includes the following in its definition of medical tourism: medical care, sickness and well-being, rehabilitation and recuperation.

India is the land of myriad experiences and exotic locales. It is a world of resplendent colours and rich cultural locales, be it magnificent monuments, heritage temples or tombs. The Country's ancient cultural heritage is inextricably linked to its technology driven present existence. The co-existence of a number of religions and cultures, together with an awe-inspiring topography makes it the perfect place for a complete holiday experience. The Indian medical tourism industry, growing at an annual rate of 30 percent, caters to patients chiefly from the US, Europe, West Asia and Africa. Although in its nascent stage, the industry is outsmarting similar industries of other countries such as Greece, South Africa, Jordan, Malaysia, Philippines and Singapore.

In 2006, over 1,50,000 medical tourists have visited India and is growing by 15% a year. The medical tourism industry in India is presently earning revenues of $450 million. Encouraged by the incredible pace of growth exhibited by the industry, the Confederation of Indian Industry (CII) and McKinsey have predicted that the industry will grow to earn additional revenue of $2.2 billion by 2012. India, touted as the favourite destination for information technology majors, is currently emerging as a preferred destination for medical or health tourism. The Government of India, State tourism boards, travel agents, tour operators, hotel companies and private sector hospitals are exploring the medical tourism industry for tremendous opportunities.

They are seeking to capitalize on the opportunities by combining the country's popular leisure tourism with medical tourism. The factors that make India as one of the favourable destination for health tourism starts with low medical cost which is one-tenth of the costs in western countries, for example, a heart surgery costs $ 6,000 in India as against $30,000 in the US, Similarly a bone marrow transplant costs $26,000 in India as compared to $2, 50,000 in the US. Foreign patients throng Indian hospitals to pass up the long waiting lists and queues in their native countries. Globalization has promoted a consumerist culture, thereby promoting goods and services that can feed the aspirations arising from this culture. This has had its effect in the health sector too. There are number of reasons for the growth of the service economy and these can be categorized into three main areas such as: ***Social Trend Demographic Trends New Services to meet New Demands***

The new services to meet new demand may include the "medical tourism". Merging healthcare and tourism an industry has been evolved in many developing countries like Greece, South Africa, Jordan, India, Malaysia, Philippines and Singapore. Medical tourism where foreigners travel abroad in search of low cost, world-class medical treatment is gaining popularity in India. India's medical tourism industry could yield as much as $3 billion in annual revenue by 2012. Indian government hopes to encourage a budding trade in medical tourism, selling foreigners the idea of travelling to India for low cost but world class medical treatment. According to the confederation of Indian industry India has the potential to attract 1 million tourists per annum, which could contribute to $6 billion to the economy. India must leverage its competitive edge, especially its cost advantage. It is only one fifth of the costs in the west. Cost savings may not be enough to foster a trade in medical tourism. Unfairly or not, most foreigners would not think of India as a land of good health. The sight of the countries overcrowded public hospitals; open sewers and garbage littered streets would unsettle most visitors' confidence about public sanitation standards in India.

Private healthcare providers argue that foreigners can be sheltered from such nastiness and that the qualities of India's corporate hospitals are world class. Currently medical tourists or medical travellers from developed industrialized countries are travelling in large numbers abroad where the quality of healthcare is equal to or even better than the standards in their own country and yet the cost is significantly lower.

These healthcare destination countries also offer numerous options for escapes to vacation touring trips, sight-seeing, shopping, exploring journeys and lounging on sun drenched exotic beaches for medical health care travellers. A combination of many factors has lead to the recent increase in the popularity of medical tourism or Medical value travel. Exorbitant cost of basic health care and medical insurance cover, high cost of modern medical facilities in advanced countries, ease and affordability of international travel, favourable currency exchange rates in the global economy, rapidly improving technology and high standards of medical care in the developing countries, best medical health care education at the medical schools, proven safety of healthcare in select foreign nations, international accreditation of foreign hospitals and access to U.S., U.K. and Australian board certified surgeons operating in select foreign countries have all contributed their share to this rapid development of global medical tourism or medical health care outsourcing.

Health care tourism or medical health care value travel has also emerged as a most popular form of vacationing mixing a broad spectrum of overseas medical health care services with leisure, a visit to health care resort or a health SPA abroad, fun and relaxation together thereby maximizing the value of vacation travel abroad, a holiday retreat with wellness and health care. Most of the foreigners treated in India come from other developing countries in Asia, Africa or the middle east where top quality hospitals and health professionals are often hard to find. Patients from the United States and Europe are relatively rare not only because of the distance they must travel but also hospital executives acknowledge because India continues to suffer from an image of poverty and poor hygiene that discourages many patients.

Medical Tourism Industry and India

India has always been a regional health care hub for the health care tourists from the neighbouring countries like Afghanistan, Bangladesh, Pakistan, Nepal, Bhutan, UAE and Maldives; recently India has emerged as one of the most important Global destination for medical tourism or health care travel. Now international patients from the developed countries like USA, Canada, UK, Europe etc. travel to India for the low-cost medical surgery treatments like knee joint replacement, total hip replacement, hip resurfacing, weight loss procedures-gastric lap band, RNY gastric bypass, heart procedures, elective surgeries and also for rejuvenation therapies promised by yoga and Ayurveda. However, a nice blend of top-class medical expertise at attractive prices is helping more and more corporate hospitals in India to lure global foreign patients for high end surgeries like organ transplants.

As more and more patients from Europe, North America and other affluent nations with very high medical costs and long wait lists look for effective options of immediate, low-cost, affordable treatments, medical health care travel to India is definitely on the cards for most of them and the fast growing Indian corporate health sector is fully geared to meet that need. Medical tourism to India is not just cost savings or the high standard of medical care facility, but also the waiting time for medical surgery treatment procedures in India is much lower than in any other country. India offers a growing number of private centres of excellence where the quality of care is as good as or better than that of big-city hospitals in the United States or Europe.

The medical care sector in India has witnessed an enormous growth in infrastructure in the private and voluntary sector. The private sector, which was very modest in the early stages, has now becoming a flourishing industry equipped with the most modern state of the art technology at its disposal. It is estimated that 75% of healthcare services and investments in India are now provided by the private sector. Health and medical tourism is perceived as one of the fastest growing segments in marketing destination India today. India could earn $2 billion annually and create 60 million new jobs by subcontracting work from the British National Health Service, the head of India's largest chain of private hospitals.

The Emerging Market for Medical Tourism

Medical tourism is growing and diversifying. Estimates vary, but McKinsey & Company and the Confederation of Indian Industry put gross medical tourism revenues at more than $40 billion worldwide in 2004. Others estimate the worldwide revenue at about $60 billion in 2006. McKinsey & Company projects the total will rise to $100 billion by 2012. According to the confederation of Indian Industry India has the potential to attract 2 million tourist per annum which could contribute to $ 5 billion to the economy. India must leverage its competitive edge especially cost advantage. It is only one fifth of the cost in the west. India enjoys a unique position as it offers holistic medicinal services.

With yoga, meditation, ayurveda, allopathic and other systems of medicines, India offers a unique basket of services to an individual that is difficult to match by other countries. Also, clinical outcomes in India are at par with the world's best centres besides having internationally qualified and experienced specialists. The equation in India to promote the industry is first world treatment at third world prices. A CII–McKinsey report last year, postulating the opportunities in health tourism industry states that the medical tourism market in the country pegged a 30 percent growth in 2000 and it has been growing at the rate of 15 percent for the past five years. The report says by 2012, if medical tourism were to reach 25 percent revenues of private up market players up to Rs.10000 crore will be added to the revenues of these players.

Scope

There is no doubt that the Indian medical industry's main appeal is low cost treatment. Most estimates claim treatment costs in India start around a tenth of the price of comparable treatment in leading countries of the world. AIIMS is a destination for patients from Nepal, Bangladesh, Bhutan, Myanmar, Mauritius and Pakistan. Besides regular patients from the Middle East, and an occasional patient drop from US and other European countries. Patients from Pakistan, especially children with heart affiliation, have been regularly coming to all India medical science. When baby Noor Fatima, a two and a half year old Pakistani girl, successfully underwent an open heart surgery in India, she opened news vistas reminding the potential of medical tourism.

In 2003 the number of patients who visited the hospital was 5000 and about 1500 was hospitalized. Along with providing treatment, the stay of the foreign patients is taken care of by the hospital itself. CII along with IHCF is working with tour operators to promote attractive packages for medical tourism. Last year, according to rough estimates, India was able to attract approximately 2.5 lakh patients to the country, but has potential for much more. CII and IHCF will suggest a list of reputed hospitals in major cities having good air connectivity, with details of their service to the government. The trade body will also suggest uniform price band in major specialities, which are indicative pricing. This would facilitate foreign patients seeking treatment in India. The Indian government predicts that India's $20 billion a year healthcare industry could grow 13 percent in each of the next six years, boosted by medical tourism, which industry watchers say is growing at 35 percent annually. In India, the Apollo group alone has so far treated 100000 international patients, many of whom are of Indian origin Apollo has been a forerunner in medical tourism in India and attracts patients from Southeast Asia, Africa and the Middle East. The group has tied up with hospitals in Mauritius, Tanzania, Bangladesh and Yemen besides running a hospital in srilanka and managing a hospital in Dubai. Another corporate group running a chain of hospitals, escorts claims it has doubled its number of overseas patients from 1000 in 2000 to 3000 this year. In India the strong tradition of traditional systems of healthcare in Kerala, for example is utilized. Kerala Ayurveda centres have been established at multiple locations in various metro cities, thus highlighting the advantages of Ayurveda in health management.

Kerala-the pioneer state Kerala or Gods own country as its corporate slogan goes has pioneered health and medical tourism in India. They have made a concentrated effort to promote health tourism in a big way which has resulted in a substantial increase of visitor arrivals into the state. Maharashtra offers tremendous potential to develop medical tourism. The latest addition in Mumbai is the Asian Heart Institute at Bandra Kurla complex, which offer State of the art facilities for all types of heart complications and even offers preventive cardiological treatment to avoid heart ailments and also to keep under control a host of heart problems. The government of Karnataka reportedly setting up a Bangalore International Health city corporation to attract patients for all sorts of healthcare and treatments. Karnataka produces the maximum number of doctors, nurses and medical technicians in the country. Karnataka is an ideal health tourism destination with the best healthcare facilities and tourist destinations. The state also boasts of having the unique property, golden palms Spa& resort, which is the one and only resort in the country where a guest can have a complete range of pathological, dental, electro-cardiograms, X-rays and even sonography tests.

Growth of the Medical Tourism Industry

The countries where medical tourism is being actively promoted include Greece, South Africa, Jordan, India, Malaysia, Philippines and Singapore. India is a recent entrant into medical tourism. According to a study by McKinsey and the Confederation of Indian Industry, medical tourism in India could become a $1 billion business by 2012. The report predicts that: "By 2012, if medical tourism were to reach 25 per cent of revenues of private up-market players, up to Rs 10,000 crore will be added to the revenues of these players". The Indian government predicts that India's $17-billion-a-year healthcare industry could grow 13 per cent in each of the next six years, boosted by medical tourism, which industry watchers say is growing at 30 per cent annually. In India, the Apollo group alone has so far treated 95,000 international patients, many of whom are of Indian origin. Apollo has been a forerunner in medical tourism in India and attracts patients from Southeast Asia, Africa, and the Middle East. The group has tied up with hospitals in Mauritius, Tanzania, Bangladesh and Yemen besides running a hospital in Sri Lanka, and managing a hospital in Dubai. Another corporate group running a chain of hospitals, Escorts, claims it has doubled its number of overseas patients-from 675 in 2000 to nearly 3000 this year. Recently, the Ruby Hospital in Kolkata signed a contract with the British insurance company, BUPA.

The management hopes to get British patients from the queue in the National Health Services soon. Some estimates say that foreigners account for 10 to 12 per cent of all patients in top Mumbai hospitals despite roadblocks like poor aviation connectivity, poor road infrastructure and absence of uniform quality standards. Analysts say that as many as 150,000 medical tourists came to India last year. However, the current market for medical tourism in India is mainly limited to patients from the Middle East and South Asian economies. Some claim that the industry would flourish even without Western medical tourists. Afro-Asian people spend as much as $20 billion a year on health care outside their countries-Nigerians alone spend an estimated $1 billion a year. Most of this money would be spent in Europe and America, but it is hoped that this would now be increasingly directed to developing countries with advanced facilities. Promotion Of Medical Tourism.

The key "selling points" of the medical tourism industry are its "cost effectiveness" and its combination with the attractions of tourism. The latter also uses the ploy of selling the "exotica" of the countries involved as well as the packaging of health care with traditional therapies and treatment methods. Price advantage is, of course, a major selling point. The slogan, thus is, "First World treatment' at Third World prices". The cost differential across the board is huge: only a tenth and sometimes even a sixteenth of the cost in the West. Open-heart surgery could cost up to $70,000 in Britain and up to $150,000 in the US; in India's best hospitals it could cost between $3,000 and $10,000. Knee surgery (on both knees) costs 350,000 rupees ($7,700) in India; in Britain this costs £10,000 ($16,950), more than twice as much.

Dental, eye and cosmetic surgeries in Western countries cost three to four times as much as in India. The price advantage is however offset today for patients from the developed countries by concerns regarding standards, insurance coverage and other infrastructure. This is where the tourism and medical industries are trying to pool resources, and also putting pressure on the government. We shall turn to their implications later. In India the strong tradition of traditional systems of health care in Kerala, for example, is utilized. Kerala Ayurveda centres have been established at multiple locations in various metro cities, thus highlighting the advantages of Ayurveda in health management. The health tourism focus has seen Kerala participate in various trade shows and expos wherein the advantages of this traditional form of medicine are showcased.

A generic problem with medical tourism is that it reinforces the medicalised view of health care. By promoting the notion that medical services can be bought off the shelf from the lowest priced provider anywhere in the globe, it also takes away the pressure from the government to provide comprehensive health care to all its citizens. It is a deepening of the whole notion of health care that is being pushed today which emphasizes on technology and private enterprise.

The important question here is for whom is 'cost effective' services to be provided. Clearly the services are "cost effective" for those who can pay and in addition come from countries where medical care costs are exorbitant-because of the failure of the government to provide affordable medical care. It thus attracts only a small fraction that can pay for medical care and leaves out large sections that are denied medical care but cannot afford to pay.

The demand for cost effective specialized care is coming from the developed countries where there has been a decline in public spending and rise in life expectancy and non-communicable diseases that requires specialist services. In India, the Apollo group alone has so far treated 95,000 international patients, many of whom are of Indian origin. Apollo has been a forerunner in medical tourism in India and attracts patients from Southeast Asia, Africa, and the Middle East. The group has tied up with hospitals in Mauritius, Tanzania, Bangladesh and Yemen besides running a hospital in Sri Lanka, and managing a hospital in Dubai. Another corporate group running a chain of hospitals, Escorts, claims it has doubled its number of overseas patients-from 675 in 2000 to nearly 1,200 this year.

Recently, the Ruby Hospital in Kolkata signed a contract with the British insurance company, BUPA. The management hopes to get British patients from the queue in the National Health Services soon. Some estimates say that foreigners account for 10 to 12 per cent of all patients in top Mumbai hospitals despite roadblocks like poor aviation connectivity, poor road infrastructure and absence of uniform quality standards. Analysts say that as many as 150,000 medical tourists came to India last year. However, the current market for medical tourism in India is mainly limited to patients from the Middle East and South

Asian economies. Some claim that the industry would flourish even without Western medical tourists. Afro-Asian people spend as much as $20 billion a year on health care outside their countries-Nigerians alone spend an estimated $1 billion a year. Most of this money would be spent in Europe and America, but it is hoped that this would now be increasingly directed to developing countries with advanced facilities.

Promotion of Medical Tourism

The key "selling points" of the medical tourism industry are its "cost effectiveness" and its combination with the attractions of tourism. The latter also uses the ploy of selling the "exotica" of the countries involved as well as the packaging of health care with traditional therapies and treatment methods. Price advantage is, of course, a major selling point. The slogan, thus is, "First World treatment' at Third World prices". The cost differential across the board is huge: only a tenth and sometimes even a sixteenth of the cost in the West. Open-heart surgery could cost up to $70,000 in Britain and up to $150,000 in the US; in India's best hospitals it could cost between $3,000 and $10,000. Knee surgery (on both knees) costs 350,000 rupees ($7,700) in India; in Britain this costs £10,000 ($16,950), more than twice as much. Dental, eye and cosmetic surgeries in Western countries cost three to four times as much as in India. The price advantage is however offset today for patients from the developed countries by concerns regarding standards, insurance coverage and other infrastructure. This is where the tourism and medical industries are trying to pool resources, and also putting pressure on the government. We shall turn to their implications later. In India the strong tradition of traditional systems of health care in Kerala, for example, is utilized. Kerala Ayurveda centres have been established at multiple locations in various metro cities, thus highlighting the advantages of Ayurveda in health management.

The health tourism focus has seen Kerala participate in various trade shows and expos wherein the advantages of this traditional form of medicine are showcased. A generic problem with medical tourism is that it reinforces the medicalised view of health care. By promoting the notion that medical services can be bought off the shelf from the lowest priced provider anyv here in the globe, it also takes away the pressure from the government to provide comprehensive health care to all its citizens. It is a deepening of the whole notion of health care that is being pushed today which emphasizes on technology and private enterprise. The important question here is for whom is 'cost effective' services to be provided. Clearly the services are "cost effective" for those who can pay and in addition come from countries where medical care costs are exorbitant-because of the failure of the government to provide affordable medical care. It thus attracts only a small fraction that can pay for medical care and leaves out large sections that are denied medical care but cannot afford to pay. The demand for cost effective specialized care is coming from the developed countries where there has been a decline in public spending and rise in life expectancy and non-communicable diseases that requires specialist services

World Class Clinical Efficiencies

Among the few providers of quaternary care for complicated medical conditions, Apollo saves millions of lives everyday Touched the lives of over 10 million patients till date. Over 4,00,000 Preventive Health checks done. Has the largest and the most sophisticated sleep laboratories in the World. Has pioneered orthopedic procedures like Total Hip and knee replacements, the Illizarov procedure, and the Birmingham Hip Resurfacing technique. Has performed over 750,000 major surgeries and over 10,00,000 minor surgical procedures till date.

Has performed over 49,000 cardiac surgeries at a 98.5% success rate. Has performed over 2,00,000 angiograms, 16,200 angoplasties (PTCA) and 3,500 mitral balloon valvuoplasities. First heart transplant patient is alive, 7 years after the operation. Has performed over 9,400 renal transplants. 130 Bone Marrow Transplants performed at high success rates. Over 30 Liver transplants done.

International Affiliations

Apollo Hospitals is recognized as a training centre by the National Board of Examination in India for post-graduate training in 16 medical departments. The Department of Radiology at Apollo is recognized by the Royal College of Radiologists, United Kingdom for training for fellowship examinations like FRCR. Recognized as a centre for conducting research work leading to Ph.D. of the Anna University, Chennai, in medical physics and digital signal processing. Apollo Hospitals is recognized by the Royal College of Physicians and Surgeons in Edinburgh for training postgraduates in radiology, surgery and trauma care.

Apollo Hospitals is the only International training organization for the American Heart Association Technical support from Texas Heart institute and Minneapolis Heart Institute for Cardiology and Cardio Thoracic surgery. Apollo Hospitals has exchange programs with the Hospitals in the US and Europe. Apollo Hospitals have an association with Mayo Clinic & Cleveland Heart Institute, USA. Apollo Hospitals is also associated with Johns Hopkins University.

Procedure	***US (USD) Approx***	***India (USD) Approx***
Bone Marrow Transplant	USD 2,50,000	USD 69,200
Liver Transplant	USD 3,00,000	USD 69,350
Heart Surgery	USD 30,000	USD 8,700
Orthopedic Surgery	USD 20,000	USD 6,300
Cataract Surgery	USD 2,000	USD 1,350
Smile Designing	USD 8,000	USD 1,100
Metal Free Bridge	USD 5,500	USD 600
Dental Implants	USD 3,500	USD 900
Porcelain Metal Bridge	USD 3,000	USD 600
Porcelain Metal Crown	USD 1,000	USD 100
Tooth Impactions	USD 2,000	USD 125
Root Canal Treatment	USD 1,000	USD 110
Tooth Whitening	USD 800	USD 125
Tooth Coloured Composite	USD 500	USD 30
Fillings/Tooth Cleaning	USD 300	USD 90
Open Heart Surgery	USD 18,000	USD 4,800
Cranio-Facial surgery and skull base	USD 13,000	USD 4,500
Neuro-surgery with Hypothermia	USD 21,000	USD 6,800
Complex spine surgery with implants	USD 13,000	USD 4,600
Simple Spine Surgery	USD 6,500	USD 2,300
Simple Brain Tumor :		
-Biopsy	USD 4,300	USD 10,000
-Surgery	USD 1,200	USD 4,600
Parkinsons:		
-Lesion	USD 6,500	USD 26,000
-DBS	USD 2,300	USD 17,800
Hip Replacement	USD 13,000	USD 4,500

Has over 4,000 specialists and super specialists, 3,000 medical officers spanning 53 clinical departments in patient care.

Less (or No) Third-Party Payment

Markets tend to be bureaucratic and stifling when insurers or governments pay most medical bills. In the United States, third parties (insurers, employers and government) pay for about 87 percent of health care. So patients spend only 13 cents out of pocket for every dollar they spend on health care. As a result, they do not shop like consumers do when they are spending their own money, and the providers who serve them rarely compete for their business based on price. A much higher percentage of private health spending is out of pocket in countries with growing, entrepreneurial medical markets. For instance, patients pay 26 percent of health care spending out of pocket in Thailand, 51 percent in Mexico and 78 percent in India. When patients control more of their own health care spending, providers are more likely to compete for patients based on price. Consequently, these countries have more competitive private health care markets.

Challenges

CII has also suggested that government should encourage medical tourism by increasing air connectivity linking major cities like Delhi, Chennai, Bangalore, Hyderabad and Kolkata and create health support infrastructure. CII says that it is also essential to establish the Indian healthcare brand synonymous with safety, trust and excellence. There is a need to undertake an international marketing campaign targeted at select countries besides establishing one stop centres in key markets to facilitate the inflow of foreign patients. There is also a need to streamline immigration process for medical visitors. The quality of healthcare for the poor in India is undeniably low. If India develops its infrastructure to international levels, it will be able to benefit medical services sector and more over help the world access the Indian medical services. The sight of the countries overcrowded public hospitals; open sewers and garbage littered streets would unsettle most visitors' confidence about public sanitation standards in India. Patients from the United States and Europe still are relatively rare not only because of the distance they must travel but also hospital executives acknowledge, because India continues to suffer from an image of poverty and poor hygiene that discourages many patients.

Cost comparisons of different treatments in India with the developed countries.

Sl No	*Treatment*	*Cost in the best hospitals of India*	*Cost in developed country*
1	Complex heart operation	$8500 including airfare	$45000 in USA
2	preventive health screening	$90	$600
3	Heart Surgery	$6500	$35000
4	Bone marrow transplant	$30000	$300000 in US
5	Open heart surgery	$15000	$200000 in US $75000 in Britain
6	Knee Surgery	$8000	$18500
7	Dental, Eye & Cosmetic Surgery	$y	$5y
8	Replacement of bulky heart valve	$12000	$300000
9	MRIS	$70	$850
10	Hip Resurfacing	$6000	$35000

Conclusion

Global competition is emerging in the health care industry. Wealthy patients from developing countries have long travelled to developed countries for high quality medical care. Now, a growing number of less-affluent patients from developed countries are travelling to regions once characterized as "third world." These patients are seeking high quality medical care at affordable prices. Reports on the number of patients travelling abroad for health care are scattered, but all tell the same story. An estimated 500,000 Americans travelled abroad for treatment in 2005. A majority travelled to Mexico and other Latin American countries; but Americans were also among the estimated 250,000 foreign patients who sought care in Singapore, the 500,000 in India and as many as 1 million in Thailand. Global competition is emerging in the health care industry. Wealthy patients from developing countries have long travelled to developed countries for high quality medical care. Now, growing numbers of patients from developed countries are travelling for medical reasons to regions once characterized as "third world." Many of these "medical tourists" are not wealthy, but are seeking high quality medical care at affordable prices. To meet the demand, entrepreneurs are building technologically advanced facilities outside the United States, using foreign and domestic capital.

They are hiring physicians, technicians and nurses trained to American and European standards, and where qualified personnel are not available locally, they are recruiting expatriates. The medical industry on a commercial platform with tourism is a new and up coming industry and needs to be explored. States like Karnataka, Kerala, Delhi, West Bengal and Maharashtra are trying their best to woo foreign patients to India and to be amongst the most favourable health destination. There is a need for constant endeavour for other states to try their best to nurture themselves in this field and contribute to GDP by providing quality service. For example the FICCI and CII have taken the lead by setting up a task force for the promotion of health and medical tourism in Maharashtra. According to CII India has the potential to attract 2 billion tourists per annum which could contribute $ 5 billion to the economy. India is not having only the expertise professionals but also has strong infrastructure to support the medical tourism industry. There is not doubt that India can be the leader in providing medical tourism by 2012.

Medical Tourism in Kerala

Kerala is not only a beautiful destination in Southern India known for its scenic beaches and serene backwaters. Of late Kerala has gained international attention for Medical Tourism and is becoming a popular international medical tourism destination. Kerala is famous for its alternative medical therapies such as Ayurveda, which help to rejuvenate and revitalize the body. What many tourists have now discovered is that Kerala has a pool of trained doctors and nurses and an excellent network of hospitals that offer international standard treatments at very affordable prices. Previously Indians working abroad, such as residents of Kerala working in the Persian Gulf countries, would return to India for medical treatment. Now International patients too have realized the advantages of travelling to Kerala and the medical tourism industry has begun to take off in a big way.

Faced with exorbitant fees for procedures such as cardiac surgery, dentistry and cosmetic surgery in their home countries, patients from the West and the Middle East have begun looking at India and Kerala in particular.

Indian doctors have established themselves as highly skilled and conscientious caregivers worldwide. Many doctors who have trained or worked abroad have returned to India to work here. Their reputation has led to the growth of the Medical Tourism industry in Kerala. Kerala Travel Tourism offers tour packages that combine medical treatment with a restful holiday in Kerala India. The world-class hospital facilities, pre and post-operative care and pleasant climate make your medical treatment and recovery in Kerala a positive experience. Some Medical Tourism options in Kerala are given below.

What is Medical Tourism?

The term "medical tourism" isn't as luxurious as you might at first believe. While some people associate tourism with "vacations" and "trips" the term actually applies to individuals who travel to foreign countries to obtain health care that is either not available or unaffordable in their own country.

There are several different reasons to use medical tourism in order to obtain health care. Some people, especially celebrities, prefer to have cosmetic surgeries done far from home because they want to be out of the public spotlight while they recover. In other case, some patients may find alternative treatments being utilized in other countries that are not available in their home country. In many cases, the main reason for participating in medical tourism is cost.

RSS Individuals have travelled across international borders for joint replacement, dental work, psychological care, and even hospice treatments. Just about every area of the medical profession welcomes medical tourism in some country. Today there are approximately 50 countries around the Risks Associated with Medical Tourism.

Those who decide to participate in medical tourism are taking quite a few risks. It is important to realize that the culture in every country is different. The natural immunity you have built up towards diseases in your home country may not protect you from foreign diseases in the place you visit. You're opening yourself up to infection not only from your procedure, but from amoebic dysentery, paratyphoid, tuberculosis, HIV, and even hepatitis.

One of the reasons people flock towards medical tourism is because the costs associated with care in other countries are often much less than the cost of care in their own homes. For example, the cost of healthcare in the United States is so expensive because it is heavily regulated by government agencies who are concerned with quality control. If the doctor makes a mistake in a foreign country you may have no recourse and, even if you did sue, the doctor is not very likely to pay you.

Medical Tourism in Kerala

The Indian state of Kerala focuses on Ayurveda as its traditional medicinal system and is heavily promoted as a medical tourism destination because of these classical treatments. That's not to say that Kerala is solely focused on Ayurveda, though. The state prides itself on having highly trained doctors from all areas of the medical profession and is believed to have some of the finest medical facilities in the world.

Indian doctors have gained recognition around the world. They're known for being very skilled and caring and several of the finest Indian doctors return to India after touring and training abroad. The Indian medical system also includes world-class pre-and post-operative care – meaning you won't be rushed out of your hospital bed because of corporate or bureaucratic red tape.

The types of medical care available in Kerala include:

- Ayurveda
- Cardiac
- Dental
- Transplant Surgery
- Ophthalmology
- Orthopedic
- Neurosurgery
- Fertility Treatment
- General Surgery, and
- Other alternative practices.

Kerala is popular amongst medical tourists for a number of reasons. Aside from providing high-quality medical care for low prices, the area is relatively easy to access and boasts a temperate climate year round. Visitors will be able to communicate easily with their doctors and the public and will have the finest amenities available, both in the hospital and in their hotels.

Medical tourism is, of course, not something that should be taken lightly – whether you plan to travel to Kerala or some other country. Make sure you conduct thorough research before deciding to take a trip overseas for a procedure you could have had done back home. Do the benefits outweigh the risks?

Kerala Medical Travel Tips

With a gradual increase in the influx of medical tourists to Kerala, it is imperative to have some travel tips available for medical tourism in Kerala. These tips travelling tips for medical tourism will be useful in your trips.

Do a search on the appropriate hospital and the hospital of choice according to their needs. Make sure you get the best quality medical care available at a price. Consult fully on the hospital which includes its reputation, facilities, technology, procedures of treatments offered and the specialists of the hospital. Have a prior appointment with the doctors and keep doctors informed about everything.

Check out the weather before starting your trip to the doctor Kerala. Keep all medical documents in the proper order as the roles of its history, previous doctor's prescription of (possibly) record of health, etc. of X rays. You should always have the information about the embassy of the destination, their friends and relatives (if any) in the city of destination.

Come prepared to stay and have treatment for a longer length or shorter time. Consult on medical tourism packages, special course of business health or discounts. It is advisable to buy some local currency at the time of arrival so that you have the hard cash for some further continuations. Keep photocopies of your documents relating to the current visa and passport. The medical tourism vacation general form is somewhat different as a little more caution and preparation gives you a happy experience in their medical trips.

Modern Medical Tourism in Kerala

Health Vacation in Kerala

The health vacation phenomenon is one of the hottest new trends at the moment, and Kerala, India currently receives a surprising number of foreign tourists who desire high-end wellness solutions. Although Kerala has long been synonymous with ancient Ayurvedic healing, the region's focus on modern medical tourism is what accounts for the bulk of visitors these days.

According to Dr. Philip Augustine, CEO of Lakeshore Hospital, the number of tourist coming into the state for a health vacation was 16,000 in 2006. It is estimated that this number could rise up to 100,000 by 2010 thanks to Kerala's world-class doctors and excellent infrastructure. The bulk of medical tourists come from the Middle-East, the U.S, the UK, and the Maldives.

Medical Tourism and Its Dangers

An international conference on medical tourism, organized jointly by the Kerala Tourism Department and the Confederation of Indian Industry (CII), would focus on attracting doctors, hospitals, and tour operators while further honing strategies to advance the benefits of medical tourism. Nawaz Meeran, President of the CII Kerala chapter, points out that the number of medical tourists arriving in Kerala rose by 30% to 40% after last year's summit. CII has also declared 2006-2007 as medical tourism year in Kerala. Part of their mission is to address the perceived dangers of medical tourism by promoting the accreditation, certification, and training of their hospital staff and personnel. They also hope to reduce the potential dangers of medical tourism by eliminating travel fatigue and prematurely expedited recovery processes.

Affordable Costs of Medical Tourism

Kerala's emergence as a top class medical tourism destination has attracted international insurance companies and third party managers. The *Guardian of London* states that the health vacation phenomenon is on an upswing with tourists from developed countries since medical tourism combines affordable wellness solutions with personalized attention. Many also throw in a brief vacation for good measure. *The Guardian* further quotes the competitive treatment costs such as:

- Heart Bypass UK £15000, France £13000, US £13250, India £4300
- Hip-replacement UK £9000, US £15900, France £7600, India £1350.

As a medical tourist Wayne Steinard says ""I still cannot believe that expenses on the surgery, other hospital charges, airfares and hotel stay do not add up to US $10,000." This sentiment is starting to spread as more and more tourists from abroad realize the many benefits of medical tourism in India.

Kerala as a Medical Tourism Destination:

Kerala is a major medical tourism destination in India because of a variety of factors like

* Well connected road, rail and air transportation,
* Sophisticated hospitals of World class standards which provides treatment for almost all medical conditions,
* Moderate climate conditions throughout the year,
* Renowned doctors specialised in all major disciplines,
* High standard Resorts and Hotels,
* Easy communication with the general public,
* Low cost packages for all treatments,
* Cardiac Surgery, Cosmetic treatments and Dentistry are well available for cheap costs.

Cardiac Care, General Surgery, Ayurveda, Dental Care, Fertility Treatment, Transplant Surgery, Neurosurgery, Ophthalmology and Orthopedic Treatment are also available in Kerala hospitals.

Ayurveda: Ayurveda is a traditional form of healing developed in India. There are many renowned Ayurvedic treatment centres in Kerala like Kottakkal Arya Vaidya Sala, Vaidyaratnam Thykkattu Mooss Oushadasala, Kerala Ayurvedic Pharmacy, S N A Oushadasala and many more.

Cardiac Care: Cardiac Care is a branch of medicine which attracts a lot of tourists from all over the world. Some of the hospitals that offer world-class cardiac care in Kerala, are the Trichur Heart Hospital, Sree Sudihindra Medical Mission Hospital in Cochin and Sri Chitra Thirunal Institute in Thiruvananthapuram.

General Surgery: General Surgery for various medical conditions are available in Kerala's high quality hospitals at a lower cost. This attracts a lot of patients from across the globe. Some of the hospitals which offer general surgery are Amrita Institute of Medical Sciences & Research Centre, Ernakulam, Specialist's Hospital, Ernakulam, Atingal Multispeciality Hospital, Trivandrum and many others.

Dental Care: Dental Care in Kerala is a cost-effective alternative for residents of western countries and nations in the Middle East. Tourists can avail world class dental care in Kerala for minimal costs. Almost all major hospitals offer dental care.

Fertility Treatment: Fertility treatment is offered at a large number of hospitals across Kerala. This is offered as a specialised treatment. Couples who are unable to conceive can have biological children with the help of modern technologies. Advanced techniques such as GIFT (Gamete Intra Fallopian Transfer) and ZIFT (Zygote Intra Fallopian Transfer) are offered at well-equipped Fertility centres in Kerala.

Transplant Surgery: Renal transplant surgery (Kidney transplantation), Liver Transplant, Bone Marrow transplant and Corneal transplant are the major transplant surgeries performed in Kerala hospitals. Amrita Institute of Medical Sciences & Research Centre, Ernakulam, Medical Trust Hospital, Cochin and Calicut Medical College are the major hospitals in Kerala for transplant surgery.

Neurosurgery: Neurosurgery is performed in Kerala for the brain and spinal conditions. Neurosurgery covers a range of surgeries including brain surgery for tumours, aneurysms and head injuries. Spinal Cord Surgery includes micro-discectomy, laminectomy, corpectomy and spinal fusion.

Ophthalmology: Many patients from neighbouring countries and the Middle East, travel to Kerala for ophthalmology treatment. Ophthalmology includes treatment of various eye problems like Cataract and myopia. LASIK treatments, Cataract surgery and corneal transplant surgery are all performed in the hospitals.

Orthopedic Treatment: Orthopedic treatment involves the diagnosis and treatment of medical conditions affecting the skeletal system. Disorders of the bones and joints, and conditions of the spine are treated at orthopedic centres in Kerala.

Tourism in Kerala

Kerala, a state situated on the tropical Malabar Coast of southwestern India, is one of the most popular tourist destinations in the country. Named as one of the *ten paradises of the world* by the National Geographic Traveller, Kerala is famous especially for its ecotourism initiatives. Its unique culture and traditions, coupled with its varied demography, has made Kerala one of the most popular tourist destinations in the world. Growing at a rate of 13.31%, the tourism industry is a major contributor to the state's economy.

Until the early 1980s, Kerala was a hitherto unknown destination, with most tourism circuits concentrated around the north of the country. Aggressive marketing campaigns launched by the Kerala Tourism Development Corporation—the government agency that oversees tourism prospects of the state—laid the foundation for the growth of the tourism industry. In the decades that followed, Kerala Tourism was able to transform itself into one of the niche holiday destinations in India. The tag line *Kerala-God's Own Country* was adopted in its tourism promotions and became synonymous with the state. Today, Kerala Tourism is a global superbrand and regarded as one of the destinations with the highest brand recall. In 2006, Kerala attracted 8.5 million tourists–an increase of 23.68% in foreign tourist arrivals compared to the previous year, thus making it one of the fastest growing tourism destination in the world.

Popular attractions in the state include the beaches at Kovalam, Cherai and Varkala; the hill stations of Munnar, Nelliampathi, Ponmudi and Wayanad; and national parks and wildlife sanctuaries at Periyar and Eravikulam National Park. The "backwaters" region—an extensive network of interlocking rivers, lakes, and canals that centre on Alleppey, Kumarakom, and Punnamada—also see heavy tourist traffic. Heritage sites, such as the Padmanabhapuram Palace, Hill Palace, Mattancherry Palace are also visited. Cities such as Kochi and Thiruvananthapuram are popular centres for shopping and traditional theatrical performances.

The state's tourism agenda promotes ecologically sustained tourism, which focuses on the local culture, wilderness adventures, volunteering and personal growth of the local population. Efforts are taken to minimise the adverse effects of traditional tourism on the natural environment, and enhance the cultural integrity of local people.

Historical Context

Since its incorporation as a state, Kerala's economy largely operated under welfare-based democratic socialist principles. This mode of development, though resulted in a high Human Development Index and standard of living among the people, lead to an economic stagnation in the 1980s (growth rate of 2.3% annually) This apparent paradox—high human development and low economic development — lead to a large number of educated unemployed seeking jobs overseas, especially in the Gulf countries. Due to the large number of expatriates, many travel operators and agencies set shop in the state to felicitate their travel needs. However, the trends soon reciprocated with the travel agencies noticing the undermined potential of the state as a tourist destination.

By 1986, tourism had gained an industry status. Kerala Tourism subsequently adopted the tagline *God's Own Country* in its advertisement campaigns. Aggressive promotion in print and electronic media were able to invite a sizable investment in the hospitality industry. By the early 2000s, tourism had grown into a fully fledged, multi-billion dollar industry in the state. The state was able to carve a niche place for itself in the world tourism industry, thus becoming one of the places with the 'highest brand recall'. In 2003, Kerala, a hitherto unknown tourism destination, became the fastest growing tourism destination in the world.

Today, growing at a rate of 13.31%, Kerala is one of the most visited tourism destinations in India.

Major Attractions in Kerala

Beaches

Flanked on the western coast by the Arabian Sea, Kerala has a long coastline of 580 km (360.39 miles); all of which is virtually dotted with sandy beaches.

Kovalam beach near Thiruvananthapuram was among the first beaches in Kerala to attract tourists. Rediscovered by back-packers and tan-seekers in the sixties and followed by hordes of hippies in the seventies, Kovalam is today the most visited tourist destination in the state.

Other popularly visited beaches in the state include those at Alappuzha Beach, Nattika beach, Vadanappilly beach [Thrissur], Cherai Beach, Kappad, Kovalam, Marari beach, Fort Kochi and Varkala. The Muzhappilangad Beach at Kannur is the only drive-in beach in India.

Backwaters

The backwaters in Kerala are a chain of brackish lagoons and lakes lying parallel to the Arabian Sea coast (known as the Malabar Coast). Kettuvallam (Kerala houseboats) in the backwaters are one of the prominent tourist attractions in Kerala. Alleppey, known as the "Venice of the East" has a large network of canals that meander through the town. The Vallam Kali (the Snake Boat Race) held every year in August is a major sporting attraction.

The backwater network includes five large lakes (including Ashtamudi Kayal and Vembanad Kayal) linked by 1500 km of canals, both manmade and natural, fed by 38 rivers, and extending virtually the entire length of Kerala state. The backwaters were formed by the action of waves and shore currents creating low barrier islands across the mouths of the many rivers flowing down from the Western Ghats range.

Hill Stations

Eastern Kerala consists of land encroached upon by the Western Ghats; the region thus includes high mountains, gorges, and deep-cut valleys. The wildest lands are covered with dense forests, while other regions lie under tea and coffee plantations (established mainly in the 19th and 20th centuries) or other forms of cultivation. The Western Ghats rises on average to 1500 m elevation above sea level. Certain peaks may reach to 2500 m. Popular hill stations in the region include Devikulam, Munnar, Nelliyampathi, Peermade, Ponmudi, Vagamon, Wayanad and Kottanchery Hills.

Wildlife

Most of Kerala, whose native habitat consists of wet evergreen rainforests at lower elevations and highland deciduous and semi-evergreen forests in the east, is subject to a humid tropical climate. However, significant variations in terrain and elevation have resulted in a land whose biodiversity registers as among the world's most significant. Most of Kerala's significantly biodiverse tracts of wilderness lie in the evergreen forests of its easternmost districts.

Kerala also hosts two of the world's Ramsar Convention-listed wetlands: Lake Sasthamkotta and the Vembanad-Kol wetlands are noted as being wetlands of international importance. There are also numerous protected conservation areas, including 1455.4 km^2 of the vast Nilgiri Biosphere Reserve.

In turn, the forests play host to such major fauna as Asian Elephant (*Elephas maximus*), Bengal Tiger (*Panthera tigris tigris*), Leopard (*Panthera pardus*), and Nilgiri Tahr (*Nilgiritragus hylocrius*), and Grizzled Giant Squirrel (*Ratufa macroura*). More remote preserves, including Silent Valley National Park in the Kundali Hills, harbour endangered species such as Lion-tailed Macaque (*Macaca silenus*), Indian Sloth Bear (*Melursus (Ursus) ursinus ursinus*), and Gaur (the so-called "Indian Bison" — *Bos gaurus*).

More common species include Indian Porcupine (*Hystrix indica*), Chital (*Axis axis*), Sambar (*Cervus unicolor*), Gray Langur, Flying Squirrel, Swamp Lynx (*Felis chaus kutas*), Boar (*Sus scrofa*), a variety of catarrhine

Old World monkey species, Gray Wolf (*Canis lupus*), Common Palm Civet (*Paradoxurus hermaphroditus*). Many reptiles, such as king cobra, viper, python, various turtles and crocodiles are to be found in Kerala—again, disproportionately in the east.

Kerala's avifauna include endemics like the Sri Lanka Frogmouth (*Batrachostomus moniliger*), Oriental Bay Owl, large frugivores like the Great Hornbill (*Buceros bicornis*) and Indian Grey Hornbill, as well as the more widespread birds such as Peafowl, Indian Cormorant, Jungle and Hill Myna, Oriental Darter, Black-hooded Oriole, Greater Racket-tailed and Black Drongoes, bulbul (*Pycnonotidae*), species of Kingfisher and Woodpecker, Jungle Fowl, Alexandrine Parakeet, and assorted ducks and migratory birds.

Additionally, freshwater fish such as *kadu* (stinging catfish — *Heteropneustes fossilis*) and brackishwater species such as *Choottachi* (orange chromide — *Etroplus maculatus*; valued as an aquarium specimen) also are native to Kerala's lakes and waterways.

Ayurveda

Medical tourism, promoted by traditional systems of medicine like Ayurveda and Siddha are widely popular in the state, and draws increasing numbers of tourists. A combination of many factors has led to the increase in popularity of medical tourism: high costs of healthcare in industrialised nations, ease and affordability of international travel, improving technology and standards of care.

However, rampant recent growth in this sector has made the government apprehensive. The government is now considering introduction of a grading system which would grade hospitals and clinics, thus helping tourists in selecting one for their treatments.

Culture

Kerala's culture is mainly Dravidian in origin, deriving from a greater Tamil-heritage region known as Tamilakam. Later, Kerala's culture was elaborated on through centuries of contact with overseas cultures. Native performing arts include *koodiyattom*, *kathakali* – from *katha* ("story") and *kali* ("play") – and its offshoot *Kerala natanam*, *koothu* (akin to stand-up comedy), *mohiniaattam* ("dance of the enchantress"), *thullal*, *padayani*, and *theyyam*. Other arts are more religion-and tribal-themed. These include *chavittu nadakom*, *oppana* (originally from Malabar), which combines dance, rhythmic hand clapping, and *ishal* vocalisations. However, many of these artforms largely play to tourists or at youth festivals, and are not as popular among most ordinary Keralites.

These people look to more contemporary art and performance styles, including those employing mimicry and parody. Additionally, a substantial Malayalam film industry effectively competes against both Bollywood and Hollywood.

Several ancient ritualised arts are Keralite in origin; these include *kalaripayattu* (*kalari* ("place", "threshing floor", or "battlefield") and *payattu* ("exercise" or "practice")). Among the world's oldest martial arts, oral tradition attributes *kalaripayattu*'s emergence to Parasurama. Other ritual arts include *theyyam* and *poorakkali*.

In respect of Fine Arts, the State has an abounding tradition of both ancient and contemporary art and artists. The traditional Kerala murals are found in ancient temples, churches and palaces across the State. These paintings, mostly dating back between the 9th to 12th centuries AD, display a distinct style, and a colour code which is predominantly ochre and green.

Like the rest of India, religious diversity is very prominent in Kerala. The principal religions are Hinduism, Christianity, and Islam; Jainism, Judaism, Sikhism, and Buddhism have smaller followings. The states historic ties with the rest of the world has resulted in the state having many famous temples, churches, and mosques. The Paradesi Synagogue in Kochi is the oldest in the Commonwealth of Nations.

Recognising the potential of tourism in the diversity of religious faiths, related festivals and structures, the tourism department launched a *Pilgrimage tourism* project.

Major pilgrim tourism attractions include Guruvayur, Sabarimala, Malayatoor, Paradesi Synagogue, St. Mary's Forane (Martha Mariam) Church Kuravilangad built in 105 A.D, Attukal Ponkal and Chettikulangara Bharani

Advertising Campaigns

Kerala Tourism is noted for its innovative and market-focused ad campaigns. These campaigns have won the tourism department numerous awards, including the *Das Golden Stadttor Award for Best Commercial, 2006*, *Pacific Asia Travel Association-Gold Award for Marketing, 2003* and the

Government of India's *Best Promotion Literature, 2004*, *Best Publishing, 2004* and *Best Tourism Film, 2001*.

Catchy slogans and innovative designs are considered a trademark of brand Kerala Tourism. Celebrity promotions are also used to attract more tourists to the state. The Kerala tourism website is widely visited, and has been the recipient of many awards. Recently, the tourism department has also engaged in advertising via mobiles, by setting up a WAP portal, and distributing wallpapers and ringtones related to Kerala through it.

Threats to the Tourism Industry

With increasing threats posed by global warming and changing weather patterns, it is feared that much of Kerala's low lying areas might be susceptible to beach erosions and coastal flooding. The differing monsoon patterns also suggest possible tropical cyclones in the future.

Awards

The state has won numerous awards for its tourism initiatives. These include:

- 2005-Nominated as one among the three finalists at the World Travel and Tourism Council's 'Tourism for Tomorrow' awards in the destination category.
- Das Golden Stadttor Award for Best Commercial, 2006
- Grand award for Environment, 2006
- Gold award for Ecotourism, 2006
- Gold award for Publication, 2006
- Gold Award for E-Newsletter, 2005
- Honourable Mention for Culture, 2005
- Gold Award for Culture, 2004
- Gold Award for Ecotourism, 2004
- Gold Award for CD-ROM, 2004 and 2003
- Gold Award for Marketing, 2003
- Grand Award for Heritage, 2002
- International Award for Leisure Tourism, 2000-2001.

Government of India

- Best Performing Tourism State, 2005

- Best Maintained Tourist-friendly Monument, 2005
- Best Publishing, 2005
- Best Marketed and Promoted State, 2004.
- Best Maintained Tourist-friendly Monument, 2004
- Best Innovative Tourism Project, 2004
- Best Promotion Literature, 2004
- Best Publishing, 2004
- Best Performing State for 2003, 2001, 2000 and 1999-Award for Excellence in Tourism.
- Best Practices by a State Government, 2003
- Best Eco-tourism Product, 2003
- Best Wildlife Sanctuary, 2003
- Most Innovative Use of Information Technology, 2003 and 2001
- Most Tourist-friendly International Airport, 2002
- Most Eco-friendly Destination, 2002
- Best Tourism Film, 2001.

Outlook Traveller-TAAI

- Best State that promoted Travel & Tourism, 2000-2001.

Federation of Indian Chambers of Commerce and Industry

- Award for Best Marketing, 2003
- Award for Best Use of IT in Tourism, 2003.

Galileo-Express Travel & Tourism

- Award for the Best Tourism Board, 2006
- Award for the Best State Tourism Board, 2003.

Tourism in Kerala

Kerala is one of the most popular tourist destinations in India. It is a small coastal state on the south western tip of India, which is often addressed with its popular sobriquent, "God's own country". One gets to experience the beauty of enchanting backwaters, exotic wildlife, lush hill stations, and mouthwatering cuisine and Ayurveda health treatments during their visit to Kerala.

Climate: like most parts of India, Kerala also enjoys Tropical climate. The weather is never too cold. Summer starts from April and continues for the next four months. The temperature during this period can soar up to 35°c. Monsoon brings heavy rain in this region between June, July, August and September. Winters are extremely pleasant since the temperature does not drop down to unbearable temperatures.

Places of visit: Kerala is graced by the Arabian Sea on its West and the Western Ghats on the East. It houses many beautiful lagoons, backwaters and enchanting landscapes. There are thus several tourist destinations in Kerala.

Munnar: Munnar is one of the best hill stations of South India. It was once the summer capital of British Government in South India. Tea plantations can be found at almost every corner of Munnar. Anamudi, the highest peak in south India is also located here and is an ideal place for trekking. Mattupetty is famous for its specialized Diary Farm and Devikulum is an abode of exotic flora and fauna and has endless spaces of velvet lawns.

Aleppey: Aleppey is a district seeped in immense natural beauty. The R-block in this region is famous for its backwaters and also has beautiful stretches of paddy fields. Aleppey is world famous for its Snake Boat Race which usually takes during the festival of Onam. Beach lovers aren't disappointed as well. The Aleppey Beach is a fascinating tourist spot.

Cochin: Cochin is the commercial capital of Kerala. The places of visit include St.Francis church, Mattancherry Palace and a Jewish Synagogue. You can also take a small excursion to the cascading Athirapally Water Falls or visit the elephant training centre in Kodanad.

Thekkady: Periyar Tiger Reserve is one of the famous wildlife sanctuaries in India. The thick forest is an ideal place for viewing elephants. You can also add boating, Trekking and Plantation tour as a part of your trip.

Kovalam: Kovalam is a beautiful beach and is popular for Ayurvedic treatments especially during monsoon. You can also plan an excursion to the World-famous Kanyakumari which is a converging spot for three mighty water bodies-the Arabian Sea, the Bay of Bengal and the Indian Ocean. The sunrise and sunset views are spectacular from the beach. The Padmanabhapuram Palace is a must visit or all tourists who wish to get a taste of its unique Travancore architecture.

Silent Valley: Silent valley is the core of the Niligiri Biosphere Reserve and has the pristine glory of almost unbroken ecological history. The accommodation and transport is available from a nearby place called Mukkali. It is necessary to plan your visit to this place by making all your bookings in advance.

Waynad, Kumarakom and Varkala are other suggested places of visit.

Kerala Ayurvedic: the therapeutic massages in Kerala are famous all over the world for its rejuvenating properties. They have proved to be effective not only in relaxing the body and relieving stress but also aids in treating ailments such as arthritis, paralysis, obesity, sinusitis, migraine, premature ageing, skin ailments etc. There are numerous Ayurveda resorts in Kerala. Kerala's equable climate, natural abundance of herbs and medicinal plants and trained hands has enabled in creating a popular tradition of refreshing and relaxing Kerala ayuredic massages.

Kerala Cuisine:: Kerala has an array of cookery specialities that are exclusive to the region. Seafood and rice form the staple food of Kerala. The flavours are composed of natural herbs, local spices and coconut. It is an ideal source of healthy food because there is less use of oil and artificial additives.

Travel To Kerala: Kerala is well accessible by air, rail and road.

AIR: There are three airports in the state-Thiruvananthapuram, Kochi and Kozhikode. Thiruvananthapuram is also an international airport, connecting the state to many places in India and the world.

Thiruvananthapuram International Airport

Domestic flights (direct): From to: Delhi, Mumbai, Bangalore, Chennai.

International flights (direct): From to: Colombo, Maldives, Dubai, Sharjah, Bahrain, Doha, Ras-al-Khaimah, Kuwait, Riyadh, Fujairah and Singapore.

Karipur Airport, Kozhikode

Domestic flights (direct): From to: Mumbai, Chennai, Coimbatore.

International flights (direct): From to: Sharjah, Bahrain, Dubai, Doha, Ras-al-Khaimah, Kuwait, Riyadh, Fujairah.

Cochin International Airport, Nedumbassery

Domestic flights (direct): From to: Mumbai, Chennai, Goa, Agathi, Bangalore.

International flights (direct): From to: Sharjah, Dubai, Abu Dhabi, Bahrain, Riyadh, Muscat.

Rail: There are around 200 railway stations in Kerala connecting most of the places in the state to places in the other parts of India and inside the state. Long-distance express trains connect important places in the state to places outside Kerala like Mumbai, New Delhi, Chennai and Kolkata.

Road: An extensive network of roads connects most of the places in the state. National highways 47, 17, and 49 connect Kerala with other parts of India.

Medical Tourism in Kerala

Medical Tourism is the synergy between hospitals and the Tourism industry. The state is all set for a leap in medical tourism. More and more hospitals are joining hands with the tourism industry to benefit their services. The high priority for health in Kerala is bound to make this relatively new aspect of tourism into a multi crore industry in future.

Kerala is already being marketed as a popular health destination for its famous Ayurveda health packages. Medical tourism is marketed alongwith Ayurveda and other health packages. Major hospitals are joining hands with the govt in promoting medical tourism. Health insurance companies are beginning to play a major role in medical tourism.

Globalisation and economic liberalization have given a boost to the medical service sector, especially in Kerala. The medical treatment for various packages form part of recuperative leisure packages at world class tourist resorts. Airport pickup, hotel accommodation, transportation, food, etc. are offered along with medical treatment at the best hospitals.

Medical Tourism in Kerala India

Medical tourism in Kerala is an up coming field which is proving a windfall for the tourism sector in India. People from all over the world come here for medical treatments ranging from cardiac care, transplants and various cosmetic surgeries. Apart from that they get the chance to experience the age old Ayurveda along with the view traditional cultural heritage of the state of Kerala.

Kerala's proliferating medical tourism industry, expected to be worth atleast US$2.2 billion by 2012, is proving a jackpot for the travel and tourism sector in India. It has been recorded that Kerala attracts more than 20,000 patients from all across the world every year. Medical Tourism in Kerala has become a common form of holidaying that covers a broad spectrum of cost effective medical care in collaboration with the tourism industry for patients needing surgical and other forms of specialized treatments.

Kerala is a tourists paradise and is no exception for the tourists coming for medical tourism. Patients get the golden opportunity to enjoy the beauty of scintillating backwaters and participate in other adventure activities during their recuperation. An extensive tour to Kerala not just works as an ameliorate experience but also actively contributes to the patients recovery.

The super speciality hospitals in Kerala are true centres of excellence known for providing world-class medical services, expertise and infrastructure to the tourists. There are many factors that have contributed to the recent increase in the popularity of medical tourism in Kerala. Apart from the long waiting lists, you get the affordable medical facilities in combination with the memorable holiday at your favourite destination in India.

While being in Kerala you can opt for various medical treatments that includes neurosurgery, cardiac care, dental care, infertility, heart transplant, hip replacement and cosmetic surgery. Many international patients place their confidence in Kerala's world class health care system, and have suggested other too for the same.

Most of the tourists come to Kerala to experience the enriching power of rejuvenation treatments promised by ancient art of Yoga and Ayurveda. The government's initiative to combine tourism along with medical practices at a cost which is comparatively very low as compared to U.S. or U. K, has contributed to the rapid growth of medical tourism in the state. So what are you waiting for go for medical tour in Kerala and treat yourself with the best quality care in India.

Medical Tourism in Kerala

1. Kerala is already marketed as a health destination mainly for its Ayurveda packages.

2. Medical tourism is marketed along with Ayurveda and other health packages.
3. Major hospitals like KIMS, Trivandrum, Lake Shore and AIMS in Kochi, and MIMS, Calicut have pioneered joining hands with the Government promoting Medical Tourism.
4. Globalization and economic liberalization have given a boost to the specialized Medical Service Sector
5. Health Insurance Companies are playing a major role in Medical Tourism.
6. Medical tourism is like any leisure product where service components like airlines, hotels, travel companies, transportation, food outlets are offered and medical treatment at the best hospitals. The medical treatment for various ailments are packaged with recuperative leisure packages at world class tourist resorts.

Kerala a Medical Tourism Destination

1. Well connected by Air from major medical tourism markets in the Middle East European markets and South Asia.
2. Moderate weather throughout the year.
3. Advanced and sophisticated hospitals of International standards located in Kerala.
4. Renowned doctors specialized in almost all major disciplines.
5. Trained paramedical staff and technicians available in Kerala.
6. Easier communication with majority English speaking public.
7. The higher hygienic standards of Kerala.
8. The developed tourism industry in Kerala with its array of high quality resorts and hotels.
9. Ideal setting for an excellent recuperative holiday.
10. Medical tourism packages offered and marketed by tour operators joining hands with excellent hospitals.
11. Incredibly competitive cost for packages of medical treatment and surgery compared to other countries.
12. Honoring of medical insurance by hospitals in Kerala.
13. Marketed efficiently in source markets.

Speciality Hospitals in Kerala

A Cure for Every Problem

If you're looking at plastic surgery, correction of congenital malformation, breast reconstruction surgery and other beauty enhancing cosmetic surgeries, Kerala offers highly specialised departments and expert surgeons to take care of your needs. Dental treatments are also a priority of tourists to Kerala as even the most complex jaw replacement surgeries cost 50% lesser than international rates. Access to state-of-the-art technology and specialised orthodontic clinics are also easier in Kerala. Without leaving a dent in your budgets.

A Definitive Cost Advantage

While a hip replacement surgery costs upto US $ 12,000 outside India, the procedure would be completed in less than one third of the cost here in Kerala. On a more common level, a regular dental filling which would cost around € 400 in Austria would cost a mere €10 in Kerala.

Generally, estimates show that most surgeries in India cost just 1/10 of the costs in Western countries. And across different categories, tourists are discovering that there is an alluring cost difference of around 60-70% on medical treatments in most premium institutions here. With increasing queues at National Health Services and other Government Health Service departments and Insurance Services across Europe, it is no surprise that thousands are finding the perfect remedy in God's Own Country.

World-class Technology Meets Round the Clock Care

Kerala's internationally recognised medical institutions attract travellers from Europe, US, the Middle East and even countries like South Africa. Some of Kerala's most acclaimed speciality healthcare institutions include the Lakeshore Hospital, Kerala Institute of Medical Sciences, SUT Hospital, Amritha Institute of Medical Sciences, Malabar Institute of Medical Sciences and a few others.

Equipped with upto 20 speciality and super-speciality departments offering services of hundreds of physicians within each institution. And with state-of-the-art computerised technology, meticulous service and aesthetically furnished environments, tourists enjoy some of the best of facilities they can find anywhere in the world.

Some Health Indicators of Kerala

1. Population density-819 per sq km.
2. Annual Per capita income – Rs 17,756 (national avg-Rs 14,712).
3. Sex ratio-1036 females to 1000 males.
4. Population growth rate – 9.4 %.
5. Low infant and child mortality-Infant Mortality Rate – <12.
6. High life expectancy at birth-Life expectancy –75yrs.
7. Virtual elimination of many communicable diseases.
8. Replacement level birth rate in many districts.
9. Birth rate – 18.2 per 1000.
10. Death rate –6.2 per 1000.
11. Maternal mortality rate-<2 per 1000.
12. Per capita expenditure on health care by Kerala population-11.95 compared to the all India figure of 6 %.

Healthcare Infrastructure

1. Bed availability-377 per 1000 population.
2. Kerala spends > 9% of the State GDP on health.
3. Kerala Health Sector – Private sector dominates with 70% share on health care.
4. Health Insurance < 9 % covered.

Kerala-Gods Own Paradise in India

Kerala: Kerala is rightly referred to as God's own country. It is a state which has all the geographical features like hills, rivers, sea, backwaters, and forests. You name it and its there. Kerala is located in Southern India. People here are very inviting and loving in nature just like the place. Kochi is the capital of Kerala. A trip to the place should cover Kochi, Alleppey, Thekkady and Munnar.

Climate: The climate of Kerala is warm and humid at the coast. The hills, especially Munnar are cool. The average temperature at the plains is 28 degrees Celsius to 32 degrees Celsius. The hills are cool at 20 degrees in summers and in winters; the temperature can drop to 0 degrees Celsius also. The best time to travel to Kerala is September to May.

How to reach: Kochi city has an international airport. It has flights to the Middle East and Singapore. Kochi is well connected to all major cities in India by air. From Kochi you can hire a taxi to move around Kerala and get back to Kochi. Such packages are easily available. State transport buses also connect Kochi to Alleppey and Munnar. The ride is quite comfortable and cheap. You can also have a glimpse of the local people and their lifestyle in the journey by bus.

What to see: First you will land in Kochi. You can spend a day or two for local sightseeing by going to places like Fort Kochi, Marine Drive, Willingdon Island, Matancherry etc.

From Kochi you can take a bus or taxi to Alleppey. Alleppey or Alaphuza is a small town famous for backwaters. Here you can stay on a house boat and spend the day cruising in the beautiful backwaters of Kerala.

From here, move to Thekkady, which is on a hill. There is a wild life sanctuary here. Elephants are easily spotted here. If you are lucky you could see a tiger!

From Thekkady you can drive to Munnar. Munnar is the most beautiful hill station in India. It gets its name from Mun and Aar. Mun is three in Malyalam language and Aar is rivers. Munnar is a confluence of 3 rivers. It is famous for its tea gardens. The beautiful landscape these tea plantations create is breath taking. The panoramic views and the cool climate of Munnar makes you feel you could stay here forever. Plan such that you get at least 3 days or more in Munnar. If you have more time, you can add Kovalam and Kanyakumari to your itinerary.

Where to stay: There are a lot of Home stays throughout Kerala. You get to stay with the family who owns the house and you can have meals cooked in traditional Kerala style. You must try a home stay at least once in your trip. The people here will love you like their own relatives and you will cherish the experience. Many hotels are available here. Abad group of hotels have a hotel in every tourist place in Kerala. For mid range hotels you can stay at Hotel Volga is Kochi. In Alleppey, stay at Hotel Pagoda, which is built in traditional Kerala style architecture. In Thekkady stay at Hotel Treetop and in Munnar, stay at hotel Elysium Garden or Abad Copper Castle.

What to eat: The staple diet of the Keralites is rice and fish. So when in Kerala, gorge on various rice and fish delicacies. Try Idli, Dosa, Appam, Idiappam and Puttu for breakfast. All these are made of rice.

Try Karimein fish and Braised chicken at the Volga restaurant in Kochi and you will ask for more. Have a coconut water break in the midst of your backwater trip in Alleppey. There are small huts selling coconut water in small strips of land in the sea.

What to shop for: Shop for rosewood and sandalwood artifacts at the Khadi Gramodyog shop on M G Road in Kochi. Kairali is another shop on the same road which has a large variety of brass sculptures, wooden elephants, jute bags etc. You can buy silk saris and dress materials at Jayalakshmi store in Kochi.

Wayanad-The Green Paradise in God's Own Country-Kerala.

Kerala has been included in most of the tour operator's package as a major tourist destination. Kerala has been presented with excellent natural beauty and environment by the God Almighty. Kerala, a South Indian state is a thriving centre of tourism in India. Wayanad district, one of the fourteen districts and a hill station is located in Kerala, South India. The lofty peaks, gurgling streams and luxuriant forests welcome you to the journey up the winding roads to this hill station. Wayanad offers a golden opportunity to the tourist for better relaxation by the hilly and misty beauty of this district of Kerala, which is further hallmarked by the tribal arts of Adiyar and Paniyar tribes nestled in the hills of this region.

God's Own Country-A Paradise on Earth

A Beautiful holiday is about going away from the pressures of everyday living, just relaxing and living every moment to the fullest. The perfect blend of nature and the best of man-made luxuries can make for the best time of your life. How would you like to wake up in the morning to the chirping of birds and looking out of your window at lush greenery. Kerala, God's own country, is all this and a lot more.

Kerala, no doubt is top on the list of the world's most beautiful destinations. Rated among the world's top 50 must-see destinations by National Geographic Traveller, Kerala is truly "Paradise on Earth". It is indeed a beautiful combination of beaches, hills, scenic plantations, valleys and backwaters. The grand network of rivers makes a great addition to its scenic beauty. In the South, the gorgeous hill station Ponmudi in the State capital Thiruvananthapuram, the beautiful beaches of Kanyakumari, the heavenly picturesque Varkala with its beaches and resorts and Alleppey known for its beautiful backwaters.

Moving northwards you are greeted by the magnificence of the commercial capital of the State, Kochi, as well as Thrissur, the cultural capital and the scenic North Kerala region. Kerala has all that you look forward to on a perfect holiday. Kerala is also renowned for its Ayurvedic treatments that are both soothing and offer a range of health benefits.

They provide a heavenly experience that is calming and rejuvenating. Whether you are looking for a treatment to cure your ailments or a relaxing massage, you will find it here. The treatments offered by Ayurveda include among others pizhichil, dhara, navarakizhi, talam and talapothichil. With the help of a qualified Ayurvedic doctor you could decide on the treatment that is best suited to you according to your body type, the season and other factors. Enjoy a relaxing day with expert masseurs.

With excellent accommodation facilities, food that says it all and a panoramic backdrop, the Kerala holiday is one that you are sure to cherish for a long time.

Kerala-Paradise for Honeymooners

India, Kerala is one of the most beautiful states of India. It is popularly described as the "God's Own Country". Endowed with superb nature beauty and peaceful climate, the State has been emerged as a paradise for honeymooners or newly wedded couples. Couples find their true delights in beautiful beaches, lovely lakes, breathtaking backwaters, cheerful hill stations, ayurvedic resorts, spa centres, and wonderful houseboats. The landscapes of Kerala offer couples a world of choices for romantic honeymoon vacation in India.

There are several deserving honeymoon destinations in the state offering couples truly romantic honeymoon experience. Alleppey, Fort Kochi, Kovalam, Varkala, Munnar, Ponmudi, Periyar, Trivandrum (the capital city of the state), Kumarakom, etc. are some of very favored destinations in Kerala for honeymooners or newly wedded couples. Couples from all over the world prefer to celebrate their romantic honeymoon vacation in Kerala, God's Own Country due to its agreeable climate and catchy attractions.

Alleppey and Kumarakom are two very popular backwater destinations in the state. Both are very popular among honeymoon couples. Gifted with superb scenic beauty and breathtaking nature creates Alleppey and Kumarakom gives couples truly romantic and peaceful ambiance. There are several ayurvedic resorts and spa centres in Alleppey and Kumarakom offering couples mesmerizing honeymoon vacation experience.

Both are also popular for backwater tourism. Alleppey is an ideal destination for starting a houseboat cruise over scenic and serene backwaters of the state. A well organized houseboat cruise or a stay at luxurious houseboat can be experience of lifetime for couples. Couples find totally different but cheerful ambiance for their honeymoon vacation.

Kumarakom is also famous for houseboat cruise. A sunset cruise over the picturesque Vembanad Lake in Kumarakom adds romance to couples. Kumarakom is also known for its rich flora and fauna. There is a world famous bird sanctuary in Kumarakom – Kumarakom Bird Sanctuary, also known as the Vembanad Bird Sanctuary. Birding in the bird sanctuary can be delightful activity for honeymoon couples.

Fort Kochi is also very popular among honeymoon couples. A visit to Fort Kochi (Cochin) gives couples wonderful opportunity to explore backwater tourism and beach tourism as well. Fort Kochi is also famous for some of monument attractions like forts & palaces, colonial homes, churches, etc. A sunset watching from world famous Chinese Fishing Nets in Fort Kochi is truly a mesmerizing experience for romantic couples. Periyar is also very popular tourism destination in Kerala. It is basically known for wildlife sanctuary and superb nature.

There are also several breathtaking hill stations in Kerala offering cheerful and romantic ambiance for honeymoon vacations. Munnar, Ponmudi, Wayanad, etc. are some of popular hill stations in the state. These all hill towns are blessed with superb nature beauty and provides couples truly romantic and peaceful climate.

There are several other destinations in the state which can be attractions of honeymoon tours to Kerala, God's Own Country. With the emergence of internet, honeymooners can book their romantic honeymoon package for Kerala online.

They can find information and detail of attractive honeymoon packages by searching keywords like Honeymoon Tour Kerala, Kerala Honeymoon Package, Honeymoon to Kerala, Romantic Tour to Kerala, Romantic Vacation, etc.

Kerala-God's Own Country

Kerala was celebrated as a 'Paradise Found'-one of the ten in the world, A perfect description for a land renowned as "God's Own Country". What adds to the charm of its backwaters, beaches, Ayurveda health holidays, hill stations, wildlife, festivals, monuments and vibrant art forms, is its amazing social development indices that are on par with the developed world.

The Important Tourist Spots in Kerala

Kovalam Beach: The Kovalam beach situated 16 Km. south of Trivandrum city, is one of the best beaches in India. It's a must see destination of India. On account of it's natural location, it affords facilities for safe sea bath.

Chowra Beach: The soft white sand is what that draws visitors to this beach and it is ideal for beach volleyball. The long stretch of beach is dotted by many cattamarams; a country fishing boat, which is three logs tied together in the shape of a boat.

Alleppey (alappuzha): Alappuzha is famous for its boat races, houseboats, coir products, fish and lakes. Alappuzha remains prominent on the tourist trial of Kerala as one of the major centres for backwater boat trips.

Kumarakom: The village of Kumarakom is a cluster of little islands on the Vembanad Lake, and this small water world is part of the Kuttanad region. The bird sanctuary here, which is spread across 14 acres is a favourite haunt of migratory birds and an ornithologist's paradise.

Thekkady (Periyar): The pride of Kerala and a testimony to nature's splendour and human innovation, the Periyar Wildlife Sanctuary is situated on the banks of the Periyar lake-an artificial lake, at Thekkady. Here the high ranges of the Western Ghats are clothed in dense evergreen, moist deciduous forests and savannah grass lands. Below this thick green canopy roam herds of elephants, sambars, tigers, gaurs, lion tailed macaques and Nilgiri langurs.

Kochi (Cochin): The eventful history of this city began when a major flood in AD 1341 threw open the estuary at Kochi, till then a land locked region, turning it into one of the finest natural harbours in the world. Kochi thus became a haven for seafaring visitors from all over the world and became the first European township in India when the Portuguese settled here in the 15th century.

Munnar Hills: one of the most popular hill stations in India is situated at the confluence of three mountain streams-Mudrapuzha, Nallathanni and Kundala. Located at 1600 m above sea level, this was once the summer resort of the erstwhile British Government in South India. Sprawling tea plantations, picture book towns, winding lanes, trekking and holiday facilities make Munnar a unique experience. Munnar also has the highest peak in South India-Anamudi, which towers over 2695 m. Anamudi is an ideal spot for trekking.

Wayanad: Wayanad lies at an altitude varying from 700-2100 metres above the sea level. The district has the highest number of tribal settlements in Kerala. The sanctuary is very rich in flora and fauna. With its green highlands, lush valleys and cool clime, Wayanad is one of the most beautiful retreats of Kerala. Apart from its breathtaking natural beauty, Wayanad is also famous for the discovery of pictorial writings of the New Stone Age at its Edakkal Caves. The caves in the Ambukuthi hills, 12 km south of Sultan Bathery, are world-famous as one of the earliest centres of human habitation.

Trivandrum (Thiruvananthapuram): The Capital city of Kerala. The wooded highlands on the Western Ghats in the eastern and northeastern borders give Thiruvananthapuram some of the most enchanting picnic spots. A long shoreline, with internationally renowned beaches, historic monuments, backwater stretches and a rich cultural heritage make it a much sought after tourist destination.

Cherai Beach: This lovely beach near Kochi, bordering Vypeen island which is a major centre for commerce, is ideal for swimming. Dolphins are occasionally seen here. A typical Kerala village with paddy fields and coconut groves nearby is an added attraction of this beach.

Kerala Backwaters

The backwaters of Kerala is a unique product of Kerala and is found nowhere else in the world. Backwaters are a network of lakes, canals and estuaries and deltas of forty-four rivers that drain into the Arabian sea. The backwaters of Kerala are a self supporting eco-system teeming with aquatic life. The canals connect the villages together and are still used for local transport. Over 900 km of this labyrinthine water world is navigable. The largest backwater stretch in Kerala is the

Vembanad Lake which flows through three districts and opens out into the sea at the Kochi Port. The Astamudi lake, literarlly having eight arms, which covers a major portion of Kollam district in the south, is the second largest and is considered the gateway to the backwaters.

The most exciting thing on the backwaters of Kerala, however, is the kettuvallom (traditional houseboat) which has become the most popular tourism product in India today. In a land as waterbound as Kerala it wouldn't be an unusual sight, but for a visitor to God's Own Country a houseboat gliding along the vast green expanse of the backwaters is the most amazing spectacle in the world. Even more enchanting is a holiday in the houseboats of Kerala.

Kerala Hill Stations-Romantic Vacations

Kerala has a long chain of lush, mid-clad hill stations that are home to exotic wildlife. All the hill resorts in Kerala offer the most enchanting experience of nature in all its virgin beauty.

The major Hill resorts of Kerala are: Munnar, Ponmudi, Peerumade, Neliyampathy,, Peruvannamuzhi, Tusharagiri, Wayanad, Pythal Mala, Ezhimala, Ranipuram, Devikulam, Wagamon etc.

Munnar Hills: Munnar hills is situated in the confluence of three mountain streams-Mudrapuzha, Nallathanni & Kundala. Situated 1600 metre above sealevel, this hill station was once the summer resort of the erstwhile British Government in South India. Sprawling tea plantations, picture-book towns, winding lanes and holiday facilities make this a popular resort town.

Peeremede: Peermade is a lovely hill station, an ideal retreat in the Western Ghats and a choice break for tourists en route to the Periyar Tiger Reserve. Sprawling gardens of tea, coffee, cardamom, rubber and eucalyptus lying side by side with natural grasslands, pine forests and waterfalls make this an ideal summer resort. The summer palace of Rajas of erstwhile Travancore is today an important monument here. Peeremede and its surroundings are suitable for trekking, cycling and horse riding.

Ramakalmedu: Rolling green hills and the fresh mountain air make Ramakalmedu and enchanting retreat. The hilltop also offers a panoramic view of the picturesque villages of Bodi and Cumbum on the eastern slope of the Western Ghats. Situated at a distance of 40 km from Thekkady and 75 km from Munnar.

Echo Point: This scenic place gets its name from the natural echo phenomenon here. Echo Point is on the way to Top Station in Munnar.

Rajamala: Rajamala is the natural habitat of the Nilgiri Tahr (Hemitragas hylocres), the Eravikulam-Rajamala region is now home to half the world population – estimated at around 1300-of this endangered mountain goat. But the Tahr is only one of the reasons to make a visit to Rajamala.

Vagamon: One of the most beautiful places with a chain of three hills-the Thangal hill, the Murugan hill and the Kurisumala, important for Muslims, Hindus and Christians respectively.

Pullumedu: Velvet lawns and rare flora and fauna add to the beauty of Pullumedu. The famous Sree Ayyappa Temple at Sabarimala and the Makara Jyothi illuminations at the shrine are visible from here. The winding journey to this hill along the Periyar River, offers a stunning view of hills draped in lush greenery.

Vandanmedu: This is one of the world's largest auction centres for cardamom. A walk through the sprawling cardamom plantations of Vandanmedu is a heady experience.

Chellarkovil: This sleepy little village with its breathtaking view of the plains and cascading waterfalls is a feast for the eyes. The village slopes down to the famous coconut groves of Cumbum in neighbouring Tamil Nadu.

Vandiperiyar: The River Periyar flowing through the centre of this town nourishes its vast tea, coffee and pepper plantations. A major trade centre, Vandiperiyar is also home to a number of tea factories. The Agriculture Farm and Flower Garden have a delightful array of rose plants, orchids and anthuria.

God's Own Country- Symbiosis of Rejuvenation & Nature Tourism

Kerala is the land much acclaimed for the cultural ethos, rejuvenation therapy, backwaters, diverse geography, over whelming greenery & enchanting flora & fauna. It is invariably called "Gods Own Country". National Geography Traveller has classified it as one of the ten "Paradise Found" on earth.

What Makes Kerala so Special

Kerala enjoys unique geographical features that have made it one of the most sought after tourist destinations in the world. Arabian Sea in the west, Western Ghats towering in the east and networked by forty-four rivers all along makes Kerala a paradise on earth.

Unique Features to Explore & Enjoy in Kerala

* An equable climate.
* Long shoreline with serene beaches.
* Tranquil stretches of emerald backwaters.
* Lush hill stations & exotic wildlife.
* Waterfalls, lakes & rivers.
* Sprawling plantations & paddy fields.
* Ayurvedic health holidays.
* Enchanting art forms.
* Magical festivals.
* Historic and cultural monuments.

An Exotic Cuisine

All the above facets offer a truly unique experience. One singular advantage that is perceived is the fact that all the destinations are easily accessible and not far away from one another.

* Kerala is more than just world class hospitality.
* Besides the tourist potential and interface, Kerala is one of the most progressive Indian state with following facets.
* India's most advanced society.
* A hundred percent literacy.
* World-class health care systems.
* India's lowest infant mortality rate.
* The highest life expectancy rate in India.
* The highest physical quality of life in India.
* Peaceful and pristine environment.
* Unpolluted & high level of cleanliness.
* Conducive & secure Investment Scenario.
* World class support services & infrastructure.

Kalamachal-The Paradise, an Untouched Gift from Gods Own Country

Kerala is known as "The Gods own country", it was names in the top ten places to visit in a lifetime. Kerala has the reputation of being one of the finest places in South India.

Kerala-God's Own Country

The site Kerala Backwaters promises to take you on one of the most enjoyable holidays in Kerala, India that has been described as 'Gods own country'. The phrase 'God's own country' is perhaps the most apt way of describing Kerala, India. Kerala with its crisp and fresh air, its absolutely pure and green environs and the nature trails that take to a strikingly beautiful world, as though God picked up his painting brush and palate and created this wonderful and soothing painting for you to realize and appreciate the fact that 'life is beautiful'.

The word 'Kerala' literally means 'the land of coconuts' and during your holidays and tours to Kerala, India you'll realize the importance of this name. The entire state has a profusion of coconut palm groves, especially the beaches, the Kerala backwaters and the villages. These trees add to the natural beauty of Kerala, India and form an integral part of the coir trade in Kerala, India.

Kerala, India is known for its natural beauty and you experience the breathtaking panoramic sights during you holidays and tours to Kerala, India with the site Kerala Backwaters. All this and more makes Kerala, India 'God's own country'. Today you will arrive Cochin International Airport. Following customs, immigration formalities and baggage collection, a SITA representative will meet you as you EXIT the ARRIVALS TERMINAL building after which you would be transferred to your hotel. Kochi, or more familiarly, Cochin is a city of many parts. Around for a long, long time, Kochi played a pivotal role in the development of shipping and trade in the region. Kochi's prime location on the west coast, its fine bay and protected harbour made it popular with seafarers and merchant ships who made frequent stops to stock up on spices, coffee and wood enroute to the rich markets of Europe and West Asia. And so down the ages, Kochi prospered as a busy port city and commercial centre. Its seafront is still extremely relevant to Cochin and to India: it houses a Naval Base and one of India's busiest ports.

It's twin city, Ernakulam, is an important railhead and industrial centre. Upon arrival at the hotel, you will be accorded with a Traditional Welcome. Welcoming guest is an age-old tradition. 'Atithi Devobhava'- treat your guest as if he were God. Indian hospitality can be savored immediately as one arrives at the hotel. The guest's forehead is anointed with the traditional red 'tika' which is considered auspicious along with garlanding. Relax with a non-alcoholic welcome drink following which proceed to check in at your room. Overnight at the hotel.

Day 02: Cochin

After buffet breakfast proceed for the sightseeing tour of Cochin. You will first proceed to Mattancherry and visit the oldest Jewish Synagogue in India, built in 1568; it was destroyed by the Portuguese and rebuilt by the Dutch a century later. You will also visit The Dutch Palace (Closed on Fridays)-which was built in 1555 and its coronation hall and murals at Ramayana are noteworthy features.

Continue your drive to Chinese fishing nets. The cantilevered fishing nets line the entrance to the harbour mouth. Chinese traders are believed to have originally introduced them in the 14th century although, today parts of the nets are known by Portuguese names. Your next stop will be St. Francis Church, originally named after Santo Antonio and dedicated to him as the Patron Saint of Portugal, St. Francis Church is the first church to have been in the new European influenced tradition. Originally a wooden building was replaced by the present stone building. Vasco De Gamma died on the site in 1524 and was originally buried in the cemetery. 14 years later his body was removed to Portugal.

The church was renamed St. Francis in 1663. In the evening, you will be taken to a Kathakali dance centre where you will witness the most elaborate of the dance forms in southern India. Here you will witness the artists readying themselves up with the make up for the final performance. Kerala owes its transnational fame to this nearly 300 years old classical dance form, which combines facets of ballet, opera, masque and the pantomime. It is said to have evolved from other performing arts like Kootiyattam, Krishnanattam and Kalarippayattu. Kathakali explicates ideas and stories from the Indian epics and Puranas. Presented in the temple precincts after dusk falls Kathakali is heralded by the Kelikottu or the beating of drums in accompaniment of the Chengila (gong). Overnight at the hotel.

Day 03: Cochin-Thekkady

After buffet breakfast at the hotel you would be driven from Cochin to Thekkady, which is also known as Periyar (180 KMS/5 Hours). Upon arrival proceed to check in at your hotel In the afternoon, proceed to Periyar National Park to view the wildlife by boat. Situated within the confines of the Western Ghats in the southern Indian state of Kerala, Periyar National Park and Tiger Reserve is one of the most captivating wildlife parks in the world. The park has a picturesque lake at the heart of the sanctuary. Herds of elephant and sambar, gaur and wild pigs and wander down to the lakeside and can be observed from the launches that cruise the lake. Periyar also harbours the leopard, wild dog, barking deer and mouse deer. Return to the hotel after your boat ride. Overnight at the hotel.

Day 04: Thekkady – Kumarakom by: Surface

After buffet breakfast at the hotel, you will be driven to Kumarakom (135 KMS/04 HRS). In the lush backwaters of Kottayam in Kerala, lies a veritable paradise, which is called Kumarakom, or the 'Venice of the East'. Palm fringed narrow canals winding through the vast expanse of paddy fields, and the neat tiny hamlets lined up along either side of the canals are panoramic sights one can never forget. Kumarakom is Kerala's heartland of lagoons, palm fringed lakes, and paddy fields, inter-linked with hundreds of winding canals, with the typical low slung country boats that carry everything from people to fish, rice and coconuts to the milkman and newspaper boy, local politicians and priests to wedding parties.

Upon arrival proceed to check in at your hotel Remaining day is free for relaxation. Lie in a hammock on this lakeshore, and allow your senses to possess you. Before you is a great Vembanad Lake, rippling under the vault of an impossibly large sky. Sunlight sparkles on her waters, tearing the reflection of a passing houseboat into crystal shards. Darter birds go about their fishy business. You relax in Peace. Of course there is peace here, but not silence. Silence is not nature's way. And the Kumarakom Bird Sanctuary next door is full of raucous neighbours. You sway a little, and the image changes; to a timber and tile mansion that seems to belong to this earth, but to another time. If you left the comfort of your hammock for a closer look, you'd see that it is authentic reconstruction. Overnight at the hotel.

Day 05: Kumarakom – Houseboat

After breakfast in the hotel, you will board your Houseboat on the backwaters of Kerala. Houseboats are also known as the "Ketuvallam" or the Rice Boat. Ketuvallam ride can be the most romantic ride you can ever have with a night halt in the middle of the lake Vembanad Lake/canal. A backwater comprises of a unique web of rivers, lakes, bays, lagoons and canals extending into the villages and town of the city. Backwaters are a central part of Kerala's Tourism Synopsis, making an absolute cruiser through the twisting and meandering water streams. This backwater journey through the narrow canals crossing exquisite villages of Kerala, embellished with lush green paddy fields, tall coconut grooves makes it a most spellbinding site. Overnight at the houseboat.

Day 06: Houseboat – Marari by: Surface

After breakfast onboard you will check-out from the houseboat at the Alleppey Jetty where your chauffeur and will be driven to Marari (45 minutes). Marari Beach Resort Sprawled expansively across 25 acres of land, the resort, like its namesake, is separated from the sea by a windbreak of stretching palms. There are a mere 52 cottages, so the sense of space here is much more dramatic. The cottages are separated by generous stretches of open parkland, dotted with fruit-laden trees. The winding village pathways are a faithful echo of the originals. Rambling walls curve around corners, their rust-coloured stones smothered with trumpet flowers. Completing the picture are rippling lotus ponds, usually with a family of ducklings getting a swimming lesson out in the middle. Upon arrival proceed to check in at your hotel following that remainder of the day is at leisure. Overnight at the hotel.

Day 07: Marari

After buffet breakfast at the hotel you are free for independent activities. Overnight at the hotel.

Day 08: Marari – Cochin

Today in time a SITA representative will meet you in the hotel lobby and transfer you to International airport to board your flight for back home.

Varkala-Virgin Paradise in the God's Own

Lapping of the waves, clear blue sky or star studded nights, whiffs of brewing coffee and freshly made cakes, foot tapping melodies, beauty of the sunset, crawling time, majestic cliff, raising toasts to good times–that is Varkala in capsule for you.

Varkala is a small town with a population of less than 50,000 and is situated 55 kms north of Thiruvanathapuram, the state's capital. The nearest airport destination to Varkala is Thiruvanathapuram (Trivandrum) which has excellent air services to both national and international destinations. It is also possible to reach Varkala via myriad buses plying towards Thiruvanathapuram from other locations in Kerala. For those who wish to lap up the picturesque and serene beauty of Kerala backwaters, a boat ride from Alleppey is also an option. Though it takes longer (8-9 hours) and there are no direct boat services to Varkala. You need to go to Kollam and further by bus to a stop from where Varkala is at a distance of ½ hour by bus/auto.

We reached Varkala late evening and decided to check in at the Santa Claus resort located on the cliff with a panoramic view to the Arabian Sea and its coastline. The resort, as we were told, got its name from the owner's mother which was Shantha! The trees of araucaria fringing the entrance to this tiny resort only reaffirm its name. During off season the room tariff is Rs.650 (non AC room) and Rs.1000 (for AC room) while during the peak season (Nov-March) the rates shoot up to Rs.3000 per night. This is the case with the battery of resorts that line the cliff and the beach.

Varkala is known to be an important centre of pilgrimage for the Hindus. According to a myth, sage Narada was approached by a group of mendicants who confessed to having sinned. Narada threw his valkkalam (the bark of tree which the mythical sages used to wear) into the air, and the place where it landed was subsequently named Varkala. The mendicants were directed by Narada to offer their prayers in the newly created place by the seashore. The place where they prayed for redemption came to be known as the Papanasam Beach. Besides, there is the local Janardhana temple that attracts many a devotees. The final resting place of Sree Narayana Guru, the great social reformer of Kerala, is also near Varkala atop a hill named Sivagiri.

There are two other beaches besides the Papanasam-Thiruvambady Beach and the Kappil Beach; all of them having one thing in common, sheer silence and pristine beauty.

Coconut trees form the periphery of the towering cliffs facing the

Thiruvambady beach. If you are an early riser you can catch the daily activities of the local fisherman with their catch of the day. Though a small town, this place is extremely getting touristy. Our bet would be that it might be next Goa in making. Come morning you will find tourist hailing from different countries bathing in the sun and sea.

To tickle your taste palate the cliff is outlined by numerous cafes and eateries. With English speaking and courteous staff, open/semi-open air seating, warm ambience, salty breeze from the pure sea, lively music; these joints can be your perfect sit-out while you relax with a hot cappuccino or a cold beer. Divine feeling better understood when experienced, (Our pick: Sunshine Cafe and Cafe Delmar). To further relax your mind, body and soul, one can avail the Ayurveda programs and services offered by most resorts in Varkala.

Kerala – a Tourists' Paradise

Just before the turn of the century, National Geographic Traveller, in a special collection issue, selected Kerala as one of the 50 destinations of a lifetime. This selection assumes added significance consideringe the fact that the only other destination selected in India was the Taj Mahal in the World Wonder Section. Kerala was aptly described as a paradise found – one of the 10 in the world. This was a fitting description for a land known as 'God's Own country'.

According to a popular legend, Kerala, the land of '*Cheras*' or the land of '*Kera's* (coconuts), was a gift of *Parasurama*, one of the ten incarnations of Lord *Vishnu*. It is believed that Parasurama threw his battle-axe into the sea repenting for the sin of killing generations of *Kshatriyas*, and the sea receded thereby creating Kerala.

History

There is no ancient history of Kerala as a whole because the State was formed only in the month of November 1956 by combining three regions, namely Travancore, Cochin and Malabar. These three regions have distinct histories of their own with cultural and social variations. Malabar was a part of the Madras Presidency and it came under British rule first. The princely States of Travancore and Cochin came under British regency later. However, these three regions have many things in common like language, customs and manners, food habits, dress, art forms, religion and festivals. A Sanskrit work, '*Kerala Mahatmyam*' and a Malayalam work *'Keralotpathy'* give some insight into the early history of Kerala.

Kerala has an area of 38,863 sq.kms. and a population of more than three crore. The capital city is Thiruvananthapuram and the principal language is *Malayalam.* The width of Kerala State varies from 35 kms to 125 kms in between the Arabian Sea in the West and the Western Ghats in the East. The State has 14 districts. These are Thiruvananthapuram, Kollam, Alapuzha, Idukki, Pathanamthitta, Thrissur, Ernakulam, Palakkad, Malappuram, Kozhikode, Kottayam, Wynad, Kannur and Kasaragod.

Tourists' Paradise

Kerala is an enchanting land of exciting charm. Even during the earlier times the magnetism of this land had attracted many foreigners like the Chinese, Arabs, the Portuguese, the Dutch, the British and the French; all of them left their indelible imprint on the architectural scene of Kerala. While Kerala was willing to accept the positive aspects of various ancient civilizations, it was equally adamant in retaining its rich cultural traditions.

Kerala is also a land of communal harmony. People belonging to different faiths live here in perfect peace and tranquillity. In the capital city of Thiruvananthapuram, there is a temple, a mosque and a church, all situated within a distance of one furlong.

In one of the most popular pilgrim centres at Sabarimala, people belonging to different faiths undertake pilgrimage and worship the deity of Sri Ayyappa. Ayyappa's Muslim friend, Vavar, is also worshipped there. As far as variety in the place of worship is concerned, you can see a snake temple at Mannarsala, a Jewish synagogue at Mattancherry and a temple without an idol at Ochira.

The beautiful beaches, the misty mountains and the far away forests, all add to the charm of the land. At Kovalam beach near Thiruvananthapuram, one can swim safely in the sea or take a sun bath at the beach or just sit and watch the waves sing lovely lullabies in hushed tones. There are beaches at Varkala, Sanghumugham too. To get a scenic view of majestic mountains, one can visit Munnar, Wynad, Ponmudi and Peermade. The misty mornings here give invigorating moments to people with a 'poetic heart'

Cultural Scene

Kerala is a land of festivals. Onam is the biggest festival. It is an occasion for all Keralites irrespective of caste, creed or religion to rejoice. It is a festival of flowers, songs, dances and feasts.

Kerala's cuisine boasts of a mouth watering menu. For breakfast, Keralites have a wide variety of items like *idli, vada, dosa, puttu, upma, idiyappam* and *vellayappam.* For lunch there is rice with a number of curries like *sambar, puliseri, rasam, thoran, avial, pachadi, pappad* and many pickles. The finishing touch is given by *payasams* – sweet porridges cooked in milk. For the non-vegetarians, there are different types of fish and meat preparations.

The articulate and educated Malayali has a number of art forms of his own. *Koothu, Koodiyattam, Ottamthullal, Kathakali, Thira, Theyyam,* are Kerala's own art forms, which have won international recognition. Since most of the year Kerala enjoys sunshine and blue sky, the dress best suited is light tropical clothing. Monsoon comes to Kerala twice a year, in May June and in October-November. The Kerala monsoon is normally gentle and enjoyable.

The ABC of Kerala tourism is *Ayurveda*, Backwaters, and Culture. *Ayurveda* is an ancient Indian health system, developed through centuries of research by sages. It means "Knowledge of Life". It is not only a system to cure diseases but also to maintain perfect health. *Ayurveda* cares for physical, mental and spiritual life. There are many renowned *Ayurveda* centres in Kerala which give effective treatment in their own special ways like *pizichil, dhara, navarakizhi, shirovasthi, snehapaanam* and *nasyam.*

Kerala backwates stretch about 2,000 kms. They flow over land giving good harvest to paddy fields, transportation facility to the traveller's and bathing ghats and even drinking water amenities for the whole villages. The backwaters of Kerala include the entire network of canals, lakes and canal – like water ways. There are about 44 rivers in Kerala, including 41 west-flowing and east-flowing three rivers. The important backwaters are Vembanad Lake, Anjengo, Ashtamudi, Veli, Kodungallur, Chettuva, Snake Boat races held in some of these backwaters present an unusual visual extravaganza.

Kerala's unique culture is the sum total of its religion, customs and manners, Dance, theatre and music traditions folklore, martial art and architecture. The very articulate and educated Keralites have made hospitality a way of life.

In no other place in the world, can one see so many tourist spots within such a short distance. The total area of Kerala is only about 1.03 per cent of India's total area and the total length from South to North is only 574 kms. There are three airports in Kerala, one each at Thiruvananthapuram, Cochin and Kozhikode, of which the first two are international airports. There is an effective road transport system managed by the Kerala State Road Transport Corporation. Private buses also ply in plenty. Most of the important towns are connected by rail. The task of tourism development is being handled by Tourism Department and the Kerala Tourism Development Corporation under the State Government. There is a chain of hotels owned by KTDC, which cater to the needs of Indian and foreign tourists at various places of tourist attraction.

Some important places of interest for the tourists are Sri Padmanabha Swamy Temple, the zoo and museum at Thiruvananthapuram, Kovalam beach, Neyyar dam, Ponmudi resorts, Varkala Beach and temple, backwaters in Alapuzha, Krishnapuram Palace, and Kumarakam Tourist complex. Other places worth seeing are Adirappalli water falls, Kalady, the birthplace of Sri Sankara, Jewish Synagogue, St. Francis Church and Dutch Palace in Cochin, Thekkady wildlife sanctuary, Vadakkumnathan temple at Thrissur and Sri Krishna temple at Guruvayur, Palaruvi Water falls, Malampuzha dam, Beypore, Wyand, and the National Park at Silent Valley. Kerala which is a tourists paradise, has been aptly described as "God's Own country".

6

Sustainable Health Tourism

Sustainable tourism is an industry committed to making a low impact on the environment and local culture, while helping to generate income and employment for local people.The aim of sustainable tourism is to ensure that development is a positive experience for local people; tourism companies; and tourists themselves. But sustainable tourism is not the same as 'ecotourism'.

Overview

Global economists forecast continuing international tourism growth, ranging between three and six percent annually, depending on the location. As one of the world's largest and fastest growing industries, this continuous growth will place great stress on remaining biologically diverse habitats and indigenous cultures, which are often used to support mass tourism. Tourists who promote sustainable tourism are sensitive to these dangers and seek to protect tourist destinations, and to protect tourism as an industry. Sustainable tourists can reduce the impact of tourism in many ways, including:

- informing themselves of the culture, politics, and economy of the communities visited.
- anticipating and respecting local cultures' expectations and assumptions.
- contributing to intercultural understanding and tolerance.
- supporting the integrity of local cultures by favouring businesses which conserve cultural heritage and traditional values.
- supporting local economies by purchasing local goods and participating with small, local businesses.

- conserving resources by seeking out businesses that are environmentally conscious, and by using the least possible amount of non-renewable resources.

Increasingly, destinations and tourism operations are endorsing and following "responsible tourism" as a pathway towards sustainable tourism. Responsible tourism and sustainable tourism have an identical goal, that of sustainable development. The pillars of responsible tourism are therefore the same as those of sustainable tourism – environmental integrity, social justice and economic development. The major difference between the two is that, in responsible tourism, individuals, organisations and businesses are asked to take responsibility for their actions and the impacts of their actions. This shift in emphasis has taken place because some stakeholders feel that insufficient progress towards realising sustainable tourism has been made since the Earth Summit in Rio. This is partly because everyone has been expecting others to behave in a sustainable manner. The emphasis on responsibility in responsible tourism means that everyone involved in tourism – government, product owners and operators, transport operators, community services, NGO's and CBO's, tourists, local communities, industry associations – are responsible for achieving the goals of responsible tourism.

Responsible Tourism

Responsible Tourism can be regarded as a movement. It is more than a form of tourism as it represents an approach to engaging with tourism, be that as a tourist, a business, locals at a destination or any other tourism stakeholder. It emphasises that all stakeholders are responsible for the kind of tourism they develop or engage in. Whilst different groups will see responsibility in different ways, the shared understanding is that responsible tourism should entail an improvement in tourism. Tourism should become 'better' as a result of the responsible tourism approach.

Within the notion of betterment resides the acknowledgement that conflicting interests need to be balanced. However, the objective is to create better places for people to live in and to visit. Importantly, there is no blueprint for responsible tourism: what is deemed responsible may differ depending on places and cultures. Responsible Tourism is an aspiration that can be realised in different ways in different originating markets and in the diverse destinations of the world.

Focusing in particular on businesses, according to the Cape Town Declaration on Responsible Tourism, it will have the following characteristics:

- minimises negative economic, environmental, and social impacts.
- generates greater economic benefits for local people and enhances the well-being of host communities, improves working conditions and access to the industry.
- involves local people in decisions that affect their lives and life chances.
- makes positive contributions to the conservation of natural and cultural heritage, to the maintenance of the world's diversity.
- provides more enjoyable experiences for tourists through more meaningful connections with local people, and a greater understanding of local cultural, social and environmental issues.
- provides access for physically challenged people and
- is culturally sensitive, engenders respect between tourists and hosts, and builds local pride and confidence.

Sustainable tourism is where tourists can enjoy their holiday and at the same time respect the culture of people and also respect the environment. It also means that local people (such as the Masaai) get a fair say about tourism and also receive some money from the profit which the game reserve make. The environment is being damaged quite a lot by tourists and part of Sustainable tourism is to make sure that the damaging does not carry on.

There are many private companies who are working into embracing the principles and aspects of Responsible Tourism, some for the purpose of Corporate Social Responsibility activities, and others such WorldHotel-Link, which was originally a project of the International Finance Corporation, have built their entire business model around responsible tourism, local capacity building and increasing market access for small and medium tourism enterprises.

Responsible Hospitality

As with the view of Responsible Tourism, Responsible Hospitality is essentially about creating better places for people to live in, and better places for people to visit. This does not mean all forms of hospitality are also forms of tourism although hospitality is the largest sector of the tourism industry. As such we should not be surprised at overlaps between Responsible Hospitality and Responsible Tourism. In the instance where place of permanent residence is also the place where the hospitality service is consumed, if for example a meal is consumed in a local restaurant, this does not obviate the requirement to improve the place of residence. As such, the essence of Responsible Hospitality is not contingent upon touristic forms of hospitality.

While Frideman (1962) famously argued that, admittedly within legal parameters, the sole responsibility of business was to generate profit for shareholders the idea that businesses' responsibility extends beyond this has existed for decades and is most frequently encountered in the concept of corporate social responsibility. There are numerous ways businesses can and do engage in activities that are not intended to benefit shareholders and management, at least not in the short term. However, often acts of corporate social responsibility are undertaken because of the perceived benefit to business. Usually in hospitality this relates to the cost reductions associated with improved energy efficiency but may also relate to, for example, the rise in ethical consumerism and the view that being seen to be a responsible business is beneficial to revenue growth. As per the Capetown Declaration on Responsible Tourism, Responsible Hospitality is culturally sensitive. Instead of then calling for the unachievable, Responsible Hospitality simply makes the case for more responsible forms of hospitality, hospitality that benefits locals first, and visitors second. Certainly, all forms of hospitality can be improved and managed so that negative impacts are minimised whilst striving for a maximisation of positive impacts.

Coastal Tourism

Many coastal areas are experiencing particular pressure from growth in lifestyles and growing numbers of tourists. Coastal environments are limitea in extent consisting of only a narrow strip along the edge of the ocean. Coastal areas are often the first environments to experience the detrimental impacts of tourism. A detailed study of the impact on coastal areas, with reference to western India can be an example.

The inevitable change is on the horizon as holiday destinations put more effort into sustainable tourism. Planning and management controls can reduce the impact on coastal environments and ensure that investment into tourism products supports sustainable coastal tourism.

Some Conceptual Models in Coastal Tourism

Some of the recent studies have led to some interesting conceptual models applicable for coastal tourism. The 'inverted funnel model' and the 'embedded model' can be good metaphors for understanding the interplay of different stake-holders like government, local community, tourists and business community in developing tourist destinations.

Community-based Management

There has been the promotion of sustainable tourism practices surrounding the management of tourist locations by locals or more concisely, the community. This form of tourism is based on the premise that the people living next to a resource are the ones best suited to protecting it. This means that the tourism activities and businesses are developed and operated by local community members, and certainly with their consent and support.

Sustainable tourism typically involves the conservation of resources that are capitalized upon for tourism purposes, such as coral reefs and pristine forests. Locals run the businesses and are responsible for promoting the conservation messages to protect their environment.

Community-based sustainable tourism (CBST) associates the success of the sustainability of the ecotourism location to the management practices of the communities who are directly or indirectly dependent on the location for their livelihoods.

A salient feature of CBST is that local knowledge is usually utilised alongside wide general frameworks of ecotourism business models. This allows the participation of locals at the management level and typically allows a more intimate understanding of the environment. The use of local knowledge also means an easier entry level into a tourism industry for locals whose jobs or livelihoods are affected by the use of their environment as tourism locations. The involvement of locals restores the ownership of the environment to the local community and allows an alternative sustainable form of development for communities and their environments that are typically unable to support other forms of development.

Stakeholders

Stakeholders of sustainable tourism play a role in continuing this form of tourism. This can include organizations as well as individuals.

Non-governmental Organizations

Non-governmental organizations are one of the stakeholders in advocating sustainable tourism. Their roles can range from spearheading sustainable tourism practices to simply doing research. University research teams and scientists can be tapped to aid in the process of planning. Such solicitation of research can be observed in the planning of Cat Ba National Park in Vietnam.

Dive resort operators in Bunaken National Park, Indonesia, play a crucial role but developing exclusive zones for diving and fishing respectively, such that both tourists and locals can benefit from the venture.

Large conventions, meetings and other major organized events drive the travel, tourism and hospitality industry. Cities and convention centres compete to attract such commerce, commerce which has heavy impacts on resource use and the environment. Major sporting events, such as the Olympic Games, present special problems regarding environmental burdens and degradation. But burdens imposed by the regular convention industry can be vastly more significant.

Green conventions and events are a new but growing sector and marketing point within the convention and hospitality industry. More environmentally aware organizations, corporations and government agencies are now seeking more sustainable event practices, greener hotels, restaurants and convention venues, and more energy efficient or climate neutral travel and ground transportation.

Additionally, some convention centres have begun to take direct action in reducing the impact of the conventions they host. One example is the Moscone Centre in San Francisco, California, which has a very aggressive recycling program, a large solar power system, and other programs aimed at reducing impact and increasing efficiency.

Tourists

With the advent of the internet, some traditional conventions are being replaced with virtual conventions, where the attendees remain in their home physical location and "attend" the convention by use of a web-based interface programmed for the task. This sort of "virtual" meeting eliminates all of the impacts associated with travel, accommodation, food wastage, and other necessary impacts of traditional, physical conventions.

Travel over long distances requires a large amount of time and/ or energy. Generally this involves burning fossil fuels, a largely unsustainable practice and one that contributes to climate change, via CO_2 emissions.

Air travel is perhaps the worst offender in this regard, contributing to between 2 and 3% of global carbon emissions. Given a business-as-usual approach, this could be expected to rise to 5% by 2015 and 10% by 2050. Car travel is the next worst offender.

Mass transport is the most climate friendly method of travel, and generally the rule is "the bigger the better"-compared to cars, buses are relatively more sustainable, and trains and ships are even more so. Human energy and renewable energy are the most efficient, and hence, sustainable. Travel by bicycle, solar powered car, or sailing boat produces no carbon emissions (although the embodied energy in these vehicles generally comes at the expense of carbon emission).

Introduction Of Sustainable Tourism

There are a myriad of definitions for Sustainable Tourism, including eco-tourism, green travel, environmentally and culturally responsible tourism, fair trade and ethical travel. The most widely accepted definition is that of the World Tourism Organisation. They define sustainable tourism as "*tourism which leads to management of all resources in such a way that* economic, social and aesthetic needs can be fulfilled while maintaining cultural integrity, essential *ecological processes, biological diversity and life support systems.*" In addition they describe the development of sustainable tourism as a process which meets the needs of present tourists and host communities whilst protecting and enhancing needs in the future.

Tourism is one of the world's largest industries. For developing countries it is also one of the biggest income generators. But the huge infrastructural and resource demands of tourism can have severe impacts upon local communities and the environment if it is not properly managed.

To reach this current state, we have witnessed an exponential growth in global tourism over the past half century. 25 million international visitors in 1950 grew to an estimated 650 million people by the year 2000. Several factors have contributed to this rise in consumer demand in recent decades. This includes an increase in the standard of living in the developed countries, greater allowances for holiday entitlements and declining costs of travel. Tourism is an important export for a large number of developing countries, and the principal export for about a third of these. Statistics for domestic tourism are not so easily available. However it is certain that domestic tourism is also growing rapidly in many Asian and Latin American countries.

. World Travel and Tourism Council (WTTC) estimates show that in 2002 travel, tourism and related activities will contribute 11% to the world's GDP, rising to 12% by 2010. The industry is currently estimated to generate 1 in every 12.8 jobs or 7.8% of the total work force. This percentage is expected to rise to 8.6% by 2012. Tourism is also the world's largest employer, accounting for more than 255 million jobs, or 10.7% of the global labour force (WTTC 2002).

It is clear that ecotourism, in the strictest sense of the word, still only accounts for a small proportion of the total tourism market. Current estimates are between 3-7% of the market (WTTC, WTO, Earth Council 1996). Taking the WTO's full definition of tourism, there's a risk that ecotourism alone will fail to fully realise the potential to support more sustainable development across the entire sector – suggesting that there may be real benefits trying to make all of the Travel and Tourism industry more sustainable.

Current Global and Regional Trends

Tourism and Travel Statistics and Trends

The magnitude of the tourism industry can be clearly seen from the World Travel and Tourism Council (WTTC) statistics. The WTTC estimates that in the year 2002, travel, tourism and related activities will contribute to approximately 10% of the world's GDP, growing to 10.6% by 2012. The industry is currently estimated to help generate 1 in every 12.8 jobs, 7.8% of total employment. This will rise to 8.6% by 2012 (WTTC 2002). Tourism has helped to create millions of jobs in developing countries. For example official estimates for 2002 suggest China has 51.1 million jobs associated to tourism and India 23.7 million jobs. In terms of the relative importance of different sectors for job creation, the largest contributors in travel and tourism employment are found in island states and destinations-ranging from 76.3% of the total number of people employed in Curacao, to 34.6% employment in Antigua and Barbuda. The top ten countries with greatest expected relative growth in employment over the next ten years are all developing countries. Vanuatu is predicted an annual growth rate of 8.8% in employment and tops the list. The balance of bene-fits begins to tilt toward the developed countries in terms of visitor exports and capital investments, in absolute terms.

The top ten list for visitor exports is led by the US. The rest are all European countries, except for China.

On capital investments, US receives an estimated investment of US$ 205.2 million-far ahead of all other countries. Japan with an investment of US$ 42.7 million and China with US$ 42.5 million follow. The expected growth rates for capital investments over the next ten years are significant for developing countries. Turkey has an annualised growth rate of 10.4% (WTTC 2002). Whilst it can be argued that tourism creates an incentive for environmental conservation, tourism is also responsible for damage to the environment. The phenomenal growth of the sector has been accompanied by severe environmental and cultural damage. The projected growth for the industry frequently occurs in destinations that are close to or have exceeded their natural carrying-capacity limits. The consequences are that short term economic gain clearly incurs long term environmental and social costs. Beyond these environmental aspects, other issues of a more social, cultural and rights-based nature have gained increased attention since the mid-1990's. These include financial leakages, disruptive impacts to local livelihoods and culture, gender bias, sexual exploitation, formal vs. informal sector, domestic vs. international tourism, the growth of "all-inclusive" package tours. Some of the key issues and challenges related to these problems are outlined in the sections below.

Issues: Progress and Challenges

Tourism and the Environment

The natural environment is an important resource for tourism. With increasing urbanisation, destinations in both industrialised and developing countries with significant natural features, scenery, cultural heritage or biodiversity are becoming increasingly popular sites for tourist destinations. Efforts to preserve and enhance the natural environment should therefore be a high priority for the industry and for governments.

But the reality is not quite as clear cut. Environments where past human interaction has been minimal are often fragile. Small islands, coastal areas, wetlands, mountains and deserts, all now popular as tourist destinations, are five of the six 'fragile ecosystems' as identified by Agenda 21 that require specific action by governments and international donors. The biophysical characteristics of these habitats often render them particularly susceptible to damage from human activities. As the scale of tourism grows, the resource use threatens to become unsustainable. With a degraded physical environment, the destination is in danger of losing its original attraction, increasing the levels of cheaper mass tourism and forcing more "nature-based" tourism to move on to new destinations, which are likely to be even more inaccessible and fragile. Mainstream "ecotourism", as promoted after the Rio Earth Summit, hasn't always enjoyed a good reputation. Tour operators have used the concept merely as a "greenwash" marketing tool. In reality it often meant introducing unsustainable levels of tourism into fragile areas, having scant regard for either the environment or for the residents of the destination areas. As the International Council for Local Environmental Initiatives (ICLEI) pointed out:

"*Tourism in natural areas, euphemistically called "eco-tourism," can be a major source of degradation of local ecological,* economic and social systems. The intrusion of large numbers of foreigners with high-consumption and high-waste habits into natural areas, or into towns with inadequate waste management infrastructure, can produce changes to those natural areas at a rate that is far greater than imposed by local residents. These tourism-related changes are particularly deleterious when local residents rely on those natural areas for their sustenance. Resulting economic losses can encourage *socially deleterious economic activities such as prostitution, crime, and migrant and child labour*" (ICLEI 1999).

Some of the different kinds of impacts that tourism development and operational activities can have include:

* Threats to ecosystems and biodiversity – e.g loss of wildlife and rare species, habitat loss and degradation,
* Disruption of coasts – e.g shoreline erosion and pollution, impact to coral reefs and fish spawning grounds,
* Deforestation – loss of forests for fuel wood and timber by the tourist industry also impact on soil and water quality, bio-diversity integrity, reducing the collection of forest products by local communities,

* Water overuse – as a result of tourism/recreational activities e.g. golf courses, swimming pools, and tourist consumption in hotels,
* Urban problems-Congestion and overcrowding, increased vehicle traffic and resultant environmental impacts, including air and noise pollution, and health impacts,
* Exacerbate climate change – from fossil fuel energy consumption for travel, hotel and recreational requirements,
* Unsustainable and inequitable resource use-Energy and water over consumption, excessive production of wastes, litter and garbage are all common impacts.

Further study could be carried out regarding the negative relationship between tourism and environment, however the many examples across the globe indicate this scenario is quite typical and widely recognised, emphasising the need to identify more mutually beneficial approaches in tourism development.

Tourism and Economics

Economic gains have been a major driving force for the growth of tourism in developing countries. The initial period of growth happened in the late 1960's and 1970's, when tourism was perceived as a key activity for generating foreign ex-and employment by both development institutions, such as the World Bank, as well as by governments. Despite the negative economic impacts of tourism (such as inflation; dominance by outsiders in land and property markets; inward-migration eroding economic opportunities for domestic industry including the poor) the demand for travel and tourism continues to grow. The WTTC has estimated there was an approximate 40% cumulative growth in tourism demand between 1990 and 2000. This demand was largely driven by economic gains at all levels, including in the communities in remote, and hitherto relatively isolated, destinations. There is significant scope for enhancing the possible gains through addressing a number of issues that can help improve opportunities for entrepreneurs and the communities in the destinations, for the poorer sections within these communities, as well as at the macro level for the national economy. Some of these are options are discussed below.

Financial leakages: Powerful trans-national corporations (TNCs) continue to dominate the international tourism market. Estimates suggest that about 80% of international mass tourism is controlled by TNCs. These companies have an almost unhindered access to markets and use this to drive down the cost of supplies. The result is high levels of financial leakage, and limited levels of revenue retention in the destination or host countries. Financial leakages tend to occur due to various factors, including importation of foreign building material, skilled labour and luxury products, and packaged travel arranged with TNCs. This is as opposed to locally sourcing the necessary resources. It has been estimated that, on average, at least 55% of tourism expenditure flows back out of the destination country, rising to 75% in certain cases e.g. the Gambia and Commonwealth Caribbean.

During the seventh UN Commission on Sustainable Development (CSD) meeting (1999), financial leakages was identified as a key area for stakeholders to take action and work together in order to try and assess the situation, as well as seek solutions to better support local communities in host/developing countries. The CSD called upon the UN and the World Tourism Organization, in consultation with major groups, as well as other relevant international organizations, to jointly facilitate the establishment of an ad-hoc informal open-ended working group on tourism to:

* Assess financial leakages and determine how to maximize benefits for indigenous and local communities,
* Prepare a joint initiative to improve information availability and capacity-building for participation, and address other matters relevant to the implementation of the international work programme on sustainable tourism development (UN CSD 1999).

Impacts on livelihoods in destination communities: In most tourist destinations of developing countries, the livelihood impacts of tourism, takes various forms. Jobs and wages are only a part of livelihood gains and often not the most significant ones. Tourism can generate four different types of local cash income, involving four distinct categories of people:

* Wages from formal employment.
* Earnings from selling goods, services, or casual labour.
* Dividends and profits arising from locally-owned enterprises.
* Collective income: this may include profits from a community-

run enterprise, dividends from a private sector partnership and land rental paid by an investor.

Waged employment can be sufficient to lift a household from an insecure to a secure footing, but it may only be available to a minority of people, and not the poor. Casual earnings may be very small, but more widely spread, and may be enough, for instance, to cover school fees for one or more children. Local participation in the industry can be categorised into three different categories; the formal sector (such as hotels), the informal sector (such as vending) and secondary enterprises that are linked to tourism (such as food retail and telecommunications). Experience from Asia suggests that:

* As a destination is developing, accommodation for tourists can be as simple as offering home stays at the early stage, with lodges, guest houses and hotels replacing more basic options as tourism grows, and some of these may include foreign companies. Once luxury resorts start to develop, the scenario becomes more complex with international investors beginning to play a much more dominant role.
* Transport tends to fall into a grey area between formal and informal sectors. Most destinations have taxis, jeeps or other motorised forms of transport, often driven by the owners. As things expand organised associations of owners, operating on a rota system become more common.
* Data about employment in the formal sector is scattered and collection is often not very systematic. There are references of cases where high-status jobs in resorts typically go to non-locals, expatriate staff or foreign-trained nationals. However, there is almost no analysis of who is employed in middle and lower ranking jobs. The potential for employment of local staff seems to improve as one moves away from the luxury resorts into less established areas.
* The informal sector includes activities such as vending, running stalls and collecting fuel wood for the tourist industry. The informal sector often provides an easy entry into the industry for the poor, especially for women. The incomes can be substantial but unreliable as it is often a seasonal activity. However it can still provide a substantial boost to the income

of the poor. Towards Earth Summit 2002 Economic Briefing No. 4· The informal sector tends to get the least attention when interventions are planned, and interventions such as planning permissions are frequently detrimental to this sector. However, there are cases where initiatives such as flexible licensing systems and cooperatives and associations have helped the sector.

* Causal labour and self-employment provide major opportunities for local communities to enhance their livelihood opportunities from tourism. Unlike formal employment, self-employment tends to highlight the entrepreneurial spirit of village communities. Villagers are used to stringing together a livelihood from a diverse variety of sources, often giving them a knack for enterprise. Causal labour includes porters, cooks, guides, launderers, cleaners, caterer and entertainers. Nepal, for instance, has a well-organised labour market to employ porters, cooks and guides on a seasonal basis. An estimate made in 1989 showed that trekking alone generated 0.5 to 1 million person days of employment in a year in Nepal.
* Significant gains also accrue from economic linkages between tourism and other economic sectors such as agriculture, horticulture, animal husbandry and handicrafts.

There continues to be fairly poor quantitative data available regarding the economic gains that can be generated from travel and tourism, particularly data that quantifies the impacts to formal, informal and indirect activities as touched upon above. There is a need for a standardised framework and guidelines for the collection and analysis of comparative data sets, to better identify the possible economic impacts for different segments of the market, as well as to develop policies which better reflect the needs of the informal as well as formal tourism ventures. Another gap in research about tourism relates to understanding how domestic tourism benefits formal and informal segments in a country and the degree to which the extreme poor gain at all from the industry.

* Domestic or regional tourists are particularly important clients for self-employed sellers and owners of small establishments (the skilled poor and not-so-poor). Studies in Yogyakarta (Indonesia) and elsewhere in South East Asia show that domestic

and other Asian tourists tend to buy more from local vendors than Western tourists.

* Budget and independent tourists, particularly back packers are also more likely than luxury tourists to use the cheaper guest houses, home-stays, transport and eating services provided by local people. They tend to stay longer at a destination than groups of tourists and interact more with the local economy, but also spend less per day, often bargaining over prices.
* Nature-based tourism (including 'eco-tourism') does not necessarily provide more opportunities for the poor than 'mass tourism'. Nature tourism does offer some potential advantages however. It takes place in less developed areas, often involves smaller operators with more local commitment. It involves a higher proportion of independent travellers, and if marketed as 'eco-tourism' can stimulate consumer pressure for ensuring domestic socioeconomic benefits. But it remains a niche in the market, can be heavily dependent on imports, and can spread disruption to less developed areas.
* Mass tourism is highly competitive, and usually dominated by large suppliers who have little commitment to a destination. They are less likely to use local suppliers. However the segment does generate jobs and negative impacts are not always spread beyond immediate localities. Further knowledge is needed about how local economic opportunities can be expanded under such circumstances, as well as to identify how the negative impacts can be minimised in the mass tourism segment.
* Cruises and 'all-inclusives' are rapidly growing segments of the market, but by their nature are unlikely to generate few economic linkages. Some governments are trying to actively reduce this, for example the Gambian Government has recently decided to ban 'all-inclusives' in response to local demands.
* The informal sector is where opportunities for small-scale enterprise or labour by the poor are maximised. For example, at Bai Chay, Ha Long Bay in Vietnam, almost a dozen local families run private hotels, but local involvement in tourism spreads far beyond this, to an estimated 70–80% of the population. Apart from those with jobs in the hotels and restaurants, local women share the running of noodle stalls,

many women and children are walking vendors, and anyone with a boat or motorbike hires them out to tourists. However, the informal sector is often neglected by planners.

Tourism and Society Culture

Tourism developments often stop people from having the right of access to land, water and natural resources. NGO's such as Tourism Concern and Rethinking Tourism have reported on examples worldwide where the articles in the UN Declaration of Human Rights are flouted, and where indigenous rights are lost or exploited. Adverse social impacts also include poor working conditions, low wages, child labour and sex tourism. The International Labour Organisation and International Confederation Free Trade Unions (ICFTU) note that some parts of the tourist industry still degrades labour and drives workers to the lowest levels, exhibiting the worst side of unsustainable production.

Cultural transformation: Fears of tourism threatening local cultures can be misplaced and many cultures have proved resilient enough to be able to take rapid changes required by tourism in their stride. However it is true that popular destinations are typically transformed at a very rapid pace. Buzzing small towns can replace sleepy one lane bazaars. Areas where once only officials rode in motorised vehicles become a familiar site for traffic jams, and dealing with unknown faces can become a daily occurrence for people whose previous focus had been confined to a few score square kilometres to their home and work.

Communities visited by tourists can (or have to!) adapt surprisingly quickly. For example, they rapidly adopt businesslike attitudes to maximise profits. They are creative in inventing and staging events to entertain and provide information on their culture. These attractions, while usually not explicitly developed to protect back regions (i.e. areas of a host society reserved only for local residents, where tourists are not welcome), can function to deflect the tourist gaze from private space and activities. Host communities take specific, active measures to protect their values and customs.

This can either be covert action such as private communal functions, fencing off of domesticities but also overt action such as organised protests and even aggression to protect their interests. Tourism development in remote areas can be positive however, bringing with it infrastructure, health services and education facilities. It could be a by-product, or a result of increased incomes, or as is happening increasingly, a result of corporate and customer social responsibility. Nevertheless, rapid tourism development can come at a price and often creates its own unique problems. Tourism activities can degrade the social and natural wealth of a community. The intrusion of large numbers of uninformed foreigners into local social systems can undermine pre-existing social relationships and values. This is particularly a problem where tourism business is centred in traditional social systems, such as isolated communities or indigenous peoples (ICLEI 1999). There are also examples in ecotourism segment, of communities becoming marginalised and forced out of traditional lands as protected areas and destinations become established. Involving host and particularly local communities in all stages of tourism development, from planning right through operations, will help to alleviate some of these issues- if their needs and perspectives are properly taken into account. There is growing amount of work in this area and an expanding body of good practice examples but such approaches need to extended. In addition, programmes which aim to train and assist communities adversely affected by tourism development i.e. providing a social safety net need to be openly assessed for their suitability, and promoted where appropriate.

Tourism and Child Prostitution: On the darker side to global tourism, the sex trade and drug tourism remain areas that are poorly reported or regulated, especially where it concerns children. The root causes behind these growing problems may not wholly lie with growth in tourism, but it is significant and should be a real cause for concern throughout the sector. In recent years the industry has started to try and tackle such problems. In 1998 it collaborated with ECPAT (End Child Prostitution and Trafficking in Children for Sexual Purposes) to draw up a Code of Conduct for tour operators in relation to child prostitution and tourism.

Signatories to ECPAT's Code of Conduct commit themselves to:

* working against child exploitation in their policy documents;
* training staff on how to combat child exploitation;
* provision of information to customers;
* putting pressure on suppliers by including a clause against the commercial sexual exploitation of children in the contract (with hotels, for example);

* provision of information to key local people and organizations by creating a network in destinations to raise awareness amongst local people.

The Fritidresor Group (FRG), a subsidiary of Thomson Travel Group, has risen to the challenge by following up on this initiative in a systematic manner. Since 1999 it has designed and conducted workshops, developed an elaborate customer information programme and initiated pilot programmes in five destinations where child abuse is common (Brazil, Cuba, Dominican Republic, India and Thailand). Feedback from ECPAT from one of the pilots has been positive, e.g. the number of paedophiles in Thailand is decreasing. There are concerns, however, that this is happening at the expense of other countries, especially in Central America, where ECPAT has a weaker presence (Tour Operators Initiatives for Sustainable Tourism Development).

Gender: Gender dis-aggregated data for the tourism sector are not easily available. Using the data for restaurant, catering and hotels as proxy, the Gender and Tourism Report prepared by Stakeholder Forum for the CSD in 1999, reached some tentative conclusions.

The general picture suggests that the formal tourism industry seems to be a particularly important sector for women (46% of the work force are women, compared to 34-40% in other general labour markets). However the proportion of women in the tourism work force varies greatly – from as low as 2% in some countries and up to over 80% in others, depending upon the maturity of the tourism industry. For example, in countries where there is a mature industry, women generally accounted for around 50% of those employed in the industry. Using data from 39 countries, the proportion of women's working hours compared to men's working hours was 89%. Whilst the proportion of women's wages to men's wages is 79% (based on data available from 31 countries).

This suggests that women continue to receive disproportionately lower wages than their male counterparts – often in equivalent positions of status in an organisation. Furthermore the statistics, typically do not include the contribution of women employed in the informal sector. Several studies have indicated, whilst this area is frequently ignored, it also tends to be a significant contributor, particularly in developing countries.

Solutions and Partnerships –Towards Sustainable Tourism

Tourism was only specifically mentioned in a few sections of 1992 Rio Agenda 21, despite its huge economic significance. Agenda 21 for the Travel and Tourism Industry was written in 1996 by the World Trade Organisation, the World Travel and Tourism Council and Earth Council to try and fill this gap. It noted that with a growing standing in the world economy the tourism industry has "a moral responsibility in making the transition to sustainable development. It also has a vested interest in doing so.". The document highlights the vital importance of the environment as the main base upon which the market relies.

These and other activities have supported a growing awareness of the positive and negative impacts of tourism, including a growing realisation of the impact that a degrading environment has on the livelihoods of communities living in destination areas. This has contributed towards the initiation of positive actions for mitigating and minimising the more negative aspects. Various different approaches have been explored, especially in the last couple of decades. Emerging from these efforts is a better recognition of the importance of the role of local communities, their valuable knowledge base and understanding of local circumstances, as well as their strong vested interest in preserving a sustainable system. Establishing partnerships with local communities is being increasingly recognised as necessary for sustainable tourism. The trend now is moving towards more integrated approaches, which include communities working with governments. Some broad proposals and responses for moving towards more sustainable tourism, from various stakeholders, are outlined below.

International Institutions, Agreements and Action Plans

International institutions such as UNEP are working in a number of ways (often in partnership) to promote sustainable tourism. This includes a proposal by UN Economic and Social Council to the UN General Assembly to designate 2002 the "UN International Year of Ecotourism". Though facing some controversy regarding the definition and breadth of the term "ecotourism", the idea was that the year would aim to recognise tourism's potential benefit as both a tool for environmental protection and development. For ecotourism, it is particularly seen as a means to advance three basic goals of the UN Convention on Biological Diversity: To conserve biological diversity;

2. To promote sustainable use of biodiversity to generate income, jobs and business opportunities in ecotourism etc.; 3. To share the benefits of ecotourism developments equitably with local communities & indigenous peoples). Other groups like the World Tourism Organisation do work to try and encourage good practice in the sector. For example the World Tourism Organisation has produced a "Global Code of Ethics for Tourism in 1999 (an extension of the WTO "Manila Declaration on the Social Impacts of Tourism" 1997), as well as a "Compilation of good practices in sustainable tourism", and a practical guide for the development and application of indicators of sustainable tourism, "What Tourism Managers Need to Know".

Business Activities and Tourism

The Rio Earth Summit 1992 was a major turning point for the tourism industry. Environmental issues subsequently became an important part of the agenda for the industry. However, the approach has not yet generally been an integrating one. Instead the focus has been on minimising environmental impacts that the industry is directly responsible for.

There is growing support by lead companies throughout the private sector to implement principles of Corporate Social Responsibility (CSR), Environmental Management and Auditing Systems (EMAS), "Triple Bottom Line" accounting procedures (Environment, Society and Economics) and Sustainability Reporting. Measures are predominately based on adopting a voluntary approach to tackling impacts rather than having regulations/legislation imposed on business by governments.

The action plan for the industry, "Agenda 21 for the Travel & Tourism Industry: Towards Environmentally Sustainable Development" contains a number of priority areas for action and suggested steps to achieve them. The importance of partnerships between government, industry and NGOs is stressed, along with the enormous benefits that will be ob-tained by making the tourism industry more sustainable. The document warns the industry not to under-estimate the challenge which requires "fundamental reorientation". However it also makes it clear that the long-term costs of inaction will far outweigh those for starting to act now. Companies are encouraged to set up systems and procedures to incorporate sustainable development issues into core management functions and to identify actions needed to bring sustainable tourism into being. A long-term communications programme was initiated after the document launch to increase awareness and promote regional implementation (WTTC). The 10 priority areas for action are:

* Waste minimization, re-use and recycling,
* Energy efficiency, conservation and management,
* Management of freshwater resources,
* Waste water treatment,
* Hazardous substances,
* Transport,
* Land-use planning and management,
* Involving staff, customers and communities in environmental issues,
* Design for sustainability,
* Partnerships for sustainability.

Another major voluntary activity highlighted by many companies is the use of codes of conduct and certification. However, even the voluntary codes lag far behind activities for environmental performance in the area of social responsibility (UNED 1999). The World Tourism Organisation recently produced a study "Voluntary Initiatives for Sustainable Tourism" examining 104 schemes worldwide and gives recommendations to improve the conditions for voluntary initiatives and achieve better effectiveness in the operation and support of voluntary initiatives. In addition it gives a checklist for the planning and assessing of your own voluntary initiatives and makes recommendations for eco-labelling. The report states that voluntary practice has not yet had a significant impact on the mass market. The report recognises that "their current impact has been minimal across the sector as a whole". It finds that 78% of tourism certificates focus on tourism within Europe and not further afield. However the report also says that:

> *"they are revealing tremendous potential to move the industry towards sustainability, but not without careful nurturing and support from key industry partners" (WTO 2000).*

When it comes to building more mainstream corporate responsibility, the vast majority of tourist companies state that whilst they would like to do something they feel they are unable to do so because of being faced with 'cut throat' business competition. They argue that the costs involved in acting more responsibly would drive them out of the market, especially if they take unilateral action without wider industry support. Industry surveys have identified the need for establishing mandatory regulations, making it compulsory for everyone to meet the same standards and thereby incur similar costs. Legal and fiscal regulation of corporate sector includes market-based tools such as carbon trading, as supported through the Kyoto Protocol of the UN Framework Convention for Climate Change. Also environmental standards legislated by governments on water quality and waste management, labelling standards, are growing but need to be more widely implemented and effectively enforced.

NGOs are increasingly engaging with the travel sector. They have been playing an active role in addressing problems such as financial leakages and in trying to encourage greater corporate responsibility. Key activities involve consumer education about the potential impacts of tourism and about how local communities might benefit more from the industry.

They actively lobby policy-makers on associated issues of trade liberalisation, fair trade and globalisation. There has also been a concerted effort to set up common certification standards, independent of the industry, along the lines of Fair Trade certification or eco-labelling. Initiatives include the International Fair Trade in Tourism Network, established by Tourism Concern in 1999 and a feasibility study for setting up a Sustainable Tourism Stewardship Council being conducted by the Rainforest Alliance, New York.

Initiatives for Assisting Local Communities to Realise Tourism Opportunities

During the 1990's a number of initiatives emerged which aimed to help communities in destination countries make the most from opportunities provided by tourism. Many have been self initiated, locally and have continued to expand under their own steam, sometimes attracting external technical and/or financial assistance on their own terms. In others, external agents have acted as catalysts. The nature of the activities have been broad, ranging from small one-village initiatives for organising handicrafts production to building powerful networks of small accommodation providers and creating a marketing network for them. Over time, and by learning from experience and sharing knowledge, these initiatives have tended to become more complex and inclusive. Effective multi-stakeholder processes have evolved from the ground. Backed with success and experience at the ground level and on a significant scale, lessons learnt here have the potential for wide and rapid replication. This also requires support from the international community for creating space and resources to assist the players who have been the active leaders of these processes so far to take the lead in formulating a strategy.

Local Authorities: A World Tourism Organisation report on the role of local authorities noted that local authorities have a key role to play in many aspects of tourism development and operations. As countries becomes more decentralised, they are taking on more in this area and realising that the sector may assist local areas in achieving development. Community involvement is referred to as a key part of this process – ensuring participation in planning and development, therefore increasing the possibility of achieving more local benefits from tourism e.g. employment, income, establishing tourism related enterprises.

The report notes that many local authorities lack in experience for planning, nurturing and developing tourism however. This can result in wasted resources and opportunities. The report states that proper planning, efficient implementation and effective management are all essential to optimise the benefits of tourism (WTO 1998). The statement by the International Council for Local Environmental Initiatives (ICLEI) during the seventh session of the CSD said that "*in addition to their direct roles in the development process, perhaps the most important role that local authorities* can play in a global economy is that of facilitator among the diverse interests seeking to influence the direction *of local development*". ICLEI also stated that "*solutions to adverse tourism impacts are to be found in the shared interest* of local communities, tourism businesses, and tourism consumers to maintain the natural wealth and social heritage of *the tourist destination*". Thus a major challenge for "sustainable tourism" will be the creation of tangible and working local partnerships. One way to approach this will be through the principles espoused in Local Agenda 21. These principles should be applied, through partnerships, to evaluate and improve efforts to address sensitive tourism development issues, including:

- Inequitable distribution of tourism revenues and "financial leakages",

* Displacement of pre-existing local settlements by tourism developments
* Equal access to local coastal and recreational resources,
* Conflict over use and long-term protection of those areas,
* Concerns related to lack of foreign tourist sensitivity to cultural traditions and sites.

Governments: It is fairly disappointing to say that many Governments have been slow to take the lead in ensuring the progress of sustainable tourism and much more work could be done by them to engage more pro-actively with this sector than in the past. Further engagement includes action at all levels, from international forums and negotiations, down to development of tourism plans and policy, and the enforcement of key regulation at national and local levels. A study for the European Union made some useful recommendations for governments to take action in support of sustainable tourism.

In addition, it recommends production of regional and national tourism strategies, as well as the development and exchange of knowledge through regional networks on sustainable tourism, engaging stakeholders as well as government ministries. PPT is an approach that gaining recognition by national governments and local authorities. Although PPT is still relatively new and has not been widely applied in practice, existing case studies reveal a number of lessons. These include:

* Diverse activities-beyond community tourism it includes product development, marketing, planning, policy, and investment.
* A lead advocate for PPT is useful, but involving other stakeholders is critical. PPT can be incorporated into the tourism development strategies of government or business.
* Location: PPT works best where the wider destination is developing well.
* PPT strategies often involve development of new products, particularly products linked to local culture. These products should be integrated with mainstream markets where possible.
* Ensuring commercial viability is a priority. This requires understanding demand, product quality, marketing, investment in business skills, and involving the private sector.
* Economic measures should expand both formal and casual earning opportunities.

* Non-financial benefits (e.g. increased community participation, access to assets) can reduce market vulnerability.
* PPT is a long-term investment. Expectations must be prudent and opportunities for short-term benefits investigated.
* External funding may be necessary to cover substantial transaction costs of establishing partnerships, developing skills, and revising policies.

Opportunities for Mutual Gain and Partnership

Conserving and documenting biodiversity: The scientific community has played a role in promoting conservation and research on biodiversity through tourism. One example is Earthwatch, an organisation that supports scientific research through volunteer tourists and funding. In the UK, Earthwatch has a programme which sponsors teachers to be volunteers, and as a result has encouraged greater environmental education in schools in the UK. Another example is the Monteverde Cloud Forest Preserve (MCFR) in Costa Rica, a unique case of what private initiative and a spirit of internationalism can do.

Community Based Wildlife Tourism: In Africa, Community Based Wildlife Tourism (CBWT) has succeeded in conserving the environment as well as empowering communities. The principle behind CBWT is simple- the benefits to wildlife must exceed the costs. In reality this is not so straight forward. A number of the caveats and complexities necessary for success have been identified through experiences on the ground:

* The link between tourism resource and wildlife conservation is not always obvious. It has to be emphasised through education, dialogue and negotiations. Financial incentives will be ineffective in the absence of institutions and capacity for sustainable management. Hence, responsibility for wildlife management and institutional capacity should take precedence over the benefits.
* Equitable distribution of local earnings from tourism is critical and they should be widely shared within the community managing tourism resources.
* Even if tourism creates incentives for wildlife conservation, wider impacts on ecosystems or bio-diversity maintenance should also be considered.

ICT and alternative technologies: The growing use of Information Communication Technology has been cited as a way to cut down on "unnecessary travel", particularly for work-related travel e.g. through using video conferencing instead of travelling to meetings all the time (IIIEE 2002). However for recreational tourism, the main focus of this paper, the link is less obvious. There are, however, numerous examples of web-based guides and tools, aiming to support sustainable tourism, that are springing up all over the place, a few of which have been cited in this paper. A recent study, for the Global Information Society International Research Programme, identified a number of ways that ICT can support tourism as well as protection of biodiversity:

* Helping to establish global tourism/biodiversity databases to enable more effective planning and monitoring in an inter-related and comprehensive way,
* Encouraging global exchange of information and expertise among professionals and stakeholders,
* Allowing small operators and others to be included in discussion and to gain greater access to data,
* Encouraging direct dialogue, including that of marketing and promotion, between sites and tourists, and between tourist providers and tourists;
* Generally improving consumer and operator awareness of impacts and outcomes of tourism.

The study indicated that it is the immediacy of ICT, its capacity to retain and distribute information and its flexibility that are some of its strongest benefits. Another is that ICT can assist the creation of new connections and networks between practitioners, operators and tourists across the globe. Such groups are important to help learn and exchange good practice in sustainable tourism.

Alternative technologies are another important area. Organisations which combine alternative technology with "learning by living" holidays are growing in number. They include activities like agro-ecotourism, which link tourism, education and promoting traditional conservation and sustainable use practices. Tourists are taught new skills for sustainable living, such as organic farming, using alternative renewable energies, through visiting eco-villages, alternative technology centres and traditional communities (ITDG 2002).

Education, Capacity Building and Participation

Education is the key to changing tourist behaviour. Some examples, such as marketing and publicity campaigns by tour operators, have already been cited. Other opportunities also exist, such as learning about sustainability in tourism through job training. These activities should be a shared responsibility between government, private sector operators and trade associations, as well as local tourist organisations, formal training institutions, unions and representative bodies (ICFTU 1999). "*Responsible tourism is the job of everyone involved* – governments, local authorities, the tourist *industry and tourists themselves*" (UNEP 2001) Recognising the substantial impacts of tourism yet also its potential to help implementation of Sustainable Development, the CSD addressed sustainable tourism for the first time in 1999.

Many of the issues raised are already considered within this paper but a direct result was the designation of 2002 as UN 2002 UN International Year of Ecotourism (IYE). IYE has not been without its critics (e.g. Third World Network, Rethinking Tourism) who expressed real concerns about assuming that Ecotourism was already a "success", when even the World Bank (who has been supporting ecotourism for over a decade) suggests that few projects have actually generated substantial income for local communities. The Quebeç Declaration on Ecotourism is expected to become a major point of reference for future discussion about eco-tourism but "much work remains to be done, notably in the fight against poverty" (WTO 2002). Promoting a broader and more inclusive approach towards seeking sustainable tourism development and capacity building will be key. According to UNEP some of the conditions for a successful transition towards sustainable tourism include:

* Involvement of stakeholders: Increase the long-term success of tourism projects by involving key stakeholders in the development and implementation of tourism plans,
* Information exchange: Raise awareness of sustainable tourism and its implementation by promoting exchange of information, between governments and stakeholders, on best practice for sustainable tourism, and establishing networks for dialogue on implementation of Sustainable Tourism Principles,
* Promote understanding and awareness: to strengthen attitudes, values and actions compatible with sustainable development.

* Capacity Building: Ensure effective implementation of sustainable tourism, through capacity building programmes to develop and strengthen human resources and institutional capacities in government at national and local levels, and amongst local communities; and to integrate environmental and human ecological considerations at all levels.

Monitoring and Measuring Progress through Indicators

The effectiveness of sustainable tourism initiatives requires effective monitoring of progress, through collecting data around key sustainability indicators for the tourism sector. During CSD 7 participants proposed that the CSD should encourage international agencies to develop indicators to measure the environmental, cultural and social impacts of coastal tourism. The World Tourism Organisation has also done some work in this area. Their Agenda 21 for the Travel and Tourism Industry noted that indicators were a relatively new area for the industry although a number of National Tourism Authorities (including Argentina, Canada, France, Malta, Mexico, Netherlands, Spain, Turkey and the USA) had participated in the World Tourism Organization ongoing programme to develop a key set of indicators for use by national and local authorities. Also UNESCO and UNEP's Tour Operators Initiative recently signed a Memo of Understanding with the Global Reporting Initiative (GRI) to develop Sustainability Reporting Guidelines specially targeted at tour operators.

Conclusions

As we've seen ecotourism is just one approach towards seeking sustainable tourism. Responsible and pro-poor tourism are emerging as new specialist approaches. And new initiatives which aim to push the mainstream tourism industry are building. One example is a new alliance between the World Tourism Organisation and UNCTAD aimed at "poverty alleviation through tourism". The initiative was announced in July 2002 and it will be presented at the Johannesburg Summit in an attempt to gain wider support. Model projects and successful multi-stakeholder initiatives, albeit on a small-scale, are also beginning to grow. Even these few examples perhaps prove that tourism has the potential to meet many of the objectives of sustainable development – to revitalize economies, support local communities, protect the environment and even generate cost savings and efficiency gains for tourism companies.

Promotion of sustainable tourism, through the development of policy tools, capacity building and awareness-raising programmes, local involvement, guidelines for good practice and actual implementation remain essential goals. Sustainable tourism should aim to directly support poverty eradication and sustainable production and consumption – in line with the general aims of Agenda 21. Making progress on a larger scale will be a fine balancing act and will require a massive "sea-change" in approach from the entire Travel and Tourism industry but it is an approach that is clearly worthy of support from all stakeholders interested and involved in the industry.

With more than 900 million people travelling each year, the tourism industry wields tremendous economic importance, especially in areas rich in biological and cultural diversity. But unless tourism is practiced responsibly and in harmony with the environment, it can lead to unchecked development, cultural exploitation, habitat destruction, waste and pollution.

The Rainforest Alliance is working to help tourism entrepreneurs conserve their environments and contribute to local livelihoods, while improving their own bottom line. We do this by:

- Training tourism businesses to adopt more sustainable practices and encourage them to pursue voluntary certification with one of the numerous existing programs.
- Providing marketing support to certified tourism businesses, and those in the process of becoming certified.
- Working with tour operators who motivate the hotels they work with to adopt sustainable practices.
- Educating travellers to seek out certified operations as a means to differentiate legitimate eco-friendly operations from those that might make misleading claims.
- Promoting sustainability certification as a strategic conservation and business development tool within the industry and to the public.
- Supporting the efforts of the Sustainable Tourism Certification Network of the Americas and the proposed accreditation body, the Sustainable Tourism Stewardship Council, to help certification programs worldwide to develop internationally sound standards for certification programs.

- Establishing regional networks of certification programs to share resources and information.

Sustainable Tourism: Tourism, the Big Picture

Tourism is big business. According to the World Tourism Organization (WTO) tourism has grown at an amazing rate in the last 30 years. Currently, the business of travel (comprising everything from airlines to resorts to boutique organizations like Context) represents 6% of the entire global GDP and nearly 30% of the entire service economy. Total tourism receipts in 2004 were $622 billion. According to the WTO, tourism is on track to eclipse oil as the single largest industry on the planet by 2010.

Like all big industries tourism has an impact on the environment, local economies, and the social and cultural fabric of the places where it operates. If not managed properly a tourism program can easily become extractive, over time reducing the value of a destination rather than enhancing it. This is obvious in places like Rome, Paris, Venice, and Florence—European cities that are among the most touristed places on the planet and where the presence of huge crowds diminishes the meaning of monuments; tour buses emit huge amounts of air pollution; and small businesses lose out to tourist-friendly chains able to serve the lowest common denominator. Over time, mass tourism strips a place of its character and turns entire quarters of a city into mere "tourist zones."?

Context, the Small Picture

Though we didn't articulate it at the time, Context was founded on principles of sustainable tourism; that is, it was designed to tread lightly on the places where we operate. We organize only small groups of people and design our itineraries to venture off the beaten path. We've always encouraged our clients to visit local businesses and eat in authentic restaurants. And we've always considered that the soul of the traveller is important to the city: If an American comes to Rome or Paris, say, and is moved on a fundamental level by the cultural heritage here, then he or she will become a defender of that cultural heritage. An educated, impassioned tourist can be a powerful advocate.

After the National Geographic Society asked Context founder Paul Bennett to join their panel on geotourism and evaluate the sustainability of cities and tourism destinations, we began to get a lot more interested in the international "sustainable tourism"? movement. Eventually, we started honing our general philosophy into something more articulate and coherent, a vision to make our business truly sustainable, so that we can protect the places that we love while enhancing the experience of the people we serve.

Our sustainable program has three main components:

1. Reducing and mitigating the environmental footprint of our office and our programs.
2. Controlling the social and economic impact of our programs.
3. Giving back to the cities where we operate.

Environmental Impact

Greening Context involves two separate initiatives. The first concerns our offices and the daily operations of our staff. This has been pretty simple, since our offices are quite small, comprising a mere 480 square feet of space between three locations in the U.S., Rome and Paris. In each place we recycle waste, use recycled goods, and bike or use mass transit to commute. (This last is made easier by the fact that no one, including founders Lani and Paul, owns a car.) Next, we look at our programs. The majority of our seminars are organized as walking tours. When forced to go farther afield on an excursion we usually use the train system, partly because they are more efficient than the highways in Italy and France.

Beyond this, we participate in a carbon-offset program. Using carbon calculators developed by Terrapass and The Conservation Fund, we estimate that our offices produce about 11.78 tons of carbon each year, including plane travel for our staff moving between our offices in Paris and Rome and the United States. We offset this with an annual contribution to a carbon-offset program overseen by Sustainable Tourism International (STI), a non-profit organization that coordinates research and projects in sustainable tourism (and of which Context is a member).

We also measure how much carbon any of our car-assisted itineraries and car transfers produce, and offset these twice yearly. The cost of this offset is included in our prices.

Social & Economic Impact

In order to manage our impact on the social and economic fabric of our cities, we generally follow the guidelines of the Sustainable

Tourism Initiative and the National Geographic Society's Geotourism Charter. Specifically, we approach this issue from two directions.

Firstly, we look for ways that we can shape our programs so that they have a minimal footprint on the city. This includes dividing large groups into smaller subgroups and avoiding overcrowded spaces like the Eiffel Tower or Colosseum, except when absolutely necessary. Thus, we find ourselves in intimate groups in intimate settings, whether it's strolling through a hidden quarter of Paris or sitting down for a salad at a mom-and-pop trattoria in Naples. This has an obvious economic effect: Instead of directing the spending power of our clients towards touristy chains that have a negative effect on the city, we help them to invest in the health of small enterprises and the living fabric of the place. We also believe that this fosters a great rapport between the host (the local business owner) and the visitor, instead of alienating the one from the other as so often happens in crowded tourist zones. (For a clear example of the enervating effect of tourism economics on a place, spend some time watching the fake gladiators extorting tourists outside of the Colosseum.)

The second tack we take is to include some amount of discussion about the traveller's role in the social and economic life of the host city into every itinerary we run. This is an uneven and haphazard element of what we do. Since our docents don't follow a script and work independently to develop their own narrative experience of these cities, the amount of time spent talking about preserving the social fabric of Paris or encouraging our clients to venture outside the Centre Storico in Florence can vary a lot. We distribute copies of the National Geographic Society's Geotourism Principles to our clients along with a copy of our own, in-house "Six Steps to Being a Responsible Visitor" document as part of our orientation guidebooks.

Investment in Cultural Heritage

The last component of our sustainable tourism program involves donating part of our profits to the Context Foundation for Sustainable Travel, a U.S.-based 501 c.3 charity that invests projects that mitigate the impact of tourism on the seven cities where Context Travel operates. We also encourage our clients to donate to the Foundation as part of their travel experience.

The Context Foundation looks at both the negative and positive aspects of travel, aiming to mitigate the former in enhance the latter. Projects that mitigate the negative effects of travel fall into three project areas: research on tourism and its effects, cultural preservation projects, and economic development to offset the impact of tourism. The Foundation also invests in projects that seek to broaden and enhance the transformative and educational impact of travel by making it available to populations, such as inner-city youths. In 2007-8, the Context Foundation earmarked five projects for support:

- An apprenticeship program for the artisans of the Oltrarno neighbourhood of Florence. Economic changes in Florence fuelled by the tremendous rise of mass tourism have put serious pressure on the silversmiths, wood-workers, paper makers, and other traditional craftsmen who have defined the Oltrarno as a centre of Italian artisanship for more than a century. In conversations with many of these artisans, with whom Context Travel works as part of their walking seminars there, we discovered that the artisans are facing tremendous difficulties in keeping their businesses viable; and there is a very real threat that in a couple of years few traditional crafts-men will continue to practice in Florence. A major problem for these artisans is their ability to attract and retain apprentices who can learn these crafts and eventually become masters in their own right. The artisans simply can't compete with global companies, including the tour companies, as employers in Florence. The Context Foundation, in response, has set up a fund to help offset the cost of employing these apprentices. We will begin with a single shop—the Bini Brothers woodworkers, who have resided in Piazza Santo Spirito for more than 100 years. We hope to grow and develop this support for more artisans over the coming years, though it is a race against time.
- Study of the effects of tourism on Venice. As any traveller to Venice knows, tourism has a major impact there, both on the environment and on its social fabric. To the first point, wake from cruise ships, daunting garbage management issues, and pollution of various types have had a serious impact on a city that is already in a fragile state. To the second point, as tourists and tourism-focused enterprises crowd out the Venetian

population, the city is losing population at a tremendous rate. Venice as we know it—as it's been known for 1000 years—is facing serious challenges. Teaming up with the UK charity Venice in Peril, we are financing a major study of the effect of tourism on Venice by noted ecologist, Venice resident, and Context Travel docent Jane da Mosto, which promises to bring into full relief the challenges facing this city and chart a roadmap for its preservation.

- Study and promotion of Ostia Antica, outside of Rome. The ancient Roman town of Ostia is often overshadowed by Pompeii. However, for travellers to Rome it really makes better sense to visit this equally important site in-stead of making such a long (and fossil-fuel consuming) trip to Naples. Working with the Rome-based American Institute for Roman Culture, we are supporting a series of projects in Ostia, including measured drawings of its buildings and promotion of it as a more sustainable destination for Rome travellers than Pompeii.
- Restoration of La Chapelle des Petits-Augustins, Paris. La Chapelle des Petits-Augustins at the Ecole des Beaux Arts is important to the study of French art, for it was here (at the Ecole) that most of France's greatest painters studied, and the chapel became a kind of repository for their studies–mostly of Italian art, of which it is filled with scale copies. The chapel stands in great need of restoration, which the Foundation helps fund through special visits.
- Travel fellowship for economically disadvantaged youths Working with the innovative St. HOPE, which has transformed the inner-city community of Oak Park, Sacramento and established a new standard for public education and economic revitalization of urban communities in the U.S., we sponsor a yearly travel fellowship for a high-achieving student. The fellowship includes travel and accommodations in Europe, plus a week-long study trip with the scholars in the Context network. The program is intensive and includes six days of seminars, classes, workshops, and other programs, capped by a writing project. The first student for 2008 has been selected and will arrive in Rome in August.

In 2008, the Foundation will continue to investigate new projects that fit its mission in other cities–namely, London, New York, and Naples.

Resources & Notes

The World Tourism Organization (WTO) is the UN agency for tourism. They produce some of the best reports on tourism economics and also advocate for tourism as a tool for economic development. The numbers cited here are drawn from their published statistics.

Sustainable Tourism International is an American non-profit that provides education and outreach services that will lessen the toll that travel and tourism takes on the environment and local cultures. STI's blend of environmental and cultural sustainability was very influential in our thinking.

National Geographic's Geotourism program was also quite important to us and serves an important blueprint for travellers and travel businesses alike.

Treehugger, a great resource for environmental sustainability, published a good report on carbon offset programs, which influenced the course of our program.

National Geographic Society's Geotourism Program

Context has modelled its Sustainable Travel Program in part on the National Geographic Society's Geotourism program. Context founder Paul Bennett sits on the Society's panel for sustainable tourism and is a contributor to both National Geographic and National Geographic Adventure. The following is taken from NGS's geotourism website:

About Geotourism: Geotourism is defined as tourism that sustains or enhances the geographical character of a place—its environment, culture, aesthetics, heritage, and the well-being of its residents. Geotourism incorporates the concept of sustainable tourism—that destinations should remain unspoiled for future generations—while allowing for enhancement that protects the character of the locale. Geotourism also adopts a principle from its cousin, ecotourism, that tourism revenue can promote conservation, and extends that principle beyond nature travel to encompass culture and history as well: all distinctive assets of a place.

What is Sustainable Tourism?: Sustainable tourism, like a doctor's code of ethics, means "First, do no harm." It is basic to good destination stewardship.

Sustainable tourism does not abuse its product—the destination. It seeks to avoid the "loved to death" syndrome. Businesses and other stakeholders anticipate development pressures and apply limits and management techniques that sustain natural habitats, heritage sites, scenic appeal, and local culture.

It conserves resources. Environmentally aware travellers favour businesses that minimize pollution, waste, energy consumption, water usage, landscaping chemicals, and excessive nighttime lighting.

It respects local culture and tradition. Foreign visitors learn about and observe local etiquette, including using at least a few courtesy words in the local language. Residents learn how to deal with foreign expectations that may differ from their own. It aims for quality, not quantity. Communities measure tourism success not by sheer numbers of visitors, but by length of stay, distribution of money spent, and quality of experience.

What is Geotourism?: Geotourism adds to sustainability principles by building on geographical character—"sense of place"—to create a type of tourism that emphasizes the distinctiveness of its locale, and that benefits visitor and resident alike.

Geotourism is synergistic: All the elements of geographical character together create a tourist experience that is richer than the sum of its parts, appealing to visitors with diverse interests.

It involves the community. Local businesses and civic groups work together to promote and provide a distinctive, authentic visitor experience.

It informs both visitors and hosts. Residents discover their own heritage and how the ordinary and familiar may be of interest to outsiders. As local people develop pride and skill in showing off their locale, tourists get more out of their visit. It benefits residents economically. Travel businesses do their best to use the local work force, services, and products and supplies. When the community understands the beneficial role of geotourism, it becomes an incentive for wise destination stewardship.

It supports integrity of place. Destination-savvy travellers seek out businesses that emphasize the character of the locale. Tourism revenues in turn raise local perceived value of those assets. It means great trips. Enthusiastic visitors bring new knowledge home, telling stories that send friends and relatives off to experience the same thing—a continuing business for the destination.

What is Sustainable Tourism?

Sustainable tourism is tourism development that avoids damage to the environment, economy and cultures of the locations where it takes place. The aim of sustainable tourism is to ensure that development is a positive experience for local people; tourism companies; and tourists themselves. Under sustainable tourism, it may be unlikely to experience the kind of 'boom and bust' that led to the rapid growth, and then despoliation of locations such as the east coast of Spain in the 1970s.

But despite this optimistic objective, sustainable tourism is still not widely understood. For a start, 'sustainable tourism' is not necessarily 'ecotourism'. Ecotourism became popular in the 1980s as a form of tourism that focused exclusively on wildlife, nature, or exotic cultures. Recent research, however, has indicated that such tourism may not actually be good for environment, or for the people who experience this attention. Safaris in Kenya, for example, are undoubtedly 'ecotourism'. But Kenya is full of cases where lions have been forced into erratic behaviour because of excessive tourists, or where the local Masai people have failed to benefit from this kind of development. More importantly, 'ecotourism' does not involve more mainstream beach-or city-based tourism, where impacts are much greater than any nature-based tourism. Sustainable tourism, therefore, is an attempt to improve the impacts of all types of tourism, and this implies seeking ways to build partnerships between tourism companies and local governments or managers of resorts.

But how can sustainable tourism be achieved? Evidence suggests that it requires cooperation between concerned companies and the managers of destinations. It does not, however, require a marked interest from consumers. Some companies have suggested that they will only take steps to achieve sustainable tourism if they recognize a clear 'market demand' for holidays that are overtly 'green' or 'environmentally friendly'. Research, however, has indicated that few tourists want holidays that are 'green' within the mass tourism market; and that holidays that are 'green' may repeat the pitfalls of ecotourism. It may not be profitable or sustainable to encourage market demand for 'green' tourism as this demand may not occur, and also may not lead to sustainable tourism.

Instead, evidence has suggested that sustainable tourism does not have to be advertised as environmentally or culturally sensitive in order to succeed. Research has indicated that profits may be increased simply by adopting some general environmental principles, such as recycling waste, planning for long-term sustainability, and seeking local partnerships for resort management. If these actions result in cleaner, less crowded, holiday resorts, then they are in effect sustainable tourism without being labelled so.

But how can companies and resort managers achieve this kind of success? This question is more controversial. One proposal has been to increase the vertical integration of tourism companies, so that individual companies have greater control over the marketing of holidays, transportation of tourists, and then management of resorts. Such integration may help avoid the disappointment and despoliation of resorts that occurs when tourists interested in conventional mass tourism are sent to sites perhaps better suited to bird watchers or hill walkers, as has occurred in Corfu. But this suggestion, however, is occasionally opposed as it may imply that smaller tourism companies cannot enter the market. Furthermore, reducing competition from smaller companies may result in reducing the pressure for lower prices of holidays. Since the 1980s, the British tourism industry has experienced rapid cuts in prices as a result of deep competition between major companies such as Airtours, First Choice, and Thompson. But it is generally the presence of competition from smaller, less regulated, companies that leads to the rapid over-development of resorts, or the reluctance of large companies to increase their costs by attending to the long-term sustainability of locations.

Thinking Point

Do you Think the Distinction Between Sustainable Tourism and Ecotourism is Useful? Why?

The achievement of sustainable tourism, therefore depends in part on providing the right incentives for companies and resort managers to reduce the negative impacts of tourism, and then a variety of local practical steps (such as limiting numbers, or zoning land use) to reduce these impacts. But in the long term, the ultimate achievement of sustainable tourism also requires tourists and companies to think more about how tourism may impact on other people's homes and livelihoods. Marcel Proust once wrote that most tourists seem to want to travel through one hundred countries with one pair of eyes, whereas the best journey would be to travel through one country with a hundred pair of eyes.

By seeking more diversity and depth in holiday destinations, tourists may help avoid the impacts of tourism on destinations, and also achieve a more satisfying experience.

What is Sustainable Tourism?

* Its informative. Travellers not only learn about the destination, they learn how to help sustain its character while deepening their own travel experiences. Residents learn that the ordinary and familiar may be of interest and value to outsiders.
* It supports integrity of place. Destination-savvy travellers seek out businesses that emphasize the character of the locale in terms of architecture, cuisine, heritage, aesthetics, and ecology. Tourism revenues in turn raise local perceived value of those assets.
* It benefits residents. Travel businesses do their best to employ and train local people, buy local supplies, and use local services.
* It conserves resources. Environmentally aware travellers favour businesses that minimize pollution, waste, energy consumption, water usage, landscaping chemicals, and unnecessary nighttime lighting.
* It respects local culture and tradition. Foreign visitors learn about and observe local etiquette, including using at least a few courtesy words in the local language. Residents learn how to deal with foreign expectations that may differ from their own.
* It does not abuse its product. Stakeholders anticipate development pressures and apply limits and management techniques to prevent the "loved to death" syndrome. Businesses cooperate to sustain natural habitats, heritage sites, scenic appeal, and local culture.
* It strives for quality, not quantity. Communities measure tourism success not by sheer numbers of visitors, but by length of stay, money spent, and quality of experience.

* It means great trips. Satisfied, excited visitors bring new knowledge home and send friends off to experience the same thing-which provides continuing business for the destination.

Environmental Protection and Natural Resource Management

Introduction: Recent and Future Trends in Tourism

Tourism can be considered one of the most remarkable socioeconomic phenomena of the twentieth century. From an activity "enjoyed by only a small group of relatively well-off people" during the first half of the last century, it gradually became a mass phenomenon during the post-World War II period, particularly from the 1970s onwards. It now reaches larger and larger numbers of people throughout the world, and is a source of employment for a significant segment of the labour force.

Although domestic tourism currently accounts for approximately 80 per cent of all tourist activity, many countries tend to give priority to international tourism because, while the former basically involves a regional redistribution of national income, the latter has now become the world's largest source of foreign exchange receipts. According to the latest figures compiled by the World Tourism Organization (WTO), foreign exchange earnings from international tourism reached a peak of US$ 476 billion in 2000, which was larger than the export value of petroleum products, motor vehicles, telecommunications equipment or any other single category of product or service.

International tourist arrivals grew at an annual average rate of 43 per cent during the 1990s, despite major international political and economic crises, such as the Gulf War and the Asian financial crisis. According to the latest WTO figures, compiled with data received up to August 2001, the turn of the millennium recorded one of the most impressive annual growth rates in international tourism. All regions of the world recorded significant growth in international tourism in 2000, during which the number of international arrivals grew at an extraordinary rate of 7 per cent to reach almost 700 million arrivals. The September 2001 terrorist attacks in the United States, however, appear to have had a more serious impact on the tourist sector than any other major international crisis in recent decades. The attacks had a particularly severe impact on air transport, business travel and long-haul travel. Worldwide travel reservations were estimated to have dropped by 15 per cent at the end of October 2001, although not every destination nor every part of the tourism sector was badly affected. For example, while air transport and luxury hotels have suffered from considerable fall in demand, travel within the same country or region, as well as travel by rail and road, appear to have weathered the worst effects of the crisis, or even benefited from it. Nevertheless, initial forecasts of 3-4 per cent rise in international tourist arrivals for 2001, made before the September 2001 attacks, were subsequently revised downwards to around a 1 per cent increase over the 2000 figures. The latest data, released by WTO in January 2002, show that there was a sharp decline of 1.3 per cent in international arrivals, to a total of less than 690 million, in 2001. Given that the northern hemisphere summer holiday season was coming to end by the time the attacks took place, this significant drop confirms that the short-term impacts of the attacks were devastating to international tourism as a whole. The last four months of 2001, in fact, recorded a drop of almost 11 per cent in arrivals worldwide and substantial decreases in all regions of the world.

It is worth noting, however, that this considerable fall in international arrivals was caused not only by a widespread fear of travelling generated by the attacks– particularly in airplanes and to certain destinations – but also by a downturn in the world economy. The economic downturn that began in the United States during the first half of 2001 had already been affecting the tourism sector before the terrorist attacks were carried out. The attacks merely aggravated the economic slowdown already under way.

According to the most recent United Nations economic forecasts, growth of only 1.5 per cent in gross world product (GWP) is expected in 2002, as compared to 1.3 per cent last year. Such a modest improvement is linked to a number of economic uncertainties, notably the high dependency of the global economy on the recovery of the United States. Higher rates of population growth would thus make 2002 the second consecutive year with no real growth in per capita GWP.

This, in turn, is also likely to undermine the short-term prospects for a recovery in international tourism, at least until mid-2002, when the summer holiday season begins in the northern hemisphere, and probably until the end of the year. Although much will depend on the evolution of the world economy during this year, it is also likely that some destinations will experience a prolonged decline in tourism revenues regardless of any world economic improvements. In the medium and long term, however, international tourism is expected to resume its rapid growth, in view of rising living standards and discretionary incomes, falling real costs of travel, expansion and improvement of various transport modes, increasing amounts of free time and other factors. The World Tourism Organization has recently reiterated its long-term forecasts, made before the September 2001 attacks, of an average annual growth rate in international arrivals of over 4 per cent in the period up to 2020. The number of international arrivals is thus expected to reach the striking mark of 1 billion by 2010 and 1.6 billion by 2020.

Main Economic Benefits of Tourism

Tourism, as a sector that comprises an extensive range of economic activities, can be considered the largest industry in the world. International tourism is also one of the fastest growing and most ramified sectors of the global economy, covering a broad range of enterprises, sectors and stakeholders. During the 1990s, when the globalization of tourism reached unprecedented proportions, international tourism receipts had a much higher average annual growth rate (7.3 per cent) than that of gross world product. By 1999, international tourism receipts accounted for more than 8 per cent of the worldwide export value of goods and services, overtaking the export value of other leading world industries such as automotive products, chemicals, and computer and office equipment.

Tourism is also the only major service sector in which developing countries have consistently recorded trade surpluses relative to the rest of the world. Between 1980 and 1996, for instance, their travel account surplus increased from $4.6 billion to $65.9 billion, due primarily to the impressive growth of inbound tourism to countries in Africa, the Caribbean, and the Asia and Pacific regions. The 1990s also experienced a significant growth of international tourism receipts in the 49 poorest developing countries: total tourism receipts in these countries more than doubled from US$ 1 billion in 1992 to over US$ 2.2 billion in 1998. Tourism is now the second largest source of foreign exchange earnings in the 49 least developed countries (LDCs) as a whole, after the oil industry, which is concentrated in only three of these countries. Tourism has become the main source of income for the economies of an increasing number of small island developing States (SIDS) – as well as less developed regions of large countries– with a natural environment appealing to tourists. Foreign exchange earnings can, however, vary significantly among these tourism-driven economies because of 'leakages' arising from imports of equipment for construction and consumer goods required by tourists, repatriation of profits earned by foreign investors and amortization of foreign debt incurred in tourist development.

Besides export earnings, international tourism also generates an increasingly significant share of government (national and local) tax revenues throughout the world. In addition, the development of tourism as a whole is usually accompanied by considerable investments in infrastructure, such as airports, roads, water and sewerage facilities, telecommunications and other public utilities. Such infrastructural improvements not only generate benefits to tourists but can also contribute to improving the living conditions of local populations. This increase in social overhead capital can also help attract other industries to a disadvantaged area and thus be crucial to regional economic development.

The tourism sector is an increasingly important source of employment – including in tourism-related sectors, such as construction and agriculture – primarily for unskilled labour, migrants from poor rural areas, people who prefer to work part-time, and notably women. Because the sector is relatively labour-intensive, investments in tourism tend to generate a larger and more rapid increase in employment than equal investment in other economic activities. Furthermore, given that the sector provides a considerable amount of jobs for women and unskilled workers, tourism can significantly contribute to empowering women and alleviating poverty.

At the same time, available data suggests that most workers in the tourism sector, notably in hotels and catering, tend to earn less than workers in socially comparable occupations in both developed and developing countries. In addition, the differential tends to be larger in less developed countries and regions, particularly those with high rates of unemployment amongst unskilled labour. Informal employment relations in small and medium-sized enterprises, which employ about half of the labour force in the hotel and catering sub-sectors worldwide, also contribute to a relatively high proportion of child labour and non-remunerated employment in these sub-sectors in many countries.

The increasing reliance of less diversified economies on tourism also increases their vulnerability to international shocks, such as, natural disasters, regional wars and other unexpected events. The recent crisis generated by fear of international terrorism, for example, caused devastating immediate effects on tourism-dependent economies, including regional economies in large countries.

In addition, sudden changes in consumer tastes and sharp economic downturns pose significant risks to such economies, given that demand for mass tourism tends to be relatively income-elastic and can produce drastic negative responses to economic recession in source markets. Nonetheless, it is now generally recognized that tourism can make a vital contribution to employment, export receipts and national income in most countries and regions. Furthermore, tourism is often identified as the most promising driving force for the economic development of less developed countries and regions endowed with areas of natural beauty – including small island developing States – because it offers them a valuable opportunity for economic diversification.

Environmental Impacts of Tourism

While tourism provides considerable economic benefits for many countries, regions and communities, its rapid expansion can also be responsible for adverse environmental (and sociocultural) impacts. Natural resource depletion and environmental degradation associated with tourism activities are sometimes serious problems in tourism-rich regions. The management of natural resources to reverse this trend is thus one of the most difficult challenges for governments at different levels.

The fact that most tourists chose to maintain their relatively high patterns of consumption (and waste generation) when they reach their destinations can be a particularly serious problem for developing countries and regions without the appropriate means for protecting their natural resources and local ecosystems from the pressures of mass tourism. The main environmental impacts of tourism are (a) pressure on natural resources, (b) pollution and waste generation and (c) damage to ecosystems. Furthermore, it is now widely recognized that not only uncontrolled tourism expansion is likely to lead to environmental degradation, but also that environmental degradation, in turn, poses a serious threat to tourism.

Pressure on Natural Resources

In addition to pressure on the availability and prices of resources consumed by local residents – such as energy, food and basic raw materials – the main natural resources at risk from tourism development are land, freshwater and marine resources. Without careful land-use planning, for instance, rapid tourism development can intensify competition for land resources with other uses and lead to rising land prices and increased pressure to build on agricultural land.

Intensive tourism development can also threaten natural landscapes, notably though deforestation, loss of wetlands and soil erosion. Tourism development in coastal areas – including hotel, airport and road construction – is a matter for increasing concern worldwide as it can lead to sand mining, beach erosion and land degradation.

Freshwater availability for competing agricultural, industrial, household and other uses is rapidly becoming one of the most critical natural resource issues in many countries and regions. Rapid expansion of the tourism industry, which tends to be extremely water-intensive, can exacerbate this problem by placing considerable pressure on scarce water supply in many destinations.

Water scarcity can pose a serious limitation to future tourism development in many low-lying coastal areas and small islands that have limited possibility for surface water use and storage, and whose ground-water may be contaminated by saltwater intrusion. Over-consumption by many tourist facilities – notably large hotel resorts and golf courses – can limit current supplies available to farmers and local populations in water-scarce regions and thus lead to serious shortages and price rises.

In addition, pollution of available freshwater sources, some of which may be associated with tourism-related activities, can exacerbate local shortages. Rapid expansion of coastal and ocean tourism activities, such as snorkelling, scuba diving and sport fishing, can threaten coral reefs and other marine resources. Disturbance to marine aquatic life can also be caused by the intensive use of thrill craft, such as jet skis, frequent boat tours and boat anchors.

Anchor damage is now regarded as one of the most serious threats to coral reefs in the Caribbean Sea, in view of the growing number of both small boats and large cruise ships sailing in the region. Severe damage to coral reefs and other marine resources may, in turn, not only discourage further tourism and threaten the future of local tourist industries, but also damage local fisheries.

Pollution and Waste Generation

Besides the consumption of large amounts of natural and other local resources, the tourism industry also generates considerable waste and pollution. Improper disposal of liquid and solid waste generated by the tourism industry has become a particular problem for many developing countries and regions that lack the capacity to treat these waste materials properly. Disposal of such untreated waste has, in turn, contributed to reducing availability of the above-mentioned resources at the local level. Apart from the contamination of freshwater from pollution by untreated sewage, tourist activities can also lead to land contamination from solid waste and the contamination of marine waters and coastal areas from pollution generated by hotels and marinas, as well as cruise ships. It is estimated that cruise ships in the Caribbean Sea alone produced more than 70,000 tons of liquid and solid waste a year during the mid-1990s. The fast growth of the cruise sector in the region may have exacerbated this problem in recent years. Furthermore, a particular cause of concern for coastal areas and small islands is the illegal disposal of sewage, solid waste and cargo residues by merchant ships, which cause marine and beach pollution.

In addition, relatively high levels of energy consumption in hotels – including energy for airconditioning, heating and cooking – as well as fuel used by tourism-related transportation can also contribute significantly to local air pollution in many host countries and regions. Local air and noise pollution linked to exhaustive tourism development or urban congestion can sometimes even discourage tourists from visiting some destinations.

Damage to Ecosystems

Intensive tourism activity in natural areas can interfere with fragile vegetation and wildlife and cause irreversible damage to ecosystems, particularly if the infrastructure in those areas is not adequately prepared to absorb mass tourism. Uncontrolled tourism activities can lead to the severe disruption of wildlife habitats and increased pressure on endangered species. As it has been widely documented, it can also disrupt wildlife behaviour, such as, tourist vehicles in Africa's national parks that approach wild cats and thus distract them from hunting and breeding; tour boat operators in the Caribbean Sea that feed sharks to ensure that they remain in tourist areas; and whale-watching boat crews around the world that pursue whales and dolphins and even encourage petting, which tends to alter the animals' feeding and behaviour.

Tourism can also lead to the indiscriminate clearance of native vegetation for the development of new facilities, increased demand for fuelwood and even forest fires. Ecologically fragile areas, such as rain forests, wetlands and mangroves, are also threatened by intensive or irresponsible tourist activity. Moreover, as will be discussed below, it is increasingly recognized that, the rapid expansion of nature tourism (or 'ecotourism') may also pose a threat to ecologically fragile areas, including natural world heritage sites, if not properly managed and monitored.

In many countries, coastlines are becoming overbuilt due to tourism development until the damage caused by environmental degradation – and the eventual loss of revenues arising from a collapse in tourism arrivals – becomes irreversible. As mentioned above, intensive tourism development and recreational activities in coastal areas can not only lead to beach destruction and coastal degradation, but can also threaten coral reefs and other marine ecosystems.

The delicate ecosystems of most small islands, together with their increasing reliance on tourism as a main tool of socioeconomic development, means that these environmental impacts can be particularly damaging since the success of the sector in these islands often depends on the quality of their natural environment. In addition, pollution of coastal waters – in particular by sewage, solid waste, sediments and untreated chemicals – often leads to the deterioration of coastal ecosystems, notably coral reefs, and thus harms their value for tourism. The equally fragile ecosystems of mountain regions are also threatened by increasing popular tourist activities such as skiing, snowboarding and trekking.

One of the most serious environmental problems in mountainous developing countries without appropriate energy supply is deforestation arising from increasing consumption of fuelwood by the tourism industry. This often results not only in the destruction of local habitats and ecosystems, but also in accelerating processes of erosion and landslides. Other major problems arising from tourist activities in mountain regions include disruption of animal migration by road and tourist facilities, sewage pollution of rivers, excessive water withdrawals from streams to supply resorts and accumulation of solid waste on trails.

Environmental Threats to Tourism

In many mountain regions, small islands, coastal areas and other ecologically fragile places visited by tourists, there is an increasing concern that the negative impacts of tourism on the natural environment can ultimately hurt the tourism industry itself. There is now plenty of evidence of the 'life-cycle' of a tourist destination, that is, "its evolution from discovery, to development, to eventual decline, … attributed to a site's overuse and the subsequent deterioration of key attractions or facilities." In other words, the negative impacts of intensive tourism activities on the environmental quality of beaches, mountains, rivers, forests and other ecosystems also compromise the viability of the tourism industry in these places.

In addition, tourism in many destinations could be particularly threatened by global environmental problems, notably the potential threat of 'global warming'. There is increasing scientific evidence that human activity has begun to change the average temperature on the Earth's surface. According to the authoritative United Nations Intergovernmental Panel on Climate Change (IPCC), this process of global warming has been caused by several factors associated with the intensification of economic activities, including the emissions of 'greenhouse gases', such as carbon dioxide produced by burning fossil fuels and forests.

According to the Third Assessment Report of IPCC, it is expected that the globally averaged surface air temperature will have warmed between 1.4 and 5.8 degrees Celsius by 2100 relative to 1990. One of the main consequences of global warming will be sea-level rise: according to IPCC, it is projected that the globally averaged sea level will have risen between 9 and almost 90 centimetres by 2100. Global warming is also expected to increase climate variability and to provoke changes in the frequency and intensity of extreme climate events, such as tropical windstorms and associated storm surges and coastal flooding.

Significant rises in sea level could cause serious problems to tourism activities, particularly in low-lying coastal areas and small islands. According to IPCC, because of their high degree of environmental vulnerability, small island States are likely to be among the countries most seriously affected by global warming. The likely impacts of sea-level rise and coastal flooding on small islands and in some coastal areas would include: (a) increased coastal erosion, (b) loss of land and property, including tourist facilities, (c) dislocation of people, (d) increased risk from storm surges, (d) saltwater intrusion into scarce freshwater resources and (e) high financial costs associated with attempts to respond and adapt to these changes. Severe negative impacts on coastal ecosystems, such as bleaching of coral reefs and deterioration of mangroves, are also expected to threaten tourism in many destinations around the world. In fact, global warming is expected to severely disrupt tourism activities not only in coastal areas and small islands, but also in mountain regions because snow conditions in ski resorts are likely to become less reliable.

Sustainable Tourism: The Way Forward

Countries and regions where the economy is driven by the tourism industry are becoming increasingly concerned with the environmental, as well as the sociocultural problems associated with unsustainable tourism. As a result, there is now increasing agreement on the need to promote sustainable tourism development to minimize its environmental impacts and to ensure more sustainable management of natural resources. The concept of sustainable tourism, as developed in the United Nations sustainable development process, refers to tourist activities "leading to management of all resources in such a way that economic, social and aesthetic needs can be fulfilled while maintaining cultural integrity, essential ecological processes, biological diversity and life support systems." These sustainability concerns are, therefore, beginning to be addressed by governments at national, regional and local, as well as international, levels. In addition, given the leading role of the private sector in the tourism industry in most countries, many initiatives have also been taken by this sector. Broadly speaking, the main policy areas regarding sustainable tourism are: (a) the promotion of national strategies for sustainable tourism development, including the decentralization of environmental management to regional and local levels, (b) the use of both regulatory mechanisms and economic instruments, (c) the support for voluntary initiatives by the industry itself, and (d) the promotion of sustainable tourism at the international level.

National and Regional Strategies for Sustainable Tourism Development

Generally speaking, the main priority for national and regional governments is to incorporate tourism planning and development effectively into overall sustainable development strategies. For example, regional development strategies for areas containing water resources that are potentially attractive to tourism, should carefully consider the availability of those resources in an integrated manner that considers all potential water users. Government policies to promote the domestic tourism industry and to attract foreign direct investment should also ensure that tourism is properly planned and managed so as to minimize adverse environmental impacts and its use of natural resources.

Since the environmental impacts of tourism development are primarily felt at the local and regional levels, national Governments need to promote decentralization of public environment management to the regional and municipal levels. Given that in many countries, local and regional governments already have important responsibilities for tourism development, central Governments should also support capacity building programmes at lower levels in order to enable local and regional authorities to better respond to the challenges of sustainable tourism development in the areas under their jurisdiction. National and local governments also need to develop clear strategies to monitor progress towards sustainable tourism.

Last but far from least, governments at all levels can greatly benefit from working in partnership with all major stakeholders, including local communities, to ensure their active participation in tourism planning, development and management, as well as in the sharing of benefits. Participation of local communities in decision-making and sharing of benefits also helps to generate better awareness of the environmental costs of tourism and thus provides strong incentives to conserve natural resources and protect local environmental assets. Governments, together with the tourism industry and other stakeholders, should also promote or support various efforts to raise public awareness about the impact of tourists on destinations, to promote respect for local communities and their cultures and to protect the environment. Such public awareness campaigns often succeed in promoting positive behavioural changes not only in tourists, but also in tourism workers and host communities as a whole.

Regulatory Mechanisms and Economic Instruments

Sustainable tourism can also be promoted by a careful mix of government policies comprising both direct regulation and market-based instruments, although financial incentives that encourage environmentally damaging activities, such as energy subsidies, should be reduced or removed. The major challenge for governments is, therefore, to formulate and effectively apply an appropriate mix of regulatory and economic instruments for both sustainable natural resources management and environmental protection. The most direct tool for promoting sustainable tourism involves the use of regulatory mechanisms, such as, integrated land-use planning and coastal zone management. In many cases, it may be necessary to protect coastlines through rigid building restrictions, such as, existing legislation in several Mediterranean countries that bans any buildings within a defined distance from the coast. It is also essential that environmental regulations be applied transparently throughout the tourism sector, regardless of business size, type of tourism activity concerned or location.

Mass tourism, in particular, should be carefully monitored, regulated and sometimes even prohibited in ecologically fragile areas. In protected areas, such as national parks and natural world heritage sites, tourism activities should be strictly subject to the preservation of biological diversity and ecosystems, not stressing their limited capacity to absorb human presence without becoming damaged or degraded. In addition to regulation, governments should also consider the use of economic instruments to promote sustainable tourism, including in remote regions where institutional capacity for environmental regulation may be limited. In fact, it can be argued that market-based mechanisms, which apply monetary values to environmental assets, are more efficient for environmental management than government regulation, even at the global level. Since the tourism industry consumes significant amounts of natural resources, economic pricing of scarce local resources – together with the phasing-out of existing subsidies that encourage wasteful consumption – will help to ensure that the true costs of these resources are adequately incorporated into tourist activities. Prices that reflect the economic value of water and energy, for example, will promote their efficient use and conservation, and provide additional revenue that can be used to improve the management of those resources. Pollution taxes can also be applied on the amounts of liquid and solid waste generated, as a means to reduce discharges and to generate funds for proper treatment and disposal. Similarly, market-based instruments can also be used effectively for the sustainable use of marine natural resources.

Economic instruments, such as user fees and tourist taxes, can actually be used to better internalise environmental costs and thus to promote broader environmental protection objectives. As it is well known, one of the main reasons why markets fail is that important environmental costs, such as pollution, are not reflected in the prices of goods and services. In a free-market economy, individual economic agents will only attempt to maximize their own utility or profit; external costs will thus not be reflected in prices. If total production costs do not incorporate full environmental costs, resources will be allocated inefficiently, both within countries and globally. One way to deal with externalities is thus to internalize them through taxes so that the full costs of production are reflected in prices.

One well-known example of charging user fees to support environmental conservation is the Bonaire protected marine areas in the Netherlands Antilles. This was one of the first protected marine parks in the Caribbean to become entirely self-financing through the levying of admission fees on scuba divers. The (private) diving industry in Bonaire was initially opposed to the levy because of its potential negative impacts on future demand and revenues, against the background of intense competition offered by many Caribbean diving destinations. The system, however, has been an unqualified success since it was introduced in January 1992 because many divers (and an increasing number of tourists in general) are willing and able to pay higher prices to support environmental protection. Fees from this scheme also support the active management of the park's coral reef and mangrove ecosystems, as well as educational activities and orientation sessions for divers.

Voluntary Industry Initiatives

As noted above, tourism services in most countries are provided primarily by the private sector, which tends to oppose greater government regulation and taxation of the industry on the grounds that they are ultimately detrimental to efficiency, competitiveness and profits. The predominantly private tourism industry has thus developed several self-regulation and voluntary initiatives to promote greater environmental sustainability. These include waste and pollution reduction schemes, voluntary codes of conduct, industry awards and eco-labels for sustainable tourism. In addition, environmental management schemes to encourage responsible practices have been promoted in various sub-sectors, including hotel and catering, recreation and entertainment, transportation, travel agencies and tour operators.

For example, the World Travel and Tourism Council (WTTC), the main international industry association, has developed an environmental management programme (Green Globe), for both travel and tourism companies and tourism destinations, aimed to raise the level of environmental awareness and to provide a low-cost practical means for improving the environmental performance of the industry. It is also responsible for ECoNETT, an internet-based tool that provides an extensive information resource on all tourism and environmental issues. Another innovative global programme is the International Hotel Environment Initiative (IHEI), led by a council of leading international hotel chains, aimed to promote environmental management in the hotel industry, which is one of the main consumers of resources and sources of waste. Such initiatives are particularly important not only because they can lead to significant reductions of water and energy consumption, as well as liquid and solid waste, but also because they promote positive behavioural changes in both tourists and employees. In addition, they can lead to improved economic efficiency and increased profitability.

At the regional level, it is worth noting the successful implementation of the Blue Flag Programme, which now extends to 18 countries in Europe, in providing an incentive to protect and improve the quality of beaches and coasts. Under this programme, environmental standards at individual beaches in Europe are assessed by measuring compliance with acceptable concentrations of a range of pollutants to ensure clean bathing water. Beaches are also judged by their compliance with guidelines dealing with litter management, the availability of sanitary and beach safety facilities, and environmental education. Beaches that meet these stringent criteria receive Blue Flag awards, which also serve as a marketing tool to attract tourists. Despite these helpful initiatives of the tourism industry to improve its standards of environmental management and protection, the very proliferation of such voluntary codes of conduct and eco-label awards at global, regional and local levels – which are not, in any case, adopted or recognized by all industry enterprises – can sometimes lead to confusion and difficulty to evaluate and compare them. While national and regional governments should fully support these voluntary initiatives and encourage the dissemination of the best practices in the private tourism industry, there is also a role for independent supervision, monitoring and comparative assessment by relevant government agencies. In addition, trustworthy codes of conduct, transparent eco-label awards and internationally agreed programmes of action for sustainable tourism are required at the international level. The international community has a particularly crucial role to play in developing a set of internationally recognized accreditation and monitoring systems for assessing the sustainability of tourism services around the world.

International Activities in Support of Sustainable Tourism

Although tourism was not specifically addressed in Agenda 21 – the international programme of action on sustainable development agreed on at the 1992 Earth Summit in Rio de Janeiro (Brazil) – its growing economic importance, significant use of natural resources and environmental impact all contributed to its gradual introduction into the international sustainable development agenda over the past ten years. One of the first concrete sectoral programmes of action arising from the increasing cooperation between the tourism industry and inter-governmental agencies was 'Agenda 21 for the Travel and Tourism Industry,' an action plan for sustainable tourism development jointly launched by the World Tourism Organization, the above-mentioned WTTC and the Earth Council in 1996.

Among its innovative key objectives are the estimation of the economic value for resources, such as wildlife, natural areas and cultural heritage, "whose conservation would otherwise be seen as having no financial value," and the establishment of "essential infrastructure, such as water treatment plants, for residents as well as visitors … (in order to) stimulate other economic activities." Many tourism-based communities and regions have also formulated their own 'Agenda 21s' at the local and regional levels.

In 1997, the United Nations General Assembly, at its special session to review the five-year implementation of Agenda 21, decided that there was a need to consider the importance of tourism in the context of Agenda 21 and to "develop an action-oriented international programme of work on sustainable tourism." This request was followed up during the seventh annual session of the United Nations Commission for Sustainable Development (CSD), held in New York in 1999, which discussed tourism as an economic sector and held a multi-stakeholder dialogue on the topic. The Commission adopted an international work programme on sustainable tourism development, which is due to be reviewed during the forthcoming World Summit for Sustainable Development in Johannesburg (South Africa) later this year, as part of the ten-year review of progress achieved since the Earth Summit. The CSD also invited the World Tourism Organization to seek further input from the private sector, non-governmental organizations and other stakeholders in the further development of its proposed global code of ethics that had been drafted in consultation with the industry over the previous two years. The final 'Global Code of Ethics for Tourism,' introduced by the World Tourism Organization in late 1999, sets a frame of reference for the responsible and sustainable development of international tourism. It includes nine articles outlining the basic rules for governments, tour operators, developers, travel agents, workers, as well as host communities and the tourists themselves. The tenth article deals with implementation and includes a proposed mechanism for conciliation, through the creation of a World Committee on Tourism Ethics made up of representatives of each region of the world and representatives of each group of stakeholders in the tourism sector, governments, the private sector, and labour and non-governmental organizations. The United Nations General Assembly adopted the Global Code of Ethics for Tourism at the end of 2001.

Although progress has been achieved over the past ten years, one of the key remaining challenges for the international community is to devise ways and means to assist developing countries to ensure that their tourism industries become more internationally competitive without damaging their natural resources and environmental assets base. This will require, amongst other things, greater technical and financial assistance, including human resources development, institutional capacity building and the transfer of environmentally sound technologies to many developing countries. The international community could also support the wider use of 'debt-fornature swaps', through which a portion of the foreign debt of developing countries is purchased at a discount by various international partners in exchange for the debtor's country investment of an agreed sum of local currency in environmental protection projects.

Conclusion

As stressed above, tourism is expected to resume its rapid growth in the future because of improved living standards, rising incomes and amounts of free time, the falling real cost of travel, and improved transportation around the world. This growth can be harnessed not only for the enjoyment of tourists themselves but, more importantly, for maximizing economic benefits and thus increasing the living standards of host communities and countries. At the same time, it is bound to have negative environmental and sociocultural impact on those communities, whose involvement in tourism planning, development and management can be crucial to minimizing the impact. The major challenge for the international community is, therefore, not only to minimize the negative impact of tourism but also to ensure that the economic benefits of tourism can contribute to environmental protection and the sustainable use of natural resources.

The International Year of Ecotourism – officially launched at the United Nations headquarters in New York on 28 January 200249 – offers an ideal opportunity not only to review ecotourism experiences around the world, but also to promote worldwide recognition of the important role of sustainable tourism in the broader international sustainable development agenda. Ecotourism is one of the fastest growing segments of the tourism sector and further rapid growth is expected in the future. There is, however, little agreement about its exact meaning because of the wide variety of so-called ecotourism activities provided by many different tour operators and enjoyed by an equally broad range of diverse tourists. Its main features include (a) all forms of nature tourism aimed at the appreciation of both the natural world and the traditional cultures existent in natural areas, (b) deliberate efforts to minimize the harmful human impacts on the natural and sociocultural environment and (c) support for the protection of natural and cultural assets and the well-being of host communities.

In other words, if carried out responsibly, ecotourism can be a valuable means for promoting the socioeconomic development of host communities while generating resources for the preservation of natural and cultural assets. In this way, ecologically fragile areas can be protected with the financial returns of ecotourism activities made by both the public and private sectors. In many developing countries, ecotourism has been particularly successful in attracting private investments for the establishment of privately owned natural parks and nature reserves. Many of such reserves are well-managed, self-financed and environmentally responsible, even when profit remains the main motivation behind the operation of a private reserve. In this way, the tourism industry can help to protect and even rehabilitate natural assets, and thus contribute to the preservation of biological diversity and ecological balance.

However, if not properly planned, managed and monitored, the concept of ecotourism can be distorted for purely commercial purposes and even for promoting ecologically-damaging activities by large numbers of tourists in natural areas. Given their inadequate physical infrastructure and limited capacity to absorb mass tourism, the fragile land and ocean ecosystems of many developing countries can be literally overwhelmed by large numbers of tourists. It is increasingly recognized, therefore, that unsustainable ecotourism activities may threaten the very natural environment upon which they depend. There is, in fact, a crucial distinction between ecotourism and sustainable tourism: while the former can be broadly defined as an alternative, nature-based type of tourism, the above-mentioned sustainability principles must be applied to all types of tourism activities and all segments of the tourism industry. At a campsite on the long trekking route to Concordia and K-2 base camp in northern Pakistan, there is a presumably 'politically correct' sign that says: "Take nothing but photos; Leave nothing but footprints." If tourists follow those instructions, but do so insensitively or in mass numbers, those seemingly inoffensive acts can disturb local cultural values and ecological balance, respectively. It should be clear by now that even ecotourism activities can cause adverse ecological impacts, particularly if they are not properly managed or if they involve tourist numbers beyond the local carrying capacity.

7

Promoting Medical Tourism in India

Promoting Health and Medical Tourism in India

Health and medical tourism is perceived as one of the fastest growing segments in marketing 'Destination India' today. While this area has so far been relatively unexplored, we now find that not only the ministry of tourism, government of India, but also the various state tourism boards and even the private sector consisting of travel agents, tour operators, hotel companies and other accommodation providers are all eying health and medical tourism as a segment with tremendous potential for future growth.

Kerala-The Pioneer State

Kerala, or God's Own Country as its corporate slogan goes, has pioneered health and medical tourism in India. They have made a concerted effort to promote health tourism in a big way, which has resulted in a substantial increase of visitor arrivals into the state. Kerala and Ayurveda have virtually become synonymous with each other. However, though Kerala has strongly focussed on Ayurveda and its wide array of treatments and medications, good facilities are also available in the other traditional forms of medicine as well as in modern medical treatment. The bias towards health tourism in Kerala is so strong that Kerala Ayurveda Centres have been established at multiple locations in various metro cities, thus highlighting the advantages of Ayurveda in health management. The health tourism focus has seen Kerala participate in various trade shows and expos wherein the advantages of this traditional form of medicine are showcased.

Karnataka's Foray into the Healthcare Sector

The department of tourism, government of Karnataka, has ambitious plans for the state. According to D B Inamdar, minister for tourism, "The idea is to make Karnataka a top health tourism destination, not only in India but internationally. We want to lure foreigners to Karnataka to avail of our sophisticated facilities and subsequently induce them to enjoy our multiple tourism offerings. This endeavour will have a positive impact on the entire economy of the state." In fact, the government is setting up a Bangalore International Health City Corporation which will cater to patients for a wide variety of health care products and treatments.

The recent operations of children from Pakistan, who have sought medical treatment in Bangalore, have not only helped to boost the state economy but more importantly, helped in fostering goodwill, peace and harmony between India and Pakistan.

Without doubt, Indian doctors are among the best in the world and given the right atmosphere and environment, they can enhance the image of Incredible India as a health and tourism destination. The state also boasts of having the unique property, Golden Palms Spa & Resort, which is the one and only resort in the country where a guest can have a complete range of pathological tests, dental treatment, electro-cardiograms, stress tests, X-rays, and even sonography tests. To crown it all, there is even a mini-operation theatre for cosmetic surgery performed by world renowned surgeons in the field.

FICCI's Focus on Medical Tourism

It is indeed gratifying to note that well established chambers of commerce are now seriously looking at medical tourism and in fact, the Federation of Indian Chambers of Commerce and Industry, Western Region Council (FICCI-WRC) has taken the lead by setting up a task force for the promotion of health and medical tourism in Maharashtra. This task force has representatives from the Maharashtra government, the medical educational institutions and the drugs department, Maharashtra Tourism Development Corporation, pharmaceutical companies, travel agents and tour companies.

Wing Cdr Anil M Gadkari, director, FICCI-WRC explained, "This is our dream project and we hope to get the support of all service providers of the industry. This project will indeed give a major boost to the tourism and hospitality of Maharashtra. We have received a positive response from MTDC who will work with us on this promotion."

Maharashtra's Unlimited Potential

This state, as a gateway to India, offers tremendous potential to develop medical tourism. The latest addition in Mumbai is the Asian Heart Institute at Bandra-Kurla Complex, which offers state-of-the art facilities for all types of heart complications and even offers preventive cardiological treatment to avoid heart ailments and also to keep under control a host of heart problems. This institute which is in collaboration with the Cleveland Institute, USA, offers 'five-star' services at reasonable prices. There are even provisions for financial assistance which is offered through various trusts associated with the institute.

There are a wide range of hospitals which help to promote medical tourism in the state. Some of these are Lilavati Hospital, Jaslok Hospital, Bombay Hospital, Hinduja Hospital, Wockhardt Hospital and Apollo NUSI Wellness Retreat. Hotels like Hyatt Regency, JW Marriott, Renaissance and Resort, also offer extensive spa facilities aimed at rejuvenating both the domestic and international tourist.

International Conference

An international health and medical tourism conference is slated to be held towards the end of this year at Bangalore, which will see delegates from various South-East Asian countries, the Middle-East and even Africa participating. This will serve as an ideal platform for Incredible India to market its health and medical tourism products and services.

Government Takes Steps to Promote Medical Tourism

New Delhi, March 4 (IANS) To promote India as a medical tourism destination, the government has taken several steps, including issuing a new visa to foreign travellers coming to the country for medical treatment. Informing this to the Rajya Sabha Tuesday, Tourism Minister Ambika Soni said to promote medical tourism in India, the government has showcased the country in overseas market through brochures, CDs, films and other publicity materials. She said the government has also introduced a new category of 'M'-visa for foreign tourists coming to India for medical treatment. In a written reply, she said a task force has been set up to promote healthcare tourism in the country. It will be headed by the health and family welfare ministry secretary has been constituted, which has members from the health department, tourism and experts from the medical field

Promoting Medical Tourism in India

Medical tourism focuses on treatment of acute illness, elective surgeries such as cardiology and cancer, among others. From October this year, the Government plans to start overseas marketing of India as a medical tourism destination. Senior Government officials say that the formalities for marketing medical facilities to a global audience have already started and they hope to complete the process of price-banding of hospitals in various cities by the third quarter of this year. The government of India is of the opinion that by marketing India as a global medical tourism destination, it could capitalise on the low-cost, high-quality medical care available in the country.

Statistics show that the medical tourism industry in India is worth $333 million (Rs 1,450 crore) while a study by CII-McKinsey estimates that the country could earn Rs 5,000-10,000 crore by 2012. Probably realising the potential, major corporates such as the Tatas, Fortis, Max, Wockhardt, Piramal, and the Escorts group have made significant investments in setting up modern hospitals in major cities. Many have also designed special packages for patients, including airport pickups, visa assistance and board and lodging, health care industry officials said.

Among the factors that make India an attractive proposition for medical treatment is cost efficiency. The estimated cost for a heart surgery in the U.S is $30,000, however the same could be performed India for about $6,000. Similarly, a bone marrow transplant could cost about $2,50,000 in the US while it could be done here for about $26,000.

New Association Promoting Medical Tourism to India

Leading Indian Hospitals, Healthcare providers (both Modern Medicine and Traditional Indian Medicine), Travel and Medical Tourism Industry providers have come together to form an industry association-Indian Medical Travel Association (IMTA) that aims to work together to make India the leading global healthcare destination. The phenomenon now popularly known as Medical Tourism is often cited as the next big opportunity for India after the IT outsourcing to earn billions of dollars in forex earnings and create jobs in the healthcare sector. So far only a select group of Indian hospitals have been making valiant attempts to market their services in international arena. More than a million overseas patients already treated at top Indian corporate hospitals like Apollo, Fortis, Wockhardt, Max, Manipal and many others have already proved to the world that the clinical quality, technology and cost proposition offered by India is unmatched. The capacity in super speciality segment Indian hospitals is expanding fast and there is no waiting period for local or overseas patients.

CII Mc'Kinsey study first reported on medical tourism as the billion dollar opportunity for India way back in 2002 and the steady growth in overseas patient arrivals has validated the potential. With a large number of new private super speciality hospitals and even integrated health cities coming up in India's top ten cities, India has the potential to become the global leader in the Medical Travel/Outsourcing industry. Indian doctors and professionals are world renowned for their skills and the country has abundance of all the inputs like talented young manpower, local high quality manufacturing base for pharmaceuticals, technology hardware and software that makes the Indian costs for high end surgical procedures so attractive. The challenge really is on the non medical side, primarily on the marketing front and also to create infrastructure and services to support the growth of medical tourism. Indian Medical Travel Association (IMTA)-a non profit body and a unified voice of the Indian healthcare (modern medicine as well as traditional Indian medicine) and travel industry is aimed at preparing India for facing the challenges of global competition and actualise the tremendous opportunity for India to become a leading global healthcare destination. Modern medicine as well as India's 5000 year old traditional therapies like Ayurveda, Siddha and Yoga can offer to the world an unbeatable healing package.

"IMTA would strive to help its members reach out in a cost effective manner to millions of our potential global consumers who reside on the other side of the globe in a different time and cultural zone and make them aware of the tremendous value that Indian healthcare offers. The fact is that prior to choosing a hospital, the international patients first decide on the country or the destination. Therefore we all must join hands to aggressively promote INDIA as a preferred global healthcare destination," Says Pradeep Thukral, Executive Director, Indian Medical Travel Association (IMTA).

The Government of India and its various arms are actively supporting the growth of medical tourism to India. Two years ago the Government of India introduced a special category of Visa called M Visa for foreigners desirous of coming to India for medical treatment. India's Ministry of Tourism has achieved phenomenal success in last five years with its much acclaimed "Incredible India "campaign that has multiplied the arrival of foreign tourists to India. The current year 2009 is being promoted by Indian Ministry of Tourism as "Visit India"' year and the ministry is keen to promote Medical Tourism. It has recently notified the Market Development Assistance (MDA) Scheme to eligible Medical Tourism players which enables them to get financial support for participation in overseas promotional events.

Emerging Trends of Medical Tourism in India

Medical tourism was a silver lining for those millions of Uninsured, underinsured and those who were forced to postpone treatments due to long waiting lists. What seemed like a boon to patients from Western countries like US, UK and Canada is now a twilight of hope for those countries who are deemed as Medical Tourism hubs. In popular medical tourism destinations like India, Singapore and Thailand, Medical Tourism is a fast growing industry where millions of dollars are being pumped in rigorously. In order to cope with the growing demand for medical care, hospitals, medical practitioners and even governments have taken measures to promote health care in India. When it comes to health care, safety is the foremost concern. The hospitals in India are well equipped with the latest technology and houses highly qualified and experienced staff who can provide timely and quality medical treatment to patients. As a move in promoting medical tourism, many hospitals are deemed as "corporate hospitals" that specially cater to the needs of medical tourists in India. Apart from offering world class treatments, they offer various services that make medical tourists' stay in India hassle free. Many hospitals in India have international accreditations that certify the quality of health care service.

Indian Government has acknowledged the growth of medical tourism in India and is now offering Medical Visas. The initial period for a medical visa may be up to a period of one year or the period of treatment whichever less, which can be extended for a further period up to one year be the State Government/FRROs on the production of medical certificate/advice from the reputed/recognized/specialized hospitals in the country. Any further extension will be granted by the Ministry of Home Affairs only on the recommendations of the State Government/FRROs supported by appropriate Medical documents. Such visa will be valid for maximum three entries during one year.

India is a big player in the medical tourism industry. In fact, it has been ranked the most popular medical tourism destination by many. Apart from the contribution of government and hospitals in improving the health care service in India, what truly gives that edge to India over other medical tourism destinations is the innumerable rejuvenation options it offers and the easiness of stay in India.

India is the birth place of Yoga, which is one of the most popular forms of exercise and rejuvenation today. There are almost an infinite number of Spa and rejuvenation centres in India that could uplift the mood and enhance health of medical tourists. India is a tourist's paradise and when in India for medical treatment, tourism comes as a co-benefit of medical tourism. Unlike other exotic destinations in the world, it is surprisingly easy to commute, stay and converse in India. People in India are extremely warm and have a sound command over English. All these factors make India the sought after destinations for medical tourism and India is now equipped to cater to the fast growing demand for health care in India.

Medical Tourism in India

Medical tourism, as the name suggests involves travelling across the border for urgent or elective medical surgeries and other specialized treatments. This is a modern 'cost effective' term coined by healthcare and tourism industries across the globe, although the phenomenon is not new as such.

Travelling across the border for medical assistance has happened for centuries. Pilgrims and patients across the Mediterranean travelled to ancient Greece to stay in the shrine of the healing god, Asklepios. Similarly, Europeans travelled from Germany to spas around the Nile in the 18th century. Today the low-cost jet rates combined with affordable health care in developing countries like India has enabled people to go beyond borders for elective procedures and complex surgeries.

More than 50 countries including India, Costa Rica, Cuba, Hungary, Israel, Malaysia, Singapore, Thailand and Belgium are actively promoting medical tourism. However, India stands as the preferred choice in terms of accreditations, government policies, cost, climate, culture and tourist destinations.

Like many countries, India also promotes medical tourism through government's official policy. According to the formulation drawn from the 'Policy Framework for Reforms in Health Care', drafted by the Prime Minister's advisory council on Trade and Industry, the National Health Policy 2002 of India states that the treatment of foreign patients/ expatriates is legally an '*export*' and the same is '*eligible for all fiscal incentives extended to export earnings.*'

Medical tourism in India is a billion dollar industry. A CII (Confederation of Indian Industries) study indicates that 150,000 medical tourist visited India in 2005. According to FICCI (Federation of Indian Chambers of Commerce and Industry) the healthcare market covering health insurance, is expected to expand up to $ 69 billion by 2012. The research also states that the Indian healthcare industry boosted by medical tourism is growing at 30 per cent annually.

Factors Promoting Medical Tourism in India

Although cost plays a major role, the reasons for medical tourism vary from patient to patient. For instance, people from US seek medical treatment that would cost one tenth of this treatment cost at home. People from other parts of the world like Canada and Great Britain are often frustrated by long waiting times at public health services. Few like to combine their surgeries with a beautiful vacation in India that offers them scenic beaches, high mountains, religious temples, historical monuments and vast deserts. On the other hand, medical tourism in India is also a boon for poor nations like Bangladesh, where treatment options are limited.

Cost Comparisons

Cost plays a major role in promoting medical tourism in India. Using competent technologies, hospitals in India are able to perform high-end treatments like liver transplantation and heart surgery at a substantially lower rate. The following figure indicates the cost of certain treatments in US and India.

Treatment	Procedure Cost (US$)	
	United States	India
Bone Marrow Transplant	2,50,000	69,000
Liver Transplant	3,00,000	69,000
Heart Surgery	30,000	8,000
Orthopedic Surgery	20,000	6,000
Cataract Surgery	2,000	1,250

Accreditations/Legal Issues

Indian government has adopted an accreditation system (National Accreditation Board for Hospitals, NABH) that ensures a guarantee of service for medical tourists. The accreditation process also recommends prices for services. In order to attain NABH's certification for medical tourism, the member hospitals must agree to dual pricing system enabling limited charges for foreigners and lower prices for domestic patients. So far, the body has approved 30 of its 120 hospital members. International Society for Quality in Health Care (ISQUA) approves India's accreditation process. ISQUA is an international body that grants approval to accreditation bodies in the area of healthcare. There are also international accreditations like JCI and TRENT that assure quality healthcare for medical tourists. Joint Commission International (JCI), is an US based accreditation group that evaluates hospitals outside United States since 1992. Trent International Accreditation Scheme is a trusted source for British and European medical tourists. The India's State and National Consumer Disputes Redressal Commission generally handle any legal disputes arising from treatments for medical tourists or Indian nationals. Currently CII is making efforts to draw standards that would address any litigation arising from such treatment to be dealt within Indian Courts.

Medical Tourism Process

Contact the medical tourism provider in India if you are seeking medical treatment here. As an initial step, the medical tourism provider will ask for your medical report covering the nature of your ailment, local doctor's opinion, medical history and diagnosis. Upon receipt of your medical report, the provider helps you get in touch with a certified medical doctor or consultant in India. He/She will advise you on the treatment/surgery required. Later you can discuss with the medical tourism provider on expenditure, choice of hospitals and tourist destinations, accommodation and duration of the stay. Ensure to sign consent bonds upon agreement. Remember to collect the recommendation letters from the consultant or medical doctors that are required for the application of medical visa. Once you arrive as a medical tourist to India, the concerned provider will assign an executive, who takes care of your treatment and accommodation.

Medical Tourism Packages

Today, most Indian private sector hospitals are very well equipped to handle a big mass of medical tourists. Backed by the strong pharmaceutical industry these private hospitals are estimated to handle a volume of 75-80% medical tourism services year on year. India is a leading drug manufacturer that exports drugs to more than 180 countries. There are a number of medical tourism providers that offer medical packages coupled with a vacation to experience the rich and glorious culture of India. Listed below are few medical packages offered by the medical tourism providers in India.

- Bone Marrow Transplant,
- Brain Surgery,
- Cancer Procedures (Oncology),
- Cardiac Care,
- Cosmetic Surgery,
- Dialysis and Kidney Transplant,
- Drug Rehabilitation,
- Gynaecology & Obstetrics,
- Health Checkups,
- Internal/Digestive Procedures,
- Joint Replacement Surgery,
- Nuclear Medicine,
- Neurosurgery & Trauma Surgery,
- Preventive Health Care,
- Refractive Surgery,
- Osteoporosis,
- Spine Related,

- Urology,
- Vascular Surgery,
- Dental Care.

Medical Institutions

India has many hospitals offering excellent and effective treatments nearly in all major medical sectors like cardiology, orthopaedics, gastroenterology, ophthalmology, urology, neurology, oncology, endocrinology, paediatric surgery, nephrology, dermatology, dentistry, plastic surgery, gynaecology, pulmonology, psychiatry, general medicine & general surgery.

Medical tourism focuses on treatment of acute illness, elective surgeries such as cardiology and cancer, among others. From October this year, the Government plans to start overseas marketing of India as a medical tourism destination.//Senior Government officials say that the formalities for marketing medical facilities to a global audience have already started and they hope to complete the process of price-banding of hospitals in various cities by the third quarter of this year. The government of India is of the opinion that by marketing India as a global medical tourism destination, it could capitalise on the low-cost, high-quality medical care available in the country.

Statistics show that the medical tourism industry in India is worth $333 million (Rs 1,450 crore) while a study by CII-McKinsey estimates that the country could earn Rs 5,000-10,000 crore by 2012. Probably realising the potential, major corporates such as the Tatas, Fortis, Max, Wockhardt, Piramal, and the Escorts group have made significant investments in setting up modern hospitals in major cities. Many have also designed special packages for patients, including airport pickups, visa assistance and board and lodging, health care industry officials said. Among the factors that make India an attractive proposition for medical treatment is cost efficiency.

The estimated cost for a heart surgery in the U.S is $30,000, however the same could be performed India for about $6,000. Similarly, a bone marrow transplant could cost about $2,50,000 in the US while it could be done here for about $26,000. Foreigners have already started trickling into India for medical treatment thus officials are hopeful that this will become a flood once the various initiatives being taken by the Government take off. The Government has also introduced various policy measures such as the National Health Policy recognizes the treatment of international patients as an export, which allows.

Opportunities in Medical Tourism in India 2007

This report "Opportunities in Medical Tourism in India (2007)" provides extensive research and objective analysis on the Medical Tourism industry in India. This report has been written to help clients in analyzing the opportunities critical to the growth of Medical tourism market in India. Detailed data and analysis will help investors to comprehend the changing dynamics of the Healthcare industry.

Key Findings

- With global revenues of approximately US$ 20 Billion (2005), the medical tourism industry is one of the world's largest industry. India's cost effective treatment makes it an important player in this industry.
- Growing Medical tourism in India will be one of the major sources for foreign exchange.
- With increasing number of non-insured population in western countries and increasing healthcare expenditure to GDP resulting in people opting for treatment choices outside their country.

Key Issues and Facts Analyzed

- What are the emerging trends in the Medical Tourism Industry in India?
- Key regulations and policy environment in the industry.
- What is the future scenario of the Medical Tourism Industry in India?
- What opportunities exist for the Medical Tourism Industry?
- What Challenges are faced by the industry?
- Who are the Key players in Indian medical tourism industry?
- Government initiatives to promote medical tourism in India.

Key Players Analyzed

This section provides the overview, key facts, financial information, future plans, and business strategies of prominent players in the Indian Healthcare market like Wockhardt Hospitals Ltd, Apollo Hospitals Enterprise Ltd, Fortis Healthcare Ltd, Max India Ltd, and SRL Ranbaxy.

Research Methodology

Information Sources

Information has been sourced from namely, books, newspapers, trade journals, and white papers, industry portals, government agencies, trade associations, monitoring industry news and developments, and through access to access to more than 3000 paid databases.

Analysis Methods

The analysis methods include the following: Ratio Analysis, Historical Trend Analysis, Linear Regression Analysis using software tools, Judgmental Forecasting and Cause and Effect Analysis

Medical Tourism in India: Winners and Losers

Promoted by the government and fuelled by the corporate boom in medical care, India is increasingly seen as the favoured destination of "medical tourists" who cross national boundaries to seek treatment that is cheaper than in their home countries. Medical tourism is a multi-billion dollar industry promoted by governments and the medical and tourism industries.

Patients who travel abroad for medical treatment do so for a variety of reasons. The elite from developing countries seek treatments not available in their own countries. Thus private hospitals in India are seeing an influx of patients from Bangladesh and the Gulf. Patients from the United States seek treatments that cost five to 10 times in their own country. And, as public-funded health insurance is unable to cope with the rising demands of an increasingly aging population, patients from countries such as the United Kingdom and Canada travel to India to beat the huge waiting period for many routine procedures.

The key selling points of the Indian medical tourism industry are the combination of high quality facilities, competent, English-speaking medical professionals, "cost effectiveness" and the attractions of tourism. The cost differential is huge: Open-heart surgery costs up to $70,000 in Britain and $150,000 in the US; in India's best hospitals it could cost between $3,000 and $10,000. Knee surgery costs Rs. 3.5 lakh ($7,700) in India; in Britain it costs $16,950. Dental, eye and cosmetic surgeries in western countries cost three to four times as much as in India. Medical tourists usually get a package deal that includes flights, hotels, treatment and, often, a post-operative vacation.

Two other major factors are the sustained growth of corporate hospitals and hospital chains across India and government patronage and promotion of medical tourism as part of public policy.

Promoted by Government Policies

While the private sector has always been prominent as a source of medical care, since 1991 neoliberal government policies supporting the private sector have created conditions for its rapid growth.

Public expenditure on health in India has hovered around 0.9 per cent of gross domestic product (GDP) in the past decade, down from 1.3 per cent. Worldwide it is ahead of only five countries-Burundi, Myanmar, Pakistan, Sudan, and Cambodia. At the same time India ranks among the top 20 countries in terms of private expenditure on health in per cent GDP terms-around 4.5-5 per cent of GDP.

A large proportion of this private expenditure is by the elite who have prospered as a result of the same neoliberal policies. This elite, while constituting less than 10 per cent of the population, is larger in absolute numbers than the elite in most rich countries. Thus the conditions for the development of a private medical sector that caters to a large enough population who can pay have been created over the past decade and a half. This has also led to a shift in the high end segment of private medical care, and the corporate sector has moved in to take advantage of its high growth potential.

Indian Medical Care: A Study in Contrasts

Medical care in India is today a study in contrasts, typical of countries that have promoted segmentation in healthcare: expensive private care catering to the elite and poor quality public-funded care for the poor. When the poor are forced to seek private medical services they face pauperisation: more than 40 per cent of patients admitted to hospitals borrow money or sell assets and 25 per cent of peasant families with a member needing in-patient care are driven below the poverty line.

Globalisation has also fostered a consumerist culture and the medical industry is sustained by this culture. It serves the fraction of the population that can pay the rates charged by the high end private medical sector.

Corporate style functioning in medical care has also introduced the need to maximise profits and expand coverage-as in the case of any commercial venture. Thus, while neoliberal policies have opened the way for the penetration of the corporate sector in medical care, the industry now needs further avenues for its continued growth as the domestic market gets saturated. An obvious target is the global healthcare industry-the world's largest industry after armaments-valued at US$2.8 trillion in 2005.

Government Patronage and Subsidy

The National Health Policy, 2002, makes it clear that government policy supports medical tourism: "To capitalize on the comparative cost advantage enjoyed by domestic health facilities in the secondary and tertiary sector, the policy will encourage the supply of services to patients of foreign origin on payment. The rendering of such services on payment in foreign exchange will be treated as 'deemed exports' and will be made eligible for all fiscal incentives extended to export earnings. "

Interestingly, this formulation draws from recommendations in the Policy framework for reforms in health care, drafted by the Prime Minister's Advisory Council on Trade and Industry headed by Mukesh Ambani and Kumaramangalam Birla.

According to industry estimates, the medical tourism market in India was valued at over $310 million in 2005-06 with 1 million foreign medical tourists visiting the country every year. The market is predicted to grow to $2 billion by 2012. These figures are significant when seen in the context of the total healthcare expenditure in the country today-$10 billion in the public sector and $50 billion in the private sector (calculated as approximately one per cent and five per cent of the country's current GDP respectively). Visitors from 55 countries come to India for treatment but the biggest growth in business is from the UK and the US. The Taj Medical Group receives 200 inquiries a day from around the world and arranges packages for 20-40 Britons a month to have operations in India. It also offers follow-up appointments with a consultant in the UK. Apollo Hospital Enterprises treated an estimated 60,000 patients between 2001 and 2004. Apollo now has 46 hospitals with over 7,000 beds and is in partnership with hospitals in Kuwait, Sri Lanka and Nigeria. The government predicts that India's healthcare industry could grow 13 per cent in each of the next six years, boosted by medical tourism which, industry watchers say, is growing at 30 per cent annually. Since 2006, the government has also started issuing M (medical) visas to patients and MX visas to the accompanying spouse.

In order to allay suspicions regarding the quality of care in a developing country, Indian corporate hospitals are getting certified by international accreditation schemes. Corporate chains such as Apollo Hospitals and Wockhardt Hospitals Group are working through agencies like IndUShealth, Planet Hospital and the Medical Tourist Company in Britain to build business across the West. The industry is also promoting the National Accreditation Board for Hospitals and has started the process of granting accreditation to about 70 hospitals across the country.

A Win-win Situation?

This is a winning ticket for the corporate medical sector and for a section of medical professionals in the country. However, if we look at the public health implications, we see an entirely different picture. The government would have us believe that revenues earned by the industry will strengthen healthcare in the country. But we do not see any mechanism by which this can happen. On the contrary, corporate hospitals have repeatedly dishonoured the conditions for receiving government subsidies by refusing to treat poor patients free of cost- and they have got away without punishment. Moreover, reserving a few beds for the poor in elite institutions does not address the necessity to increase public investment in health to three to five times the present level.

The extra revenue from medical tourism could benefit healthcare in India if it were taxed adequately to support public health. Instead the medical tourism industry is provided tax concessions; the government gives private hospitals treating foreign patients benefits such as lower import duties and an increased rate of depreciation (from 25 per cent to 40 per cent) for life-saving medical equipment. Prime land is provided at subsidised rates. The industry also gets a pool of medical professionals who train in public institutions for fees of Rs 500 a month and then move to work in private hospitals-an internal brain drain, and an indirect subsidy for the private sector of an estimated Rs 500 crore per year. Thus, the price advantage of the medical tourism industry is paid for by Indian tax payers who receive nothing in return. Let us end with a contrast. Cuba has been a pioneer in medical tourism for almost four decades. It has hospitals for Cuban residents and others for foreigners and diplomats. Both kinds are run by the government. Cubans receive free healthcare for life while tourists have to pay for it.

The Cuban government has developed medical tourism to generate income which is ploughed back to benefit its country's citizens. The Cuban example shows that there are ways to use medical tourism to really benefit our people. But we are then talking about entirely different systems and underlying philosophies.

Medical Tourism Industry Certifications

Maintaining High Quality Services in the Medical Tourism Industry

One of the primary concerns for health travellers is whether foreign providers can offer the same high-quality medical care they receive in their country of origin. This growing demand for foreign healthcare providers has prompted the Joint Commission on Accreditation of Healthcare Organizations (JCAHO), the best known healthcare accreditation group in the USA, to form an international offshoot known as the Joint Commission International (JCI).

In 1999, the JCI began surveying and accrediting hospitals and healthcare facilities outside of the USA. There are now over 220 accredited hospitals worldwide and most are providing quality services for the medical tourism industry.

Aside from the JCI, there are alternative non-profit groups providing accreditation for healthcare organizations in the USA. These include but are not limited to:

- Community Health Accreditation Program (CHAP) – The first accrediting body in the US that provides assessments for community based healthcare organizations.
- Accreditation Commission for Health Care, Inc (ACHC)– Was created by home care providers as an accreditation organization that caters to small health institutions.
- The Compliance Team, Inc – Is known for their Exemplary Provider Program. They are an accrediting body for Durable Medical Equipment (DME).

- Healthcare Quality Association on Accreditation (HQAA)– Another accreditation body working with durable medical equipment (DME).
- National Committee for Quality Assurance (NCQA)– Drives improvement in the health care system through the Healthcare Effectiveness Data and Information Set (HEDIS) which is used by 90% of health plans in the USA.

Non-US Accreditation Organizations

Aside from the accreditation bodies based in the USA, there are a number of international accreditation organizations in the medical tourism industry that are based abroad. These organizations perform a similar international role as the JCI, providing accreditation to international or regional health providers.

- Accreditation Canada-Formerly known as the Canadian Council on Health Services Accreditation (CCHSA)-focuses in improving patient safety.
- Trent Accreditation Scheme (TAS) – A UK-based non-profit accreditation organization that performs surveying and accrediting healthcare providers in the UK and around the world.
- The Australian Council on Healthcare Standards (ACHS) – The leading health care and accreditation organization in Australia. It features the Evaluation and Quality Improvement Program (EQuIP) and acts as a consultant for several countries.
- International Society for Quality in Health Care (ISQua) – With members from over 70 countries, ISQua has board members from North America, Europe and Asia-Pacific regions.
- European Society for Quality in Healthcare (ESQH) – Is dedicated to improving the quality of healthcare in Europe. It consists of 19 member countries, all of which are National Societies for Quality in Healthcare in their respective countries.
- The Society for International Healthcare Accreditation (SOFIHA) – Is a group formed by providers of international healthcare accreditation. This forum is where they discuss and share ideas geared towards developing high-quality accreditation of medical facilities worldwide.

The International Organization for Standardization (ISO) – Is an international body formed by various national standards organizations. In the healthcare industry, ISO provides a framework in the design and improvement of quality management systems for healthcare providers.

International Certification Status of Medical Tourism Providers

Destination countries for medical travellers, realizing the impact of the medical tourism business in the economies of their respective countries, strive to provide the highest quality at the lowest possible cost. These countries are openly marketing medical tourism, with governments supporting these efforts by providing better facilities and seeking international accreditation.

Part of these efforts includes hiring or training physicians with international credentials such as, professionals who train and are board certified in the USA, Australia, Canada and Europe. For example:

India – Apollo Hospitals is the largest healthcare provider and the first JCI-certified hospital in India. The Apollo Group is also tied with Johns Hopkins Medicine International on studies regarding heart diseases. On top of this, the Indian Healthcare Federation provides accreditation standards for its local providers. Another provider, Wockhardt, is affiliated with the Harvard Medical School.

Singapore – This country provides state-of-the-art hospitals, three of which are accredited by the JCI. The International Medical Centre which is also affiliated with Johns Hopkins International, is the most notable.

Panama – With several Panamanian physicians trained and certified in the United States, Panama's top hospitals are comparable to the US. Foremost is the Punta Pacifica Hospital which is affiliated with Johns Hopkins International.

Thailand – There are over 1 million medical tourists going to Thailand each year. The front-runner for Thailand's medical tourism industry is Bumrungrad International Hospital in Bangkok. They are located in a modern hospital building that complies with US standards, and an American-managed medical staff that includes 200 US board-certified doctors and surgeons. The rest of the staff members are licensed in Australia, Europe and Japan.

There are other foreign hospitals that are owned, managed or affiliated with American hospitals, healthcare providers and prestigious universities. An example is the Cleveland Clinic which owns and manages several facilities in other countries like Canada, Austria and the United Arab Emirates. The International Hospital Group which is based in Dallas, builds and operates US-standard hospitals in Mexico.

Qualification of Doctors and Surgeons in Medical Tourism Destinations

Just as many doctors in the USA undergo part of their medical training abroad, many physicians from other countries have also trained and received board-certification in the United States. Foreign hospitals boast of their US and/or internationally certified medical staff. This can boost their image in the medical tourism industry. Many of these physicians have fellowships with American medical societies and have speciality certification from an American medical board. The golden standard for certification for the medical profession in the USA is provided by the American Board of Medical Specialities (ABMS). This is the umbrella organization for 24 nationally approved medical speciality boards. The coveted Gold Star is given by the ABMS to certified local and international physicians to demonstrate their expertise in their speciality fields. Certifications by the ABMS and its Member Boards are widely referenced by healthcare organizations, law firms and insurance companies. These speciality boards include the following certification bodies:

* American Board of Allergy and Immunology,
* American Board of Anesthesiology,
* American Board of Colon and Rectal Surgery,
* American Board of Dermatology,
* American Board of Emergency Medicine,
* American Board of Family Medicine,
* American Board of Internal Medicine,
* American Board of Medical Genetics,
* American Board of Neurological Surery ,
* American Board of Nuclear Medicine,
* American Board of Obstetrics and Gynecology,

* American Board of Ophthalmology,
* American Board of Orthopaedic Surgery,
* American Board of Otolaryngology,
* American Board of Pathology,
* American Board of Physical Medicine and Rehabilitation,
* American Board of Plastic Surgery,
* American Board of Preventive Medicine,
* American Board of Psychiatry and Neurology,
* American Board of Radiology,
* American Board of Surgery,
* American Board of Thoracic Surgery.

In the UK, the prominent professional medical association is the British Medical Association (BMA). However, certification is provided by the General Medical Council (GMC), which is responsible for controlling the certification and licenses of doctors and surgeons. The GMC also liaises with medical associations and certification bodies from other countries, particularly medical tourism industry providers. The result is a mutual recognition of physician qualifications.

In Europe, the European Union of Medical Specialists (UEMS) is responsible for controlling the certification and licenses of doctors and surgeons. The GMC also liaises with medical associations and certification bodies from other countries, particularly medical tourism industry providers. The result is a mutual recognition of physician qualifications. With over 1.4 million certified medical specialists represented by the UEMS, they aim to standardize the laws and practices of the National Medical Associations from member countries. These include:

* Austria
* Belgium
* Cyprus
* Czech Republic
* Denmark
* Estonia
* Finland
* France
* Germany
* Greece
* Hungary
* Iceland
* Ireland
* Italy
* Latvia
* Lithuania

* Luxembourg
* Malta
* Netherlands
* Norway
* Poland
* Portugal
* Slovakia
* Slovenia
* Spain
* Sweden
* Switzerland
* United Kingdom.

The Leader in Community based Health Care Accreditation

The Community Health Accreditation Program, Inc. (CHAP) is the leader in improving the quality of community based health care services in the USA.

CHAP is an independent and non-profit accrediting body created in 1965.

CHAP's goal is for home care to not only prosper, but gain strength in the overall health care industry. To achieve this, CHAP is devoted to providing consultation of the highest calibre, along with a broad network of professional staff resources.

Compliance Team

Compliance Team is a leading provider of technical consulting services and resources to the pharmaceutical, biotechnology, and medical device industries.

We provide complete project teams including project management or technical resources that you manage to meet your project staffing needs. Our professionals have diverse qualifications and capabilities in commissioning, qualification, validation, engineering, quality assurance, and regulatory affairs gained from years of experience working within operating companies and making major contributions to our clients' successes on critical projects.

Our mission is to deliver commissioning, qualification, validation, and compliance consulting solutions to ensure your successful delivery of projects critical to your business success, on time and within budget. We provide fast, responsive, professional service to meet your compliance-sensitive project and technical resource needs at an exceptional value.

Compliance Team provides the right talent at the right time to help you achieve your business objectives and a higher level of compliance.

Description of the HQAA, Inc. Application and Accreditation Process

In making the decision as to which accreditor to align with and to trust, one has to believe that informed decisions are made throughout the way. It is important to fully understand and assume responsibility to start, implement and complete the journey knowing what lies before you.

As has been shared before in previous month's blogs about the HQAA process, the "application" is the first step of the journey, not the beginning of the final leg. It begins with filling out the application page found on this home page under "Click Here to Apply". The application with HQAA is the discovery phase of your organization. Here, information is collected that is used to determine the most appropriate sets of standards, your specific company information, your specific ID numbers, and your company description. This information is captured to not only report many of these items to CMS, but to then create your Workroom, or manual of standards to work through.

The HQAA "application" is, as I've stated, your first step on a journey. It is NOT an indication that you are ready for your survey. This becomes apparent as soon as the "submit" button is clicked on the application. The accreditation coach makes immediate contact and informs each customer of the expectations. The Q-torial video found within the Workroom clearly identifies the expectations and responsibilities of both the organization and the coaches.

Once the application is submitted, an online Workroom is created individually for your organization, and an accreditation coach is assigned. The purpose of the Workroom phase is to assist in preparing your policies, procedures and processes to meet compliance with the mandated Quality Standards. Coaches assist to ensure that all components critical to the Quality Standards are contained in your written, documented structure.

They do this with you one document at a time. The policy design/implementation phase is secondary to the implementation of that which you say you do on paper is what is actually performed by all employees within your organization. This implementation phase of the journey is one that is critical to a successful on-site survey. Surveyors need to observe that the processes surrounding the Quality Standards are woven in to the fabric of your organization. Three months of implementation is necessary in order to validate that the company is in compliance.

The site survey is observing the action of "where the rubber meets the road". It is allowing the surveyor the opportunity to validate that all required processes are taking place, that all mandated requirements surrounding the management of Medicare beneficiaries occur, that employees are all aware of the need to follow through consistently with these processes, and that meaningful information is collected in order to make consistent improvements to the management of all these processes within the organization. The survey is not the "end" of the process, but it is one of the final legs of the journey.

The successful outcome of the survey is a litmus test as to the implementation phase. The outcome can result in a minimal written post-survey outcomes report, a recommendation for a focused re-visit to observe demonstrated improvements in specific areas, or a complete second full survey. This second full survey is an indication that significant numbers of processes/actions have not been implemented and the organization is allowed time to ensure that they are. A second complete survey is conducted in order to validate that improvement. Following acceptance of the follow-up report, the organization's accomplishments are brought before a formal review committee for approval of the accreditation award. HQAA notifies all customers within 24 hours that their award has been approved.

Now enter this final crunch in the timeline for achieving accreditation. There have been countless articles, advertisements, presentations, statements and forums from CMS, blogs, tweets and really, an information overload that has been presented for no less than 2 years identifying the need to "get accredited". Entering in to the arena of accreditation at the last phase of time allowable has not diminished the level of responsibility that the organization has to the diligence of accomplishing all the requirements. CMS promoted a deadline of sorts in order to jumpstart the last segment of the industry to getting on board with the accreditation mandate.

The deadline that was presented, that of January 31 of this year, was intended to be a deadline to say to your accreditor that you are "ready for survey". That deadline within the HQAA process, as hundreds of customers learned, was one that said, "I'm ready to begin the documentation, planning, perfecting and implementation phase; all PRIOR to survey. It was for that reason that HQAA allowed another deadline of completion of the Workroom portion by March 15th (an internal extension of the 1-31 deadline) to be guaranteed survey in time for accreditation to occur.

I've spoken of accreditation as a journey. The complete and overall process is really a first step in and of itself. Accreditation is not the end; it is the means in which an organization says to itself, its community, and its customers that you have developed a conscientiousness that will carry your company in to the future, and to identify to your customers that you adhere to a set of best practices that focus on their treatment and care. I believe wholeheartedly that there is not any other segment of the healthcare continuum that cares any more deeply for their patients that the home care industry.

8

Medical Tourism in Different Countries

Medical Tourism and Plastic Surgery in Thailand

Whatever you wish to call it, there is no denying the significance of this trend spreading throughout the world. Medical Tourism and its electively centred cousin Cosmetic Tourism have gained recognition worldwide as a viable option to expensive surgery in one's home country.

* The Land of Smiles!!
* Where could be a better place to spend your vacation than in a country dubbed 'The Land of Smiles'?
* Come discover the nation everyone is talking about!

Discover the advantages of having your cosmetic surgery, plastic surgery, or dental surgery performed overseas. Thailand has established itself as the worldwide leader for Medical Tourism through its premium hospitals and talented plastic surgeons. Your cosmetic surgery procedure will be performed at ISO and JCI/JCAHO accredited facilities by board certified surgeons using the latest techniques. Learn about some of the exciting surgical options available here. Our wide variety of recuperation packages are individually tailored to suit your needs and lifestyle. Lavish 5 star hotels coupled with your personal liaison and on call nurse make for ideal recovery settings. Let MMR assist you in reaching your dreams. Get the fantastic results others have experienced by combining affordable plastic surgery with a relaxing holiday in amazing Thailand.

What is a Medical Tourism?

Medical Tourism, also called Health Tourism is the umbrella term used for people seeking healthcare outside of their home countries. Elective surgeries like breast enlargement or rhinoplasty surgery are usually accompanied by a brief holiday following the surgery. In most cases, in destination countries, costs of health care are far less than that of western nations. This, combined with ongoing advancements in standards and technology, has fuelled one of the fastest growing sectors in the health care industry.

Dental Tourism-Dental Procedures & Surgery

Who doesn't want that award winning 'Hollywood smile'? However, dental surgery in England and America doesn't come cheap. However, there are many countries that offer the same dental procedures at a fraction of the price.

As a bonus, these patients can recuperate in exotic destinations and pamper themselves during their stay. Many receiving inpatient procedures opt to stay in lavish facilities-the total price of which is offered at significant savings compared to dental work in their home country.

Recovery time is usually short for dental work, even when the procedure is relatively invasive. Outpatients can therefore travel, receive dental work and then spend the remainder of their time enjoying a wonderful vacation—all at a significant savings. Europeans have long been practicing dental tourism and for years been travelling to neighbouring countries, especially Hungary for their dental needs. Almost everyplace offers the standard dental cleaning, gingivitis treatment, sealants and amalgam filling. Of course, relatively inexpensive procedures like simple cleanings or cavity fillings don't usually warrant travelling outside your home country.

Medical Tourism in Thailand

Health travel, once a luxury of only the rich, can now be enjoyed by virtually all. In the days of yesteryear, hardly anyone even pondered the possibilities of going abroad to a distant foreign land to have treatment. But now, with the advent of the world becoming the one and only global village, millions are crossing international datelines in hope of achieving a 'better new life'.

One of those countries which have sprung to life as a destination for medical treatment is the south-east Asian country of Thailand. Unlike most Western countries, the cost of private medical treatment is cost-effective where hospitals do not charge a bomb. Contrary to popular belief, the standards in Thailand are of an extremely high international standard where many of the health workers have graduated in developed Western countries. Looking at it straight on, the reality is – Thailand can offer the patient the same kind of treatment as back home while enabling him or her to enjoy the holiday of a life time. The uptrend of medical tourism in Thailand is escalating to meteoric heights.

History

Thailand's first hospital was founded during the reign of King Chulalongkorn and the Medical Association of Thailand was established in 1921.

Prince Mahidol, the father of the present king Bhumibol, has much to do with developing medical schools in Thailand and goes down in Thai history as 'The Father of Modern Thai medicine'. Prince Mahidol realized the importance of bringing Western standard medical practice to Siam and so helped fund many of Thailand's doctors and nurses to go abroad to further their studies at institutes such as Harvard and MIT in the United States. And it was those health workers who planted and later sowed the seeds of a world-class medical network in Thailand.

Latest Situation

Westerners are currently arriving in Thailand, the Land of Smiles, in exhilarating numbers to undergo medical treatments at a fraction of the cost as that charged in their home countries.

On top of having treatments conducted by highly trained and skilled doctors, patients can also enjoy a marvelous holiday in one of Asia's prime tourist destinations. Many of the country's hospitals are now globally renowned for their expertise. They include Bumrungrad Hospital, Bangkok General Hospital, Samitivej Hospital and Bangkok Nursing Home Hospital.

Figures and Statistics

Thailand as a destination for medical treatment has rocketed in recent years and they have the statistics to prove it. Take just one country like the United Arab Emirates for example – over 60,000 of their citizens a year come to Thailand to enjoy treatment. Two of the Thailand's top hospitals Bumrungrad and Samitivej treat patients of whom 40% are foreign – this kind of high percentage is quite phenomenal. According to the Kasikorn Research Centre, 2005 alone attracted an unprecedented 1.28 million foreign medical travellers which generated revenue of 33 billion baht. That means therefore, that on average each patient spent 25,800 baht for their treatments. It was revealed in an article in Newsweek in 2006 that 400,000 foreign patients were treated at just Bumrungrad hospital in Bangkok. This prestigious world-class hospital has an outpatient capacity of 6,000 patients per day.

Thailand presently has a free universal health program for its citizens with more than 600 hospitals and 400 medical facilities. Today, Thailand has proudly become a medical hub for patients from the United States, Europe, the surrounding countries, and the Middle East.

Why Thailand/Reasons to Chose Thailand as the Medical Destination

There is no single reason why so many folk come to Thailand to receive medical treatment. Not only is Thailand a superb destination for stunning beaches, islands, mountains, modern infrastructure, cuisines, low costs and friendly people, there are other reasons too. Some of the Best Hospitals in the World:Thailand has, over the years, spent furtively in developing its medical tourism infrastructure and established over 30 English speaking hospitals, innumerable dentistry clinics and other alternative healing centres. Some are accredited to prestigious boards including the Joint Commission on Accreditation of Healthcare Organizations and the International Organization for Standardization.

Incredible Service: It is no joke when Westerners write on the Internet or chat in bars that the service, look and ambiance of Thailand's hospitals is similar to that of a five-star hotel. The treatment received from doctors, nurses, orderlies, administrators, and technicians is outstanding and the doctor patient ratio is as low as 1:4. Extra-ordinary value for money: Foreign patients can expect to pay just 10-50% for the cost of treatment, in comparison to what they would pay back home.

The likes of hip surgeries, teeth whitening, face lifts, x-rays, mastectomies, and heart bypasses can all be performed at very affordable prices. With the money they save they can enjoy a memorable holiday and even go back home with cash leftover. Unique Procedures: Many hospitals are offering treatments which are virtually unheard of elsewhere.

Excellent Long-lasting Outcome: Some of Thailand hospitals have been recognized for performing outstanding treatments for several procedures while producing excellent outcome with long lasting effects. Thailand is Amazing for Relaxing: After treatment, patients can experience spas and resorts which are universally famous for exceptional service and comfort, while looking over beautiful virgin beaches or remote mountains.

International Health Care System

Thailand top hospitals provide prompt and complete response in any emergency situation and are recognized outside of Thailand as having standards equivalent to that of those in the West.

Foreign Patients: The renowned Bumrungrad Hospital in Bangkok attracts on average 400,000 foreign patients per year or an average of 1,000+ a day. Other hospitals too, such as Samitivej also specialize in serving foreigners.

Regulatory Agency: Private hospitals in Thailand are accredited by the government according to standards that meet or exceed those in North America. Only four countries in the world – the United States, Canada, Australia, and Thailand – require private hospitals to meet rigorous medical and healthcare standards and be duly accredited as achieving those standards.

International Accreditation

The standard of treatment in Thailand is considered in North America of being one of the highest in the world with most of their doctors holding US professional certification. Many of the hospitals have international JCAHO accreditation; this is an organization which is the primary inspector of hospitals, nursing homes and other medical institutions in the US. All of Thailand's hospitals have to be licensed by the Health Ministry and the same applies to the doctors. In fact, some of the hospitals in Thailand have accreditation from Western medical associations. Most of the country's major hospitals also have achieved other accreditation being the International Standards Organization's ISO 9001:2000 accreditation. Many of the doctors in Thailand have graduated and trained in Europe and the US and hold medical credentials form there. The hospitals also have working relations with Western hospitals. The UK Foreign and Common Wealth Office verifies that Bangkok has "Excellent International Hospitals" and the

US State Department has stated that Bangkok also offers "Excellent facilities exist for routine long-term and emergency healthcare.

Technology

The most up-to-date state of the art developments and technologies have been introduced in Thailand to enhance medical facilities and treatment. They include:

- DSA (Digital Subtraction Angiography),
- Digital Mammogram allowing accurate diagnosis and early discovery of cancer in women.
- Green light PVP Laser for Prostate Treatment to precisely target prostate tissue with a high powered laser beam.
- PET/CT Scanner (Position Emission Tomography/Computed Tomography Scanner) assist in the earliest detection of cancers and assess heart muscle viability for the evaluation of functional brain anatomy.
- Novalis Shaped Beam Surgery System Installed and Operating helps applies doses of radiation, allowing it to destroy diseased tissue or cauterize a problem area without affecting healthy adjacent tissue. Other treatments are cancerous tumours, arteriovenous, malformations and Parkinson's disease.
- 4D Ultrasound creates a motion life-like picture with the speed of 25 volumes per second.
- magnetic Resonance Imageing (MRI-Intra Achiva 3.0T MRI) allows the detailed information necessary to detect blood circulation abnormalities and is particularly useful in the early detection of brain cancer.
- Gamma Knife Surgery makes non-invasive brain surgery possible by applying hihgly targeted gamma radiation to the treatment of tumours, arteriovenous malformations of the brain and functional disorders.
- IMRT (Intensity Modulated Radiotherapy) focuses radiation doses on tumours without damaging the surrounding tissue.
- Minimal Invasive Heart Surgery, the da Vinci Surgical System uses robotics to translate the surgeon's natural hand movements into the micro movements of a robotic arm. The surgeon is able to apply less invasive incisions with unprecedented

precision, lowering risk, accelerating recovery, and greatly reducing scarring.

Medical Tourism Thailand

Popular For: Alternative Medicine, cosmetic surgery, dental care, gender realignment, heart surgery, obesity surgery, oncology, orthopedics.

Visa Requirements: A valid passport and return ticket are required. Visa not required for stays up to 30 days.

Thailand has all but established itself as king of the castle when it comes to international medical tourism. The affordable prices combined with high levels of quality care in a country rich in culture, natural beauty and amazing food all combine to make Thailand the first choice for many seeking medical treatment abroad. In fact, Thailand is one of the world's preferred destinations for all types of treatment including medical, cosmetic and dental procedures.

Pros: Thailand stands as one of the world's top tourism destinations, which means the country is long accustomed to receiving foreign travellers. In the big cities, English is understood, especially at private clinics that will interest tourists looking for treatment. The cost of a flight ticket, food and accommodation and the procedure itself can add up to less than the price of a procedure in North America. Throw in the fact that Thailand has much to offer as a regular tourist spot, this Southeast Asian country is set to remain a favourite medical tourism destination for a long time to come.

Cons: While most medical practitioners in Thailand are experienced and well-qualified, there are some doctors whose reputations can be less than ideal. Medical tourists should shop around to make sure they're getting the best treatment possible and that the price is not the only consideration. Thailand and the rest of Southeast Asia experiences three distinct seasons, and it is important to choose the right time to come. The rainy season can be unpleasant at times, with hard downpours that regularly flood the streets of cities. The summer season can see temperatures reach uncomfortable levels along with debilitating humidity and pollution.

Medical Tourism in Thailand

Thailand is a world leader in the medical tourism industry and the country's private hospitals and clinics are able to perform all kinds of surgeries from heart procedures to hip and joint replacements and recuperative operations after injury. Bangkok has several hospitals that are used to receiving foreign patients, and the number of hospitals means that it's easy to get a second opinion and find a doctor you're comfortable with before gong under the knife.

Thailand Cosmetic Surgery

Thailand's cosmetic surgeons have profited from Thailand's reputation for medical tourism. The prices for elective surgery can be a fraction of what they would be in the west, with the quality level being consistently high. While common procedures such as face lifts, tummy tucks and breast augmentation are widely available, Thailand is also a world specialist in sex reassignment surgery. Procedures of this nature include facial feminization surgery and vaginoplasty.

Thailand Dental Tourism

Thailand is known for its masterful dentists. Many North Americas make up to three trips over the period of a year to receive extended dental surgery, and still come out saving significant amounts of money. The dental equipment used in Thailand is on par with some of the best in the world, and the dentists are very well trained. Procedures available include crowns, dentures, laser teeth whitening and bridges.

Thailand Alternative Medicine

The Thais have long been practicing alternative medicine and many practitioners using herbal medicines and holistic approaches are available. This sector is beginning to attract foreign attention, particularly the country's wellness retreats, yoga workshops and chiropractic treatments.

Thailand Health Spas

The spa industry is big business in Thailand. Thais and foreigners alike take advantage of the many spas in the cities, where saunas, steam baths and every kind of massage are available for much less than the going rate in the west. Spas here are well suited to catering to international tourists and cost-saving packages are available at every establishment.

Medical Tourism in Thailand

Private healthcare in the West is notoriously expensive and many people look to Thailand to find cost-effective solutions for their medical problems...

'Generation X' is in charge and its legacy is a world where government 'interference' in the free market and healthcare is at an all-time low. Unable to depend on state healthcare systems, people in many parts of the world have to resort to their private resources for the operations and treatments they need. Private healthcare in the West is notoriously expensive, for some, prohibitively so. Even commonplace medical areas like dentistry and orthodontics are extortionately priced, while surgery and major operations can completely drain personal finances. Given the costs, and the stakes, many people have looked beyond the shores of their native homelands to find cost-effective solutions. Many have found their solutions in Thailand, spurring a trend in 'medical tourism' within the country.

But why Thailand?

The Thai medical profession is probably one of the most advanced in the region. Successive governments have invested in ensuring the education and training Thai doctors receive is parallel to that offered elsewhere in the region. Many doctors undertake specialist training abroad, particularly the United States and Europe, and are at least equally as well qualified as physicians in the West-often more so. A qualified, experienced medical profession is though useless without proper facilities and equipment. Fortunately, Thailand's hospitals and clinics are world class. Huge investments have been made in equipment and management standards are so high that hospitals achieve ISO 9001 accreditation. Many major hospitals belong to management groups that ensure the very highest standard of medical service is available through their branch hospitals at various locations around the country. All this expertise and proficiency means that Thailand's hospitals are a secure option for those seeking medical treatment.

Thailand's medical solutions do not though rest at major surgery or treatments. A variety of cosmetic surgery options are available, as is cosmetic dentistry and laser sight correction (LASIK, etc.). Thailand is also a very popular choice for people requiring sex reassignment surgery.

In recent years, "medical tourism" has become the new buzzword for the development of Thailand's tourism industry. What this means is encouraging people to come to Thailand, have a little elective surgery, and then recuperate on some nice beach. The idea is not as crazy as it may sound. Some of Thailand's private hospitals are capable of world class healthcare, accredited according some of the toughest standards around. While they might be expensive for many Thais, these hospitals are still able to offer a high standard of care for far less than a hospital stay in most western countries will cost.

We're not talking about critical care, such as transplants. Medical Tourism is targeted at elective and non-emergency treatments, such as cosmetic surgery or hip replacements. Such are the cost savings that some insurance companies will not only cover the costs of treatment, but some of the travel costs as well, to have work done in Thailand. Thailand's low cost health care is not limited to medical treatment. Thanks to tight government price controls, most medicines cost far less than they do in western countries.

Thai Hospitals

Here's a short list of hospitals that specialize in treating foreigners. They all have staff who speak English, as well as many other languages. All of the institutions below are based in Bangkok, although some have branches in other parts of the country.

Bumrungrad International Hospital

Perhaps the most advanced and internationalized of Thailand's private hospital. Coming here can seem like a visit to a five star hotel and the United Nations all in one. Although comparatively expensive for Thais, the hospital gets many foreign visitors in search of high quality health care at reasonable cost. The web site provides an overview of the hospital's services, and the ability to make appointments online.

Bangkok General Hospital

A good general medicine hospital. The web site is available in many languages. The main services for foreign visitors are cosmetic surgery. The hospital can arrange for a variety of treatments as part of your holiday.

Samitivej Hospital

Samitivej is one of Bangkok's most respected hospitals. Its main claim to fame is the "baby friendly" natal facilities. It's probably unlikely that you would want to travel to Thailand to have your baby, but the hospital has several other services to offer as well, including extensive children's healthcare departments.

St. Carlos Hospital

This small hospital has combined traditional medicine with a full fledged spa to provide a complete range of health and beauty treatments, from cosmetic surgery to detoxifying body treatments.

Rutnin Eye Hospital

Rutnin is perhaps Bangkok's largest eye hospital, with a full range of services such as lasik corrections.

Medical Tourism Resources

Cosmetic Surgery Travel

Sort of a medical travel planner, providing a concierge type service to help you plan your trip to Bangkok for cosmetic surgery or other medical procedures. They can help you to plan your trip, select doctors and facilities, and schedule your appointments or procedures before you arrive.

Oasis Medical Tourism

Web presence of Mondial Assistance Thailand, a subsidiary of global assistance and insurance company Mondial Assistance Group. They can assist you with planning all aspects of your Thai medical experience.

Costa Rica Medical Tourism

Fast growing Medical Tourism in Costa Rica owes its existence to tourists from the US and Canada travelling primarily to get medical & surgical procedures done abroad. Many unique factors make Costa Rica healthcare a preferred medical travel destination.

Why Costa Rica as a Medical Tourism Destination?

Medical treatments are usually about 50-70% cheaper than in the US and no one has to wait their turn for surgery.

Easily accessible from US and Canada. There are frequent flights from important cities in both these countries. Also Americans, Canadians and most Europeans staying in Costa Rica for less than 90 days do not require a visa. They do need a passport that is valid for at least 30 days.

Traditionally, the procedures that have been popular with medical tourists in Costa Rica have been cosmetic and dental treatments. But with growing standards of medical care, there is rapid medical tourism demand for various other surgeries and medical procedures.

Vacationing with a Medical Trip to Costa Rica

Costa Rica's unique geographic location-it has the Pacific ocean on the one side and the Caribbean Sea on the other-has endowed it with beautiful pristine beaches, lush green mountains formed by past volcanic eruptions, dense rainforests, lakes, and rivers. All these help support one of the most diverse plant and animal life on the planet. Costa Rica also has many active volcanoes and hot springs. Most medical tourism destination are not ideal for a vacation or a touristic holiday, not in the case of Costa Rica, which is not only a great medical care destination, but also a popular tourism destination. Sometimes called 'the Switzerland of Central America', Costa Rica is famous for microclimates where in an hour's travel one may experience from very hot and humid to hot and dry to cold and rainy.

If the doctor allows it and depending on what suits your temperament, you could take a peek at one of Costa Rica's active volcanoes like Arenal or one with the widest crater in the world like Poas, and bathe in the hot water springs, or visit the rainforests, wildlife parks, or go for a hike. Not to forget, the many beaches, butterfly gardens, river or lake tours, museums, fishing or scuba diving, coffee farm tours or even a visit to the National Theatre for someone into orchestra.

Costa Rican Food

Unlike many other Latin American countries, the local food in Costa Rica is not spicy. For chicken connoisseurs, a must-try local dish is the wood *fire roasted chicken.* For those who may miss good old American fast food, there are many franchise restaurants like McDonalds, Pizza Hut, and Kentucky Fried Chicken that you can go to.

The Spirit of "Pura Vida" & Medical Tourism

Costa Rica is a foreigner-friendly country; it attracts over 2 million tourists every year. The phrase Pura Vida differently means "Full of Life", "Purified life", "This is living!" or "Going great!" and reflects the easy-going, relaxed lifestyle of Costa Ricans. Costa Rica has a special police force called 'Tourist Police' that is just to assist the tourists with directions and answering questions.

A politically stable country, Costa Rica does not have an army. It has a high standard of living when compared to that of other Latin

American countries and also a stable economy. It has a literacy rate of 96% and the lowest crime rates in the region. Many US and Canadian citizens and Europeans choose Costa Rica to lead their retired life because of the low cost of living, comfortable climate and its unspoiled natural habitats.

Health care in Costa Rica compares with the best in the world. It is no surprise then that the UNDP's 2007/2008 Human Development Report puts the average life expectancy in Costa Rica at 78.5, above that of USA's 77.9

Popular souvenirs to bring home from Costa Rica are the fresh-from-the-farm coffees and the variety of hand-crafted wooden items. It is illegal in Costa Rica to try to export any plants or animals or even sea shells or rocks.

Factors to consider-Medical Travel to Costa Rica

* Spanish is the main language in Costa Rica. But English is frequently used in tourist-frequented spots like hotels, resorts, leading hospitals and clinics. In hospitals, there are always interpreters available.
* At most places in Costa Rica, the American dollar is accepted.
* Most US cell phones do not work in Costa Rica. Before you set out from your home country, it is a good idea to check with your cell phone provider about the coverage and call rates in Costa Rica.
* Do not expect the blazing internet speeds that you may be used to in Canada or USA.
* Travellers should use licensed taxis, which are red with medallions (yellow triangles containing numbers) painted on the side. Licensed taxis at the airport are painted orange.

Medical Tourism Corporation has arranged with its network hospitals in Costa Rica to have special guest suites designed to comfortably accommodate the patient and the accompanying guest while in the hospital. Also, MTC has made special arrangements with recovery resorts that have 24 x 7 nursing for any post-hospital discharge care, with adequate arrangement for the comfort of the accompanying guest. There is always an English-speaking personal case manager at the medical destination. So, if you are looking for medical care abroad,

Costa Rica is one of the places to consider seriously. Even if you are just planning a vacation, you may go to Costa Rica for pleasure and save some money by getting any pending medical or dental care done while there! There couldn't be a better place than Costa Rica to recuperate and unwind. Thus, medical tourism in Costa Rica is a complete package of health, fun, and savings. We hope this information will be a valuable aid on deciding on Costa Rica as a medical tourism destination of your choice.

Medical Tourism in Costa Rica

Over the last decade, Costa Rica has evolved from being a mere eco-tourism destination to a country of choice for foreigners, particularly from United States and Canada, seeking quality healthcare services and surgeries at a much lower price than their home countries.

In a report from McKinsey & Company, it was highlighted that medical tourists from the United States and Canada prefer Latin American countries like Costa Rica due to the shorter travel time, affordable costs, and an opportunity for a memorable vacation.

Healthcare System in Costa Rica

Aside from its close proximity to the United States, medical tourists flock to Costa Rica due to its excellent healthcare system which is ranked by the World Health Organization even higher than the US. Costa Rica has modern hospitals and state-of-the-art clinics utilizing the latest in medical technologies and board-certified surgeons who are trained and certified in North America or Europe.

Aside from services offered to medical tourists, Costa Rica is also credited for providing a high quality public and private healthcare services with prestigious and reputable hospitals and other health facilities.

Consider the following healthcare facts:

* The World Health Organization ranked Costa Rica's health system as one of the top three Latin America countries, ranked even higher than United States and New Zealand.
* The World Bank ranked Costa Rica to have the highest life expectancy, at 78.7 years, among all countries in Latin America. This is equivalent to the level in Canada and higher than the United States by a year.

Top Hospitals in Costa Rica

Costa Rica top hospitals are accredited by the Joint Commission International like Ministro de Salud de Costa Rica (The Costa Rica Health Ministry), which offers the local license Habilitacien Hospitalaria, and local municipalities like the Municipio de Escazu in San Jose, which offers licensures like the Funcionamento. Some hospitals like the CIMA Hospitals are owned and managed by leading US hospital corporations. There are currently three JCI-accredited hospitals in Costa Rica and all are located in San Jose, the capital of Costa Rica. These hospitals include:

Hospital CIMA-San Jose, Costa Rica

Accredited by the JCI on May 2008. CIMA is also certified by the ISO and was the first hospital that was certified for Quality Processes by the Ministry of Health in Costa Rica. Other CIMA hospitals can be found in other locations in Costa Rica, like the CIMA Hermosillo, CIMA Chihuahua and the CIMA Santa Engracia, although the CIMA San Jose is the top destination for medical tourists.

Hospital Clinica Biblica-San Jose, Costa Rica

Accredited by the JCI on October 2007. It was built in 1929 by American missionaries and has grown into a high-quality medical facility with a capacity of 120 inpatients and 5000 outpatients per day. They have a dedicated Medical Tourism department with English and Spanish fluent staff and employees.

Hospital La Catolica-San Jose, Costa Rica

Accredited by the JCI on June 2009. The hospital recently built new infrastructures on top of its newly remodeled facilities which boast of its own high class hotel, the La Posada El Convento, located within the confines of the medical facilities.

Popular Treatments done in Costa Rica and Comparative Costs

Known initially for its excellent dental surgery services, medical tourism in Costa Rica has spread to a variety of other medical procedures, including:

* General and cosmetic dentistry,
* Cosmetic surgery,
* Aesthetic procedures (botox, skin resurfacing etc.),

* Bariatric and Laparascopic surgery,
* Orthopedic surgery,
* Fertility treatments,
* Addiction treatment.

The following are cost comparisons between Medical procedures in Costa Rica and equivalent procedures in the United States:

	USA	***Costa Rica***	***Average Savings***
	Medical Procedures		
Heart Bypass	Up to $130,000	$24,000	70-80%
Heart Valve Replacement	Up to $160,000	$15,000	80-90%
Angioplasty	Up to $57,000	$9,000	70-80%
Hip Replacement	Up to $43,000	$12,000	60-70%
Hysterectomy	Up to $20,000	$4,000	70-80%
Knee Replacement	Up to $40,000	$11,000	60-70%
Spinal Fusion	Up to $62,000	$25,000	50-60%
	Plastic and Reconstructive Surgery		
Facelift	$7,000-$9,000	$4,600 – $5,000	30-40%
Rhinoplasty	$8,000-$12,000	$3,500 – $3,900	50-65%
Breast Lift	$5,000-$8,000	$3,000 – $3,400	40-55%
Breast Augmentation	$5,000-$8,000	$2,700 – $2,900	50-65%
Blepharoplasty (Eyelid Surgery)	$4,000-$5,500	$2,000-$2,200	50-60%
Brazilian Butt Surgery	Up to $10,000	$3,000-$3,300	55-65%
Tummy Tuck	$6,000-$8,500	$3,900 – $4,200	45-50%
Facelift	$7,000-$9,000	$4,600 – $5,000	35-45%
Male Breast Reduction	Up to $6,000	$2000-$2600	50-60%
	Bariatric Surgery		
Laparoscopic Gastroplasty	Up to $30,000	$10,500	55-65%
Laparoscopic Roux-en-Y	Up to $35,000	$14,000	50-60%
	General and Cosmetic Dentistry		
Bridges	$1,000+ per tooth	$250 – $400 per tooth	60-70%
Crowns	$1,000+ per tooth	$250-$400 per tooth	60-70%
Implants	$3,500+ per tooth	$700 – $900 per tooth	70-80%
Porcelain Veneers	$1,500+ per tooth	$300 – $500 per tooth	65-80%
Root canal	Up to $800	$315	55-60%
Teeth whitening	Up to $700	$250	55-65%

Malpractice and Liabilities Laws in Costa Rica

Medical Tourists can receive better reassurance against malpractice in Costa Rica as compared to most medical travel destinations, as most dentists, physicians and clinics are required to have and maintain professional liability insurance during the course of their practice. Any malpractice claims can be initiated through the court system as required under the laws of Costa Rica.

Medical travellers are also encouraged to purchase comprehensive medical coverage options offered by certified international insurance companies to medical tourists and their travel companions.

Pros

The WHO ranked the quality of healthcare in Costa Rica as among the top nations in Latin America, a rank that is even better than the United States.

The close proximity of Costa Rica to the United States and Canada makes it an ideal destination for North American medical tourists.

Language will not be a barrier as hospital staff and most of the locals can speak English.

The culture in Costa Rica is family-oriented, friendly and visitors are assured that they will receive a warm and hospitable welcome not only by the hospital staff and crew but all other locals as well

The cost of medical treatments in Costa Rica ranges from a third to even a fourth of what it can cost in the United States or Canada.

As required by law, medical practitioners carry liability insurance at all times, giving patients protection and coverage from malpractice.

Costa Rica is known as a prime Eco-tourism destination so visitors are assured of majestic views, amazing destination spots and a temperate climate, which assures medical tourists of an excellent vacation experience conducive for recovery and relaxation.

Cons

Costa Rica is strict with regards to overstaying visitors and may be stringent in providing visas for anyone with previous overstaying records. They are also meticulous with regards to documentation requirements if visitors are accompanied by children.

Travelling to Costa Rica

Due to the close proximity of Costa Rica to the United States and Canada, medical travellers do not need to spend long hours on the plane.

Average estimated travel time in hours

From/To	*San Jose, Costa Rica*
New York City	4.5
Chicago	4.5
Washington, DC	4
San Francisco	6
Los Angeles	5.5
Toronto	5
Montreal	5
Vancouver	7

Entry and Exit Requirements to Costa Rica

USA and Canadian medical travellers with a valid passport and a pre-paid airline ticket do not need to get a visa and can stay up to 90-day in Costa Rica.

Should there be a need for an extension to the 90-day allotted period, particularly if required by medical procedures and recovery needs, a request for an extension can be submitted to the Office of Temporary Permits of the Department of Immigration in Costa Rica.

It is strongly advised for medical travellers to stick to this allotted period as Costa Rica may deny entry for people who have previous overstaying records in the country.

Statistics for Medical Tourism in Costa Rica

According to Promed (the Council for the Promotion of Medicine in Costa Rica), there were approximately 22,000 US citizens who visited Costa Rica in 2008 for medical procedures, mostly baby boomers or people aged over 50 who are seeking quality medical services including dental, surgical and other medical packages at very affordable rates.

Costa Rica's healthcare system is very advanced, particularly in the city of San Jose, and is considered one of the best in Latin America.

For some procedures, it ranks higher than the US. The country boasts highly-competent specialists in plastic surgery and dentistry, which are two areas of treatment most in demand. With additional recent medical advancements, heart, kidney and liver transplants are now offered, as is bone marrow transplantation. The World Health Organization gives high marks to the quality of medical care in Costa Rica.

World-renowned as a leader in eco-tourism, Costa Rica boasts tropical rainforests, stunning mountain vistas, fabulous beaches, an ideal climate and friendly, welcoming people. There is now an increasing awareness that the country is also a premier destination for quality medical treatment at amazingly low prices.

The country's specialists in cosmetic surgery procedures are fully-credentialed and are experienced in the latest surgical and non-surgical techniques available. Costa Rica's Plastic Surgery Board provides listings of physicians who are credentialed members of the national association. In addition, the board will provide information on whether a physician is currently certified or preparing for certification. Costa Rica's cost of living and the strong value of the US dollar in relation to the country's currency means medical services cost much less here than in the US. Every year, thousands of US citizens take advantage of the low cost of procedures and the high level of quality care provided by Costa Rica's cosmetic surgeons and dentists. By the early 1990s, approximately 15 percent of all visitors to Costa Rica entered the country specifically to undergo some sort of medical treatment.

Typically, a patient will plan on a week to 10 days in Costa Rica, which allows time for a procedure and a short recovery period. The actual time spent, of course, depends on the complexity of the surgery and the number of follow-up visits required. With medical tourism packages, a patient will often spend a few days sightseeing, undergo the planned treatment and then spend some time in a suitable location, such as an eco-tourist destination, for rest and additional sightseeing or recuperation.

Medical Tourism In El Salvador

El Salvador

El Salvador is a land of amazing contrasts, accented by a long string of cone-shaped volcanoes and their tranquil mountain lakes. In addition, the country's Maya ruins are considered some of the most interesting in all of Central America.

Significant points-of-interest include Cerro Verde National Park and the Santa Ana and Izalco volcanoes; the cloud forests of Montecristo National Park; Mayan ruins at Tazumal; El Espino and El Cuco beaches along the Pacific Ocean; shopping and night life venues in San Salvador; the colonial architecture, splendid churches and colorful handicraft markets spread across the country, and of course, the indigenous native celebrations and religious festivals that fill the calendar.

Over the last ten years, the country has instigated a strong move toward democracy, countrywide modernization, and an greatly improved tourism industry. They look forward to providing Americans with a medical tourism option. El Salvador is located in Central America and can be reached from most US cities within 3 to 7 hours.

Country Information

El Salvador is located in Central America. It has a total area of 8,123 square miles, making it comparable in size to the state of Massachusetts. El Salvador is the smallest country in Central America. Due to its size it is affectionately called the "Tom Thumb of the Americas". It has 123.6 square miles of water within its borders. Several small rivers flow through El Salvador into the Pacific Ocean, including the Goascoran, Jiboa, Torola, Paz and the Rio Grande de San Miguel. Only the largest river, the Lempa River, flowing from Honduras across El Salvador to the ocean, is navigable for commercial traffic.

Volcanic craters enclose lakes, the most important of which are Lake Ilopango (27 sq mi) and Lake Coatepeque (10 sq mi). Lake Guija is El Salvador's largest natural lake (17 sq mi). Several artificial lakes were created by the damming of the Lempa, the largest of which is Embalse Cerron Grande (135 sq mi).

El Salvador shares borders with Guatemala—126 miles (203 km) and Honduras—212.5 miles (342 km), and is the only Central American country that does not have a Caribbean coastline. The highest point in the country is Cerro El Pital at 8,957 feet (2,730 meters).

El Salvador's population numbers about 6.9 million people. Fully 90% are mestizo (mixed Amerindian and Spanish/European), 9% white (mostly Spanish, but also some French, German and Italian descent), and only 1% indigenous.

Language

Spanish is the official language of El Salvador. English is the second language.

Religion

Roman Catholic 83%, Protestant & other 17%.

Climate

Tropical and subtropical; dry season (November through April); rainy season (May through October); cooler in highlands. El Salvador's weather is influenced by altitude. Pacific lowlands are uniformly hot; central plateau and mountain areas more moderate. The temperature in San Salvador area ranges from a high of 74-100 degrees Fahrenheit, to a low of 54-74 degrees Fahrenheit. The wet season is from May to October. The hottest months are March and April.

El Salvador has a tropical climate with pronounced wet and dry seasons. Temperatures vary primarily with elevation and show little seasonal change. The Pacific lowlands are uniformly hot; the central plateau and mountain areas are more moderate. The rainy season, known locally as invierno, or winter, extends from May to October. Almost all the annual rainfall occurs during this time, and yearly totals, particularly on southern-facing mountain slopes, can be as high as 78 inches. Protected areas and the central plateau receive lesser, although still significant, amounts. Rainfall during this season generally comes from low pressure over the Pacific and usually falls in heavy afternoon thunderstorms. Although hurricanes occasionally form in the Pacific, they seldom affect El Salvador.

From November through April, the northeast trade winds control weather patterns. During these months, air flowing from the Caribbean has had most of the precipitation wrung out of it passing over the mountains in Honduras. By the time this air reaches El Salvador, it is dry, hot, and hazy. This season is known locally as verano, or summer. Temperatures vary little with season; elevation is the primary determinant. The Pacific lowlands are the hottest region, with annual averages ranging from 77°F to 85°F. San Salvador is representative of the central plateau, with an annual average temperature of 74°F and absolute high and low readings of 100°F and 45°F, respectively. Mountain areas are the coolest, with annual averages from 54°F to 74°F and minimum temperatures sometimes approaching freezing.

Clothing

The first thing to consider when packing for your medical travel trip is climate. The dress code in El Salvador is casual. Professionals usually wear light cotton suits. The popular "guayabera" or embroidered cotton shirt, is preferred casual wear for men, particularly in the warmer areas. As a health tourism guest, just wear very loose, comfortable clothing. .

Mobile Phones

A Subscriber Identity Module Card (SIM Card) is now available for El Salvador and foreign patients who are travelling for medical purposes. The SIM Card must be used in conjunction with a Digital GSM mobile phone within the 900-MHz range or a Digital PCN mobile phone within the 1800-MHz range.

Getting Online & Checking E-mail

All of El Salvador's leading hotels offer facsimile (fax) and e-mail services. Numerous private businesses offer such facilities, most often in conjunction with translation services. El Salvador has been expanding its information service for residents and tourists alike through the Internet system. Services are now available at El Salvador's leading hotels and at the many "cyber cafés" that are cropping up in all major tourist destinations.

Medical Tourism: Saying Goodbye to El Salvador

When I told people we were going to El Salvador their response was almost always "Why in the world would you go there?" People have the impression it's unsafe and the last place in Central America you'd want to visit. Then, tell them you're going for dental work and they are really baffled. Being a journalist, I'm not someone who would randomly hop on a plane and let someone pull my husband's teeth out. I did my homework. Planet Hospital facilitated everything and thankfully got us in contact with Dr. Lorenzana. Knowing he was trained in the U.S., speaks perfect English and is an American Board Certified Prosthodontist helped us feel confident about the quality care. The Americans we'd spoken to ahead of our own decision raved about the experience and they were right.

In all my husband had three teeth pulled, seven implants, a bone graft and a sinus lift. He also has a mouth full of beautiful temporaries.

The procedure took about 4 hours. He didn't feel a thing and never had any pain. The entire process far exceeded our expectations. Dr. Lorenzana loves what he does and he loves his country. He has a real desire to let the world know what a great place it is to visit and that the quality of care really is first class.

Hard not to fall in love with the people here. They are so kind and eager to accommodate. It makes them sad and frustrated that the country still has a reputation for being unsafe, despite the war being over for more than a decade. Ricky (Our Planet Hospital Country Host) picked us up at the hotel and took us to Dr. Lorenzana's office for our final visit before heading home. The doctor took all the stitches out of Doug's mouth and gave him the final instructions for keeping his new teeth clean. He'll need to floss and rinse with Listerine, keep his mouth healthy while the implants integrate to his bones. We'll then come back in about five months for Doug's permanent crowns.

It's bittersweet to leave. In the short time we were there we made friends for life, some now are like family. I'm sold on medical tourism as a way to save a whole lot of money and get a vacation in the process. Our original estimate here in the states: 60 thousand dollars. The cost in El Salvador 19 thousand. Add a few thousand for travel expenses and we're still saving over 30 thousand dollars. Doug's temporary teeth look like a million bucks. We can't wait to go back in July.

Hospitals In El Salvador: Zaldivar Institute, Clinica Diagnostico, Dr. Lorenzana Dental Clinic

Actual statistics from "The World Health Report 2000-Health systems: Improving performance."

The U. S. health system spends a higher portion of its gross domestic product than any other country but ranks #37 out of 191 countries according to its performance. However, the US ranks #1 in health expenditure per capita, while El Salvador ranks 115th in the overall health system performance and 83rd in the health expenditure per capita. The reason for this ranking is that El Salvador has something that resembles two distinct health care systems. The first is a completely private based system that uses qualified doctors, state of the art technology and the doctors spend ample time with their patients, which unfortunately, only the wealthy can afford. The other is a government run system that is more designed for the poor, where the doctors are overworked and don't have as much time to spend with each patient. This was largely due to a decrease of government expenditures on health programs during the war.

With the stability of government and less political unrest, El Salvador is becoming a popular gem for medical tourists. Many doctors have trained and studied in the United States, access to the latest state of the art technologies and the beauty of its people are making it a popular destination for dental and medical procedures.

El Salvador is a major coffee centre, and coffee influences the way of life, the scent in the air and the attitude of the people. Its capital San Salvador, is an attractive town with many old buildings of pronounced great architecture.

Transportation in this relatively small country is easy, and getting to famous sights will be a breeze. Lake Coatepeque and Chalchuapa are some for the famous ones while San Salvador's Pacific coast rival the best ones in the world. The natural beauty-volcanoes, coffee plantations, and isolated beaches make for a good environment to take a rest and appreciate nature too.

When you visit El Salvador, you will notice that affordable prices reflect the lower cost of living. Cosmetic surgery is common and medical tourism is safe, accepted and one of the best, there is a countrywide modernization, all of which are aimed to improve the tourism industry.

Castilian Spanish is the official language of El Salvador, while English is the second language. This makes communication a lot easier. Cuisine can be described as straightforward and tasty, centering around corn, beans, rice, tomatoes, and meat. Of course, coffee is present, and one of the more simple, but luxurious joys of the trip.

El Salvador

El Salvador is one of the most densely populated countries in Central America. A wide mix of ethnic groups dominated largely by the Spanish and expatriate refugees, give this country its unique and rich cultural heritage. The population is friendly and fun loving and welcomes tourists with open arms. With a favourable tropical climate, temperatures do not vary too much with changing seasons. The volcanic landscape is breathtaking and makes for a popular tourist attraction. The jagged mountains and calm waters of the lakes on one end are a lovely contrast to the beaches of the Pacific Ocean on the other end. Another interesting aspect of this tourist destination is the mystical ruins of the Mayan culture found in the region. This civilization is said to have been lost mysteriously in time and always fascinates casual tourists and explorers alike.

Medical care at El Salvador

El Salvador is becoming one of the medical tourism hubs in Latin America. Its proximity to America is one of the prime factors fueling this industry. It can be reached within a couple of hours from any city in the US. Countrywide modernization has also led to the establishment of state-of-the-art medical facilities and clinics across El Salvador. This country is a popular medical tourism destination for pre and post operative medical care for cosmetic surgeries and other rehabilitative treatments.

Medical Tourism Expands in El Salvador

El Salvador's foray into the medical tourism industry is backed by its government and export promotion agencies. The tour was sponsored by Export Salud, El Salvador's chamber promoting medical tourism into the country, as well as the Medical Tourism Association. Export Salud has 200 physicians and dentists and is an active member of the Medical Tourism Association.

El Salvador's Vice President, Ana Vilma de Escobar, as well as the Minister of the Exterior and the Minister of Tourism participated in discussions about the burgeoning medical tourism market in El Salvador and solicited the input of the facilitators visiting the country. Representatives of El Salvador Medical Travel toured two privately-owned hospitals that are aggressively marketing medical tourism, Hospital de Diagnostico and Hospital de la Mujer, and met with physicians and dentists who are promoting their care internationally.

Tonya Walton, CEO of El Salvador Medical Tourism, reported "El Salvador is a new player in the medical tourism industry, and I had no idea what to expect from the visit. I was impressed by the high quality hospital facilities as well as the credentials of the physicians who are providing services worldwide." Ms. Walton further indicated that El Salvador is primed to be the next major player in the booming medical tourism industry, presenting strong competition for well-known destinations such as Costa Rica and Mexico.

El Salvador Medical Tourism formalized agreements with Surgical Specialities Abroad and El Salvador Medical, two physician groups that are promoting their services to international travellers. El Salvador's medical providers offer advanced dentistry, gastroenterology and bariatric surgery, ophthalmology, general surgery, plastic surgery, and orthopedics. The physicians, many of whom were trained in the US, are able to provide services such as dental implants and full mouth restoration, gastric and weight loss surgeries, all types of ophthalmologic care including Lasik, hernia repair, myriad cosmetic procedures, as well as laparoscopic orthopedic procedures and joint replacements. Medical tourists can expect to save up to 75% over U.S. prices.

El Salvador's tourism industry is growing as word spreads about its beautiful beaches, volcanoes, archaeological sites, and mountains. About the size of Massachusetts, vacationers can travel among the attractions in 40 minutes or less. Costs are lower than other Central American destinations such as Costa Rica.

El Salvador Medical Tourism offers comprehensive services to plan and facilitate medical tourism.

El Salvador Medical Tourism facilitates travel abroad for medical, surgical, and dental care. The company focuses on safety, quality, and personalized service.

Medical Tourism Economic Report-El Salvador

El Salvador is a land of amazing beauty and has experienced much growth over the last ten years. During this period, the country has adopted the US dollar as its currency (2001), continued to move towards a free-market democracy, became the first to ratify the Central America-Dominican Republic Free Trade Agreement (CAFTA) in 2006, engaged in a countrywide modernization, and became the third largest economy in Central America despite being the smallest country (total area of 8,123 square miles [21,040 sq km], about the size of the state of Massachusetts) in that region. Most U.S. cities can reach El Salvador by airline within 2 to 7 hours, English is the second language (Spanish is the official language of the nation), and the tourism market from the U.S. and other western countries is robust.

According to a recent report by the Ministry of Tourism, El Salvador received $411,135,773 USD in foreign currency in the first half of 2008 (annualized to $822 million USD or a 22.0% growth in earnings compared to 2007). The same report indicates that were 991,874 tourists during this same period (annualized to 1.9 million tourists or a 25.8% growth rate compared to 2007). Also, for the same period, the percentage distribution of tourists by region is: Central America, 62.12%; North America, 31.64%; Europe, 2.83%; South America, 2.30%. Within the Central American market niche, the number of tourists from Guatemala (which it borders along with Honduras-which is third with 103,234 arrivals or 15.0% of the total) increased by 12.95% versus 2007. The U.S. was 2nd with 183,476 arrivals (360k when annualized) which was about 26.65% of the total number of tourists.

Recently, the country has been expanding capacity in the hospitality sector and currently has 7,282 rooms in 318 hotels throughout the country. It has some of the most interesting Mayan ruins in all of Central America, over 307 km of shoreline (with supposedly wonderful surfing!), majestic volcanoes, and beautiful cloud forests. El Salvador has a tropical climate with only two real seasons, the dry season (verano-from November to April), and the wet season (invierno-from May to October). Temperatures vary depending on the elevation in El Salvador with the coastal areas being the warmest, averaging between 22°C and 32°C throughout the year. El Salvador's central international airport, Aeropuerto Internacional Comalapa, is about 50 km southeast of San Salvador (the capital city) and is a major Central and Latin American hub (with direct flights to North American cities like Los Angeles, New York and San Francisco).

The Chamber of Exporters of Health Services of El Salvador (Exportsalud), the Export Promotion Agency of El Salvador (Exporta), the Investment Promotion Agency (Proesa), and Ministry of Tourism (Mitur) are pursuing medical tourism in this country. These include savings of up to 75% over U.S. prices and many U.S.-trained physicians in the areas of dentistry, gastroenterology, bariatric surgery, ophthalmology, general surgery, plastic surgery, and orthopedics, providing services such as dental implants, gastric and weight loss surgeries, ophthalmologic care, hernia repair, cosmetic procedures, and laparoscopic orthopedic procedures.

Economic Facts

According to the CIA Factbook, it is expected that economic growth will decelerate in 2009 due to the global slowdown and

El Salvador's dependence on exports to the US (its most important trading partner, receiving 65.4% of its exports and providing 46.3% of its imports). In addition (similar to Mexico), El Salvador leads the region in remittances per capita from Salvadorans living abroad (primarily from the U.S.) with inflows equivalent to nearly all export income (in 2005, remittances reached $2.83 billion). An estimated 1.5 to two million Salvadorans reside in the United States (estimated in 2007 as 3% of the foreign born residents), many of them illegally (in 2007, it is estimated that only 30.1% are naturalized citizens). The total population of El Salvador is estimated at 7,066,403 and growing at a slightly positive rate of 1.679%..

The GDP (using the purchasing power parity model) of El Salvador was $45.34 billion USD (using 2008 estimates) which equals out to around $6,400 per capita (PPP). GDP was growing at a 3.2% rate and GDP per capita was growing at a 2.3% rate back in 2008. In the most recent estimates from 2008, the services sector makes up 64.1% of the GDP, with industry (primarily manufacturing) making up 24.7%, and agriculture making up 11.2%. The labour force is composed of approximately 2.958 million Salvadorans (by industry in 2006 would be: services 58%, industry 23%, and agriculture 19%) and the unemployment rate is 6.3% according to 2008 official rates (there is quite a bit of underemployment in El Salvador).

Healthcare Facts

The ratio of physicians per 1,000 population in El Salvador increased in the last 5 years from. to 1.22 (but still low compared to an OECD of 3.1) and now the country has at least 7,298 registered physicians (from 2002 numbers). The ratio of nurses per 1,000 population however is which is significantly lower than the OECD average of 9.7. The number of dentists in El Salvador per 1,000 population is surprisingly high at which is comparable to Canada which has a rate of. According to WHO statistics, the total expenditures on health per capita was $387 USD and total expenditures on health as a percentage of GDP was 7.0% (in 2006). This ranks as 83rd in the world in health expenditure per capita but overall El Salvador ranks 115th in the world in health system performance.

According to some commentators, the reason for this low ranking is that El Salvador has something akin to two distinct health care systems. The first is the government run system (approximately 41.8% of the total healthcare expenditures) that is designed for the poor, employs overworked doctors, uses out of date equipment (it was estimated in 2000 that 63% of hospitals in El Salvador are over 30 years old), and don't have as much time to spend with each patient. This system was made up of 610 establishments in 2000 (30 hospitals, with a total of 4,677 hospital beds, 357 health units, 171 "health houses", 52 Rural Nutrition Centres, and 1 clinic).

The second system is a completely private based system (using a Fee For Service or FFS approach) that uses qualified doctors, state of the art technology, and the doctors spend ample time with their patients, which unfortunately, only the affluent can afford (58.2% of healthcare expenditures, with households contributing 97% out-of-pocket). Most of these private sector clinics, general and speciality hospitals are concentrated in the country's capital and other large cities. Some of the main hospitals are the Hospital de Diagnostico, Hospital de la Mujer, Centre Pediatrico, and Centre Ginecologico. The main insurers in this region are SISA, Pan American Life, ASESUISA, and Salud Total.

El Salvador is in the process of receiving recommendations from Joint Commission International, Trent Accreditation Scheme and Accreditation Canada to evaluate options for international accreditation of its hospitals and speciality clinics.

Impacts to Other Industries

An interesting aspect of the medical tourism hopes of El Salvador was the announcement by a medical tourism firm that it was working with a major insurer to design a low-cost health plan (coverage might cost a family as little as $200 USD per month) that would offer limited benefits (sometimes referred to as a "mini-med" plan) where the benefit would be a specific sum of money. Mini-med plans typically provide coverage for a limited number of physician visits each year, a limited amount of inpatient care, and some basic coverage for prescription drugs (the benefits are typically capped at a maximum of about $25,000 USD annually). Because these policies pay a relatively low amount, patients bear a significant cost-sharing amount for medical care which can provide an incentive to avoid high out-of-pocket costs.

The unique aspect of the plan was that it would reimburse patients the same amount for each particular service, regardless of where it is performed geographically. Therefore, a patient would pay significantly lower out-of-pocket costs by going abroad for treatment. The firm was planning on a health plan targeted at El Salvadorans living in the United States. These beneficiaries would receive a limited number of primary care visits (in the U.S.) and could travel to El Salvador for covered major medical needs.

Also, an interesting trend is El Salvador's market in reproductive tourism (includes IVF procedures and surrogacy options). Driving this trend are the number of fertility specialist practicing outside the U.S., the state-of-the-art facilities in countries like India, Mexico, and El Salvador, the high surrogacy costs in the U.S. ($80,000 USD or more), and the existing legal liabilities (in the U.S., there are no legal guarantees that the surrogate will not later attempt to keep the baby). It was reported in 2008 that surrogate pregnancies (currently estimated to be a $1 billion USD business in India) only cost around $25,000 USD in India (it is assumed to be similar in El Salvador), plus there are limited legal issues and the arrangements are also easier to manage.

Summary

El Salvador has a lot going for it when looking to grow the medical tourism market particularly in the beauty of its location, friendly populace, and western-trained and English-speaking providers. However, it still has some obstacles to overcome including more robust and mature competitors in other Latin American countries, the disparity in its' health system, and a reputation for violence and crime. However, there is the possibility it could carve out chunks of market share rapidly in areas like full mouth restoration and reproductive tourism, among others. Finally, medical tourism in El Salvador received a big PR boost when a Fox News Radio Anchor/Reporter (Lori Lundin) wrote a multi-piece blog (in 2008) off of the Fox News online site about her experiences in the country. Lori's husband Doug needed a full mouth restoration and was quoted a price of $60,000 USD by a U.S. dental surgeon. They then received quotes from several countries and decided upon El Salvador and paid $19,000 USD for the procedure plus a few thousand for travel expenses (a savings of over $30,000 USD!). They describe the country and the people in a very complimentary light and bemoan the fact that the country still has a reputation for being unsafe. This is a great piece and is worth its weight in gold for marketing medical tourism in this beautiful country.

El Salvador

El Salvador is the capital city of the nation of San Salvador. The valley where it is located was earlier known as "El Valle de las Hamacas" (The Valley of the Hammocks) because of its high seismic activity. San Salvador is the second largest city in Central America. Home to nearly 2.2 million people it is home to one-third of El Salvador 's population and one-half of the country's wealth.

History

The origins of the city can be traced to before the Spanish Conquest. It is near the present location of San Salvador that the Pipil tribes established their capital, Cuscatlán. Although the city was founded in the 16th century, it was rebuilt and changed locations twice afterwards. Originally founded in what is now the colonial town of Suchitoto, north of the present-day city, it was moved to the Valle de Las Hamacas, which boasted more space and more fertile land, thanks to the pristine Acelhuate River.

Culture

Spanish is the main language in El Salvador. The Roman Catholic religion plays an important role in the Salvadorian culture. Important foreign personalities in El Salvador were the Jesuit priests and professors Ignacio Ellacuria, Ignacio Martin-Baro and Segundo Montes. Painting, ceramics and textile goods are the main manual artistic expressions. Writers Francisco Gavidia (1863–1955), Salarrue (Salvador Salazar Arrue) (1899-1975), Claudia Lars, Alfredo Espino, Pedro Geoffroy, Manlio Argueta, José Roberto Cea and poet Roque Dalton are among the most important artists to stem from El Salvador.

Tourism

Parks

San Salvador has the large urban park, the "Parque de los Pericos". There is another park called Parque Cuscatlan, which is very elegant, with lights, trees and paths. Popular with locals, the beautiful botanical gardens of La Laguna showcase much native fauna. Zoologico Nacional and Parque Saburo Hirao (native plants) are in the SE part of the city by the old Presidential House. Los Planes De Renderos, 1000 meters above sea level, the mountain offers a spectacular view of San Salvador, and is a popular oasis for locals from the hectic city.

Entertainment

San Salvador has several entertainment venues. You can go to restaurants, bars, clubs, casinos, or if you are travelling with kids you can go to the cinemas, bowling, bingo, and arcades.

The trendiest night spot to visit is called Zona Rosa. Some of the best hotels are located there, including the Sheraton Presidente as well as one of the most luxurious hotels in Central America, the Hilton Princess. Although Zona Rosa doesn't cover a large area, it's home to many exclusive, upscale bars and nightclubs, and the best restaurants in town.

Beaches

Between 1996 and 2006, 7.3 million visitors mainly Central Americans and Europeans along the Pacific Oceans coast line. Most of the North American and European tourists are seeking out El Salvador's fine beaches to relax and for surfing. Among the best recommended beach resorts is the Casa de Mar Hotel & Villas, Hacienda Del Pueblo, Rancho Buena Vista and many more.

Medical Tourism Fame

Its move toward democracy and its proximity to the United States are putting El Salvador on the fast track to becoming a medical tourism hub. Private hospitals in the country have state of the art facilities and are staffed with qualified doctors who are able to spend ample time with patients. The most popular procedures sought by medical tourists are cosmetic surgery and dental treatments, both of which you can get for a fraction of the cost compared to the U.S.

Language

The official language of El Salvador is Spanish, however English is spoken by some throughout the country.

Climate

El Salvador's climate is tropical with two seasons: the wet season (May to October) and the dry season (November to April). The temperature depends on the elevation. Coastal areas tend to be hotter with average temperatures between 72°F and 90°F (22°C and 32°C) year round. The central areas have varying temperatures, which can be as high as 82°F (28°C) and as low as 66°F (19°C).

Visa/Entrance Requirements

U.S. and Canadian citizens do not need a visa in order to enter El Salvador, but you must have a passport (valid for 6 months from the date of entry). You must also buy a tourist card (valid for 30 days, but you can request up to 90 days) for $10 USD upon entry. If you leave the country by land before the expiration of the tourist card you may return without having to pay another $10.

Airlines Servicing this Destination

There is one international airport in El Salvador. It is located in San Salvador and is called the Cuscatlan International Airport (SAL).

The following airlines have flights to El Salvador:

* Delta
* Air Transat (seasonal)
* American Airlines
* Continental Airlines
* Copa Airlines
* Mexicana
* TACA.

Hotels

El Salvador has many options for the budget traveller. A private room in a hostel or guesthouse ranges from $10 to $25 USD per person per night and 3 star hotels start at $60.

There are also luxurious hotels in the country, one of which won the 2005 World Travel Award. 5 star hotels are comparatively cheaper than in the U.S. or Western Europe. They range from $95 to $200 USD.

Currency

El Salvador has two currencies:

* United States Dollar (USD).
* El Salvador Colon (SVC).

  The exchange rate of U.S. dollars to El Salvadorian colones is $1 USD to 8.75 SVC.
* The colon is no longer being printed in an attempt to make the U.S. dollar the only currency circulating in the country.

Communicating Home

The international access code for El Salvador is 503.

In order to call El Salvador from the U.S. or Canada you must dial 011 (exit code), then 503 (country code for the El Salvador), and then the phone number (eight digits. All fixed numbers start with the number 2). To call a cell phone in El Salvador from the U.S. or Canada you must dial 011 + 503 + phone number (eight digits, starts with the number seven). In order to call the U.S. or Canada from El Salvador you must dial 00 + 1 + area code + phone number.

Cyber-cafes are widely available in major cities and towns. Larger hotels and most private hospitals throughout the country offer Broadband Internet connection.

Sightseeing

El Salvador is a naturalist's paradise. La Libertad is 21 miles (34 km) south of San Salvador and is a popular tourist spot. It has beautiful beaches and offers some of the world's best surfing. Just west of La Libertad is Zunzal, where international surfing competitions are held. Other nature sites include the cloud forests of the Parque Nacional Montecristo-El Trifinio, the Volcano of San Miguel, the Laguna Botanical Gardens (in San Salvador), and many hiking trails. Fans of Pompeii and Santorini will be pleased with the Joya de Ceren Archaeological Site. In 600 AD, there was a volcanic eruption that buried the farming community of the Joya de Ceren, which was a prehispanic culture. The community is so well preserved that visitors to this site can see the day to day lifestyles and infrastructure of the Joya de Ceren people.

Shopping

San Salvador has many markets including the Mercado Cuartel, which is the busiest market in the city; the Santa Tecla Market, where you can buy many items from food to pinatas; and the Ilopango market, which is ideal for shopping for handicrafts. If the hustle and bustle of the market does not suit your style, San Salvador has many shopping malls that are frequented by middle class and wealthy Salvadorians and international travellers.

Nightlife and the Arts

Upscale nightlife is localized to the Zona Rosa area of San Salvador, which features venues for salsa dancing, live music, and Mariachi bands. Popular night spots include Senor Frog's, Stanza, Club Code, Guadalajara Grill, and La Luna. Make sure that you take a taxi to and from your hotel to the clubs. Do not walk or take public transportation, especially at night. One of El Salvador's most famous artists, Fernando Llort, who has galleries in the U.S. and Europe also has a gallery in San Salvador. Featured pieces are priced to fit all types of budgets and include original oils, ceramic tiles, tablets, prints, and framed prints. Those who enjoy a nice stroll through a museum should visit the David J. Guzman National Museum of Anthropology, The Museo de la Palabray La Imagen (the Museum of Words and Images), The Natural History Museum of El Salvador, the Zoological Park, and the Museum of Art. For theatre buffs, San Salvador is home to the National Theatre, which is the oldest theatre in Central America.

Medical Tourism Association?

The Medical Tourism Association is the first international non-profit association made up of the top international hospitals, healthcare providers, medical travel facilitators, insurance companies, and other affiliated companies and members with the common goal of promoting the highest level of quality of healthcare to patients in a global environment. Our Association promotes the interests of its healthcare provider and medical tourism facilitators members. The Medical Tourism Association has three tenets: Transparency, Communication and Education.

Transparency

The Medical Tourism Association seeks to provide transparency in both quality of care and pricing. Every day we see more and more that the globalization of healthcare has created a very flat world. We exchange technology, information, communication, physicians and patients. In order to ensure patient safety, it is our goal to create a transparency about the quality of healthcare that can be found in each country. With this, it is increasingly important to create a transparency in pricing as well so patients travelling overseas for care can be sure of what they are receiving without hidden costs or unforeseen expenses. The Medical Tourism Association is also working on the Quality of Care Project, which will change the way we look at the reporting of global healthcare statistics and the quality of care available at hospitals around the world.

Communication

The Members of the Medical Tourism Association agree that communication is the key to success, particularly with respect to ensuring positive patient outcomes. Last year, the Founders of the Medical Tourism Association polled international healthcare providers and found that each provider has the same concerns with the increasing globalization of healthcare. Why should we all try to resolve these concerns individually instead of collectively? The members of the Medical Tourism Association have agreed to put competition aside and work together to resolve the issues one by one and to work together to address them as they arise. We have created a forum for communication for all of the actors in the global healthcare environment. We have committees that work together to address issues such as legal, economic, patient financing, Errors and Omissions (E&O) insurance, communication with insurance companies, media support and more.

Education

Although we live in a world where information is at our fingertips, there are so many people who lack the information that they can receive the highest quality of care outside of their home country. Some patients in countries like the United States, Canada, and the United Kingdom have a lack of access to healthcare due to high cost and high wait times. Patients in some other regions as in some parts of Africa and the Middle East do not have access to high quality of care in their own country and need to look elsewhere. Some patients just would like to travel outside of their country for healthcare to incorporate high quality of care with a holiday and tourism. Regardless of the reason, patients need education and information to understand what they should look for in finding a provider overseas and considerations that should be taken seriously to ensure patients safety. As insurance companies continue to incorporate global healthcare and medical tourism options into their benefit plans and domestic healthcare providers are required to treat patients for aftercare when patients return to their home country, education is required to accomplish this seamlessly. The Medical Tourism Association strives to provide education to anyone with any interest in this industry using various means: the media, conferences, and through the Medical Tourism Magazine. The Medical Tourism Magazine is a monthly trade journal aimed to provide a wealth of information for anyone interested in or affected by the globalization of healthcare.

Our Mission

* To raise awareness of the high level of quality healthcare available in various countries.
* To promote positive and stable growth of the Medical Tourism and Global Healthcare Industry with a strong focus on Transparency and Communication.
* To provide an unbiased source of information for patients, insurance companies and employers about top hospitals, their quality of care and outcomes.
* To protect the reputation of Medical Tourism from disreputable hospitals and healthcare providers which may not have the same level of quality healthcare and standards.
* To serve as one voice for purposes of dealing with the government organizations and the media to protect the reputation of the Medical Tourism Association's members.
* To promote and provide a forum for communication and to increase connectivity between patients, healthcare providers, and insurance companies.
* To seek out future affiliated industries and technologies that will allow international healthcare providers to operate more efficiently in the global healthcare industry.
* To educate patients, insurance companies, agents, brokers, consultants and physicians from around the world about the growth of medical tourism and the globalization of healthcare.

Non-Profit Status

The Medical Tourism Association is an international non-profit organization which has been designated for 501(C) status by the Internal Revenue of the United States Government. Section 501(c) of the Internal Revenue Code provides for the exemption of business leagues, which are not organized for profit and no part of the net earnings of which inures to the benefit of any private shareholder or individual. The Medical Tourism Association does not have shareholders or investors.

As provided by www.IRS.gov, a business league is an association of persons having some common business interest, the purpose of which is to promote such common interest and not to engage in a regular business of a kind ordinarily carried on for profit. Trade associations and professional associations are business leagues. To be exempt, a business league's activities must be devoted to improving business conditions of one or more lines of business as distinguished from performing particular services for individual persons.

Medical Tourism Magazine

The Medical Tourism Magazine has launched its online version of the Medical Tourism Magazine at. Readers of the online version of the magazine will be able to read the full version of the magazine online for free and view past issues.

The Medical Tourism Magazine is a bi-monthly Medical Tourism industry magazine in both print and electronic versions. Readers can sign up for a free online subscription below or purchase an annual hard copy subscription, by clicking here, Annual Magazine Subscription.

The Medical Tourism Magazine will address important issues affecting the Medical Tourism industry and have a primary focus on the quality of healthcare available at leading international hospitals. Each issue of the medical tourism magazine will cover the world as a whole, but also have a special inside focus on one specific country. We are always looking for stories, articles, authors and input for our magazine.

Magazine will address issues such as;

1. Quality of Health Care Overseas,
2. Legal Issues Surrounding Medical Tourism,
3. The American, UK and Canadian Health Care Crisis and the opportunities for Medical Tourism in these countries,
4. What Foreign Patients look for in overseas hospitals and providers offering Medical Tourism,
5. Specific Country Focus each issue,
6. Issues International Insurance Companies, Employers and Healthcare companies should consider when entering the Medical Tourism Industry.

The magazines distribution is currently in the thousands and is distributed to International Hospitals, International Health Insurance Carriers in the Middle East, US, UK and Canada, healthcare providers throughout the world, the travel industry, directly to potential medical tourism patients considering going overseas for surgery, and anyone interested in the industry. The magazine also is distributed to a majority of the health plans which administer Self Funded Employer health plans in the U.S.

Medical Tourism Association's Medical Tourism Magazine Announces Issue 10 Special Issue: What Patients Are Saying About You

West Palm Beach, FL, June 05, 2009 —(PR.com)— The Medical Tourism Association is pleased to share their newly released Issue 10 Special Issue: What Patients Are Saying About You with you. Please go to the Medical Tourism Magazine website to view. Scroll down to Issue 10 Special Issue: What Patients Are Saying About You. Highlights from this Issue Include:

It's All About the Patient

From Customer Service on the hospital side and on the facilitator side, to the greater underlying issues of Trust as a whole, medical tourism offers significant opportunities for us to step back and take a look at our service offerings to patients. Only then are we ready to create marketable and successful programs. And after doing so, how do we judge our successes?

By Renee-Marie Stephano

Other articles include: Are Your Patients Wandering Over to Your Competition? 6 Action Tips to Stop Them in Their Tracks…

In an economy such as ours we need to make each patient opportunity count. That means being quicker, smarter and more caring than our competition. Below are six action tips that are guaranteed to keep your patients from falling ill to wanderlust. Because, let's face it, if we don't take care of our patients, someone else will.

By Bill Cook

Patient Survey: The Medical Tourism Association has released preliminary results from its first patient surveys in the Medical Tourism Industry. This survey is extremely important to the solid growth of the medical tourism industry by providing a better understanding why patients are travelling and where they are travelling to as well as insight. Creating Profitability Through Service Excellence ~ Do You Really Know What Your Customers Think?

In the words of Peter Drucker, widely considered the father of modern management, "Quality in a service or product is not what you put into it. It is what the client or customer gets out of it." How does the medical tourism industry measure business success? The obvious answer is through financial statements and growing patient volume.

By Tonya Walton

The Medical Tourism Magazine is a bi-monthly Medical Tourism industry magazine in both print and electronic versions. Readers can sign up for a free online subscription below or purchase an annual hard copy subscription. The Medical Tourism Magazine will address important issues affecting the Medical Tourism industry and have a primary focus on the quality of healthcare available at leading international hospitals. Each issue of the medical tourism magazine will cover the world as a whole, but also have a special inside focus on one specific country. We are always looking for stories, articles, authors and input for our magazine.

The Medical Tourism Association is the first international non-profit association made up of the top international hospitals, healthcare providers, medical travel facilitators, insurance companies, and other affiliated companies and members with the common goal of promoting the highest level of quality of healthcare to patients in a global environment. Their Association promotes the interests of its healthcare provider and medical tourism facilitators members. The Medical Tourism Association has three tenets: Transparency, Communication and Education

Medical Tourism Association Presents Health Tourism Magazine

With the increased awareness and incorporation of health and wellness into our lives and the importance of establishing a balance among one's mind, body and soul, the Medical Tourism Association, which you can find at http://www.Medical Tourism Association.com, is launching its new enlightening publication, Health Tourism Magazine. This is a bimonthly online publication, dedicated to the education and raised awareness of health, wellness, fitness, nutrition, alternative and medical wellness issues at http://www. Health Tourism Magazine.com. With our business to consumer approach to the promotion of each issue of our magazine, Health Tourism Magazine will focus on all areas of health and wellness which may not only complement the treatment plans for patients receiving surgical procedures, but also provide the opportunity for an improvement of the quality of life for both the patients and their companions.

With the same focus on quality, informative content and chic style as its "sister" magazine, Medical Tourism Magazine, each issue of the Health Tourism Magazine will cover topics such as integrative, alternative, homeopathic and preventative medicines together with overall spa and wellness topics.

The Medical Tourism Association, also known as the Global Healthcare Association, is the first international non-profit association made up of the top international hospitals, healthcare providers, medical travel facilitators, insurance companies, and other affiliated companies and members with the common goal of promoting the highest level of quality of healthcare to patients in a global environment. Our Association promotes the interests of its healthcare provider and medical tourism facilitators members. The Medical Tourism Association has three tenets: Transparency, Communication and Education. To find more information please go to http://www. Medical Tourism Association.com.

Health Tourism Magazine is a monthly online magazine, dedicated to educating and raising awareness of health, wellness, alternative and medical wellness issues. With our business to consumer approach to promoting the magazine, Health Tourism Magazine will focus on all areas of health and wellness which compliment surgical procedures. As the "sister" magazine to Medical Tourism Magazine, each issue of the Health Tourism Magazine will cover topics such as integrative, alternative, homeopathic and preventative medicines together with overall spa and wellness topics.

Monthly Medical Tourism Magazine for Thailand

The Health Travel Industry Research Society (HTRIS Thailand) has launched a monthly publication to promote Thailand's medical travel industry.

"Medica Tourism Magazine highlights the very best of Thailand's medical, hospitality, tourism, travel and wellness industries," said Secretary-General Chatree Niramitvijit. "We are working with industry representatives to inform the world about the best offerings, promotion discounts and package deals." The full-colour, 120-page glossy magazine is distributed to more than 60 countries every month through the Kingdom's embassies and consulates, chambers of commerce, trade promotion offices and tourism information centres throughout the world.

HTRIS, a non-profit private sector initiative, was established to focus on information for the improvement and promotion of Thailand's international health service industry, particularly the hospital, hospitality, tourism, travel, wellness and support industries such as transport, insurance, translation, pharmacies, information, retail and entertainment.

Medical Tourism in Singapore

The small state of Singapore is known for its very stringent laws and regulations particularly in the areas involving cleanliness. These regulations are carried over to Singapore's ultra-high quality levels in healthcare and world-class facilities, making it an ideal destination for medical travellers who are looking for modern infrastructure, a clean and structured environment, and an English-speaking populace.

Singapore Healthcare System

The World Health Organization ranked Singapore as the 6th best health system in the world, much higher than the United States and Canada. Singapore hospitals and health centres are either government or public facilities like the Singapore General Hospital, or are privately owned like the Raffles and Parkway hospitals.

These hospitals offer top-of-the-line quality healthcare services and facilities, serviced by English-speaking and internationally trained medical practitioners and staff. Singapore health facilities receive local accreditation from the Singapore Health Promotion Board, the Singapore Laboratory Accreditation System (SINGLAS), the Singapore Accreditation Council (SAC) and the Ministry of Health.

Most of these hospitals are also accredited by top international regulation and standardization bodies. Medical practitioners' standards and practices are regulated by the Singapore Medical Council, Singapore Nursing Board, Singapore Dental Board, Pharmacy Board and the Laboratory Board. The Health Sciences Authority and the Singapore Accreditation Council controls and regulates the certification of medical devices and other health products.

Singapore Top Hospitals

In 2006, there were already 29 hospitals and speciality centres catering to medical travellers, offering ultra-high quality healthcare and accommodation facilities serviced by 7,000 doctors and over 15,000 registered nurses. These medical facilities have international accreditation from the Joint Commission International (JCI), ISO and OHSAS. Singapore has a number of JCI-accredited hospitals. These include the following top hospitals:

Alexandra Hospital

First accreditation by the JCI on July 2005 and was renewed on October 2008. The facility started out as the British Military Hospital during the 1930's and was renamed Alexandra after it was handed over to the government in 1971.

National Heart Centre of Singapore

First accreditation by the JCI on October 2005 and was renewed on July 2008. It is Singapore's major health centre for cardiovascular and other cardiac needs catering to both local and foreign patients.

National University Hospital

First accreditation by the JCI on August 2004 and was renewed on July 2007. It is the only university hospital in Singapore that offers international acute tertiary care.

Parkway Hospitals Singapore Pvt. Ltd.

The Parkway Hospitals is a group of three JCI-accredited health facilities which includes the East Shore Hospital, the Gleneagles Hospital and the Mount Elizabeth hospital. These are private healthcare facilities offering local and international health services with tie-ups to healthcare institutions in the Australia, UK and the United States.

Raffles Hospital Private Limited

First accreditation by the JCI on December 2008. It is an international patient's centre that offers a full range of personalized and specialized healthcare services.

Singapore General Hospital

First accreditation by the JCI on July 2005 and was renewed on July 2008. Established in 1821, it is the flagship hospital for the public sector and is the oldest and largest tertiary hospital offering a full range of health specialities.

Institute of Mental Health/Woodbridge Hospital

First accreditation by the JCI on July 2005 and was renewed on July 2008. It is the only institution in Singapore that provides multi-disciplinary tertiary psychiatric services.

Common Treatments Done in Singapore and Comparative Costs

Singaporean hospitals and healthcare facilities offer a wide array of procedures and services for medical travellers, which include but are not limited to the following:

* Orthopedic Surgery (hip and knee replacements, etc.),
* Cardiac Surgeries (heart bypass, valve replacements, etc.),
* Cancer and Oncology,
* Diagnostic/Investigations,
* Cosmetic Surgery,
* Non-surgical Rejuvenation (botox, microdermabrasion, etc.),
* Dental Services (surgeries, dental implants, etc.),
* Bariatric Surgeries,
* Eye/Ophthalmology (LASIK, Cataract Surgeries, etc.),
* Alternative Medicine,
* Health Spas.

The following are cost comparisons between Medical procedures in Singapore and equivalent procedures in the United States:

	USA	Costa Rica	Average Savings
Cardica Surgery			
Heart Bypass	$55,000-$130,000	$13,000-$18,500	70-80%
Heart Valve Replacement	$130,000-$160,000	$12,000-13,000	90-92%
Coronary Angioplasty	$42,000-$57,000	$11,500-$13,000	70-77%
Coronary Angiography	$5,500-$6,000	$1,300-$1,500	70-75%
Orthopedic Surgery			
Hip Replacement	$24,000-$43,000	$12,000-$16,000	50-65%
Hip Resurfacing	$45,000-$50,000	$13,000-$15,000	70-75%
Hysterectomy	$19,000-$21,000	$5,500-$6,500	70-75%
Knee Replacement	$38,000-$42,000	$12,000-$13,500	65-70%
Spinal Fusion	$60,000-$63,000	$8,000-$10,000	80-85%

Plastic and Reconstructive Surgery			
Stem Cell Transplant	$200,000-$250,000	$72,000-$90,000	60-65%
Face Lift (Rhytidectomy)	$19,000-$21,000	$6,500-$7,500	60-65%
Breast Augmentation/Reduction (Mammoplasty)	$9,000-$11,000	$7,000-$9,000	18-20%
Liposuction (Lipoplasty)	$14,000-$16,000	$4,500-$5,500	60-65%
Nose Surgery (Rhinoplasty)	$6,500-$7,500	$3,500-$4,500	40-46%
Tummy Tuck (Abdominoplasty)	$8,000-$9,000	$6,000-$6,500	25-40%
Eye/Ophthalmology			
LASIK Eye Surgery	$2,000-$2,500	$1,500-$2,000	20-25%
Eyelid Surgery	$6,500-$7,500	$3,500-$4,000	45-50%
General and Cosmetic Dentistry			
Root Canal	$800-$1200	$350-$900	25-60%

Malpractice and Liabilities Laws in Singapore

Doctors in Singapore are required to carry medical malpractice insurance but these are not as expensive as compared to the US, the cost of which are recovered through the payments for medical procedures and treatments as shouldered by patients.

Pros

The WHO ranked the quality of healthcare in Singapore as 6th in the world. Singapore is a highly urbanized, orderly and spotless country so medical tourists should not expect the same chaotic environment that are typical in other Asian destinations. There are several JCI-certified hospitals and healthcare facilities in Singapore. English is one of Singapore's official languages and is spoken by all doctors and medical staff Although the cost for medical procedures in Singapore is not as low compared to India or Thailand, the prices are still lower then Western Europe and the USA.

Cons

Medical procedures and treatments done in Singapore are more expensive compared to other Asian medical tourism destinations such as Thailand, India and Malaysia. The climate in Singapore is hot and humid, which may be uncomfortable to most westerners particularly during the post-procedure and recovery stages Prices of goods, transportation and accommodation in Singapore are relatively more expensive than other Asian countries For US and Canadian medical tourists, travel times to Singapore are very long.

Travelling to Singapore

Non-stop or single-stop flights are available from various destinations to Singapore through the flagship Singapore Airlines and other international airlines.

Average estimated travel time in hours;

From/To	*Singapore*
New York City	18
Los Angeles	16
Australia (Sydney)	7
Indonesia (Jakarta)	2
Philippines (Manila)	3.5
UAE (Dubai)	7
Toronto	21
Vancouver	18
United Kingdom	14

Singapore Entry and Exit Requirements

As a general requirement for entry and exit to Singapore, all foreign visitors are required the following items: passport/travel document with a minimum validity of 6 months; a return or onward ticket; entry requirements for the visitor's next destination; sufficient funds that would support their stay and purpose in Singapore; and required applicable Visa or pass as described below.

Visiting nationals from the UK, Australia, Canada, USA and EU countries do not require a Visa upon entry and will be issued a Social Visit Pass upon arrival, provided that they comply with the general requirements as described above. The visit pass is valid for 30 days upon arrival. Other countries listed in Singapore's Assessment Level I and Level II countries are required to have either a Business Visa or a Social Visit Visa prior to entry to Singapore.

Should there be a need for an extension in stay, or if the required pre-procedure and post-procedure duration requirements would go beyond 30 days, the medical traveller should arrange for an extension pass (valid up to 90 days) from the Embassy of the Republic of Singapore or the Consulate-General of Singapore before leaving the

United States or Canada. If the need for extension is determined while already in Singapore, special permits can be arranged and obtained from the Immigrations and Checkpoints Authority of Singapore.

Medical Tourism in Hungary

Hungary has become a prime destination for health travellers from the UK, Germany, Austria, Italy, Scandinavia and other Western European countries seeking affordable dental and cosmetic procedures. The price of treatments in Hungary is usually much lower of what you would have to pay in Western Europe.

Hungary Healthcare System

Medical travellers are assured of a high-quality healthcare system in Hungary as it was patterned after the National Health System of Great Britain when it was established in 1945. The systems in place are all similar except for the long waiting times typical of what patients experience in the UK.

Doctors and medical professionals are registered with the *Orvosi Kamara* of the Hungarian Chamber of Medicine, which provides permission to these professionals to practice their trade. Dentists' and dental surgeon qualifications are controlled by the Hungarian Dental Council, which practices very stringent and comprehensive training that has longer duration than what is practiced in the UK. These qualifications are recognized by the European Union, allowing these doctors to qualify working in any of the EU countries. Unlike in other countries where dentists are specialized in only one area, Hungarian dentists are trained and qualified in all aspects of dentistry. Most top quality hospitals and clinics in Hungary are operated by the private sector although there are some prominent hospitals which are state owned. Private hospitals and clinics usually maintain modern medical equipment, facilities and technologies due to the stringent requirements set by their German and Austrian clients who have been travelling to Hungary for healthcare for over fifteen years. These hospitals, clinics are locally accredited and licensed by the Hungarian Ministry of Health and the State National Health Commission and Medical Service. Hungary is yet to have a JCI-accredited facility, although these hospitals are recognized by the Care Quality Commission in the UK and the rest of the European Union and some have been certified by the International Organization for Standardization.

Top Clinics and Hospitals in Hungary

Javorszky Odon Korhazat Hospital : Located in the municipality of Vac, the Javorszky Odon Hospital is a community hospital with 847 beds and 12 departments and 18 medical specialities that caters to more than 22,000 inpatients and 150,000 outpatients per year. It is the only health care institution in this region that provides acute care. The hospital is ISO certified and has partnered with the Novant Health Triad Region (NHTR) of North Carolina. It is considered as a model hospital for Hungary by the Ministry of Welfare.

Buda Health Centre : Located in Budapest, the Buda Health Centre is the leading institution in Hungary that caters to all aspects of spinal disease through private or state-financed healthcare options.

Aesthetica International Medical Centre : Established in 2005 in the heart of Budapest's Bank Centre, the Aesthetica International is the leading, ISO-certified medical centre offering various services in the fields of cosmetic and plastic surgeries, dermatology, mesotheraphy and other related procedures. It is a subsidiary of the Proportzia Premium Medical Centres in Israel.

FirstMed Centres Kft. : FirstMed Centres are private health facilities that are affiliated with the American Clinics International, Inc. It is a multi-disciplinary international and local health facility that offers physical, family medicine, gynecology, prenatal and orthopedic care. ProHair Transplant Clinic ProHair is located in Budapest and is the leading national institution dealing with hair loss and balding for all sexes and aims to perform extensive research and help educate the general public about the alopecia or hair loss disease. The clinic is operated by a team of leading plastic surgery and hair transplant doctors.

Common Treatments Done in Hungary and Comparative Costs

Hospitals and healthcare facilities in Hungary offer a wide array of procedures and services for medical travellers, which include but are not limited to the following:

* Plastic surgery
* Aesthetic procedures
* General Dentistry and Dental Surgeries
* Laboratory examinations
* Eye Surgery & Ophthalmology
* Dermatology

* Obesity and Weight Loss Surgery
* Hair Transplantation
* Radiological examinations
* Internal medicine
* General surgery
* Gynecology and Obstetrics.

The following are cost comparisons between Medical procedures in Hungary and equivalent procedures in Germany and the UK:

German Hospitals	***Hungary***	***Average***	***Savings***
Face Lift (rhytidectomy)	€3,800-$6,600	€2,100-€2,700	30%-60%
Breast Augmentation (Mammoplasty)	€3,100-$3,800	€1,800-€2,000	35%-50%
Nose Surgery (Rhinoplasty)	€3,400-€4,000	€1,350-€1,700	50%-65%
UK Hospitals	***Hungary***	***Average***	***Savings***
Plastic and Reconstructive Surgery			
Face Lift (rhytidectomy)	£7,300-£8,000	£2,100-£2,700	70%-80%
Breast Augmentation (Mammoplasty)	£4,800-£5,500	£1,800-£2,000	60%-70%
Tummy Tuck	£4,000-£4,800	£1,600-£1,900	50%-65%
Liposuction (lipoplasty)	£3,000-£3,700	£900-£1,000	65%-75%
Nose Surgery (Rhinoplasty)	£3,500-£4,500	£1,500-£2,300	35%-65%
Porcelain Bonded Crowns	£500	£180	60%-65%
Root Canal (per canal)	£200	£60	70%
Tooth Extraction	£90	£30	65%
Tooth Whitening	£475	£280	40%
Dental Implants	£1,900	£800	55%-60%

Malpractice and Liabilities Laws in Hungary

It is a requirement by Hungarian law that all medical and healthcare facilities should provide their doctors with insurance against malpractice claims. Although the number of cases are relatively small at 300 cases per year, these malpractice suits are for lesser sums compared to international standards. However, these figures are starting to rise in recent years, prompting insurance companies to increase their premiums on medical malpractice coverage.

Pros

* Premium dental and cosmetic surgery procedures at very cost-effective prices.
* State of the art medical, healthcare and diagnostic facilities comparable to top international standards.
* English and German speaking, highly trained and qualified medical specialists and staff.
* Affordable accommodations and favourable tourism destinations suitable for post-surgery recovery.
* Close proximity to the European and Middle Eastern countries make it a prime destination for medical travellers from these regions.

Cons

* Lack of International accreditation including the JCI in the majority of hospitals and clinics.
* There are a limited number of major hospitals catering to international patients. Most of the market is served by small clinics.
* Malpractice compensation is relatively low compared to Western Europe.

Entry and Exit Requirements to Hungary

Citizens of the European Union do not require an entry visa for a stay in Hungary of up to 90 days, as long as the passports carried by the passengers are still valid within 6 months from the date of entry.

Statistics for Medical Tourism in Hungary

Medical travellers from Austria and Germany have long been regular clients for Hungary's dental and surgical industry. A report by the BBC claimed that more than a million medical tourists from Austria go to Hungary for dental procedures each year, while 35,000 patients come from the UK.

Medical Tourism in Malaysia

Malaysia is one the fast emerging destinations for medical tourism in Asia for mostly Asian health travellers. According to the Association of Private Hospitals of Malaysia (APHM), the majority Malaysia's medical tourists come from Indonesia mainly due to the superior quality of healthcare that Malaysia offers. The same reason draws health travellers from other Asian countries like Bangladesh and Pakistan. Patients from richer Asian countries like Singapore and Japan, which are the second and third highest origins of medical travellers respectively, visit Malaysia due to lower prices of medical procedures.

Australians and people from the European Union are attracted to the low cost of medical procedures in Malaysia, while Middle Eastern medical travellers visit Malaysia for both the price and the quality of healthcare provided.

Travelling to Hungary

There are several major airline carriers travelling to Hungary from various countries of origin from across the globe. On top of that, Hungary is also accessible by land, sea and train from neighbouring European countries.

Average estimated travel time in hours

From/To	*Hungary*
London	2
Munich	1
Berlin	1
Vienna	1
Zurich	2
Geneva	2
Rome	2
Paris	2
Copenhagen	2
New York City	9

Healthcare System in Malaysia

The majority of hospitals offering services to medical tourists are privately owned institutions following internationally recognized standards in healthcare. Currently, there are at least 35 hospitals in Malaysia that are being geared for medical tourism. All are accredited locally by the Malaysian Medical Society for Quality of Health (MSQH) and are licensed by the Malaysian Ministry of Health. Most of these hospitals are accredited by international bodies including the International

Organization for Standardization (ISO) and the Joint Commissions International (JCI) among others, making them at par with medical institutions in western countries. Doctors and staff practicing at Malaysia international hospitals are English-speaking and internationally trained. Over 90 percent of these doctors were trained in the UK, USA or Australia, and in some cases are involved in international medical research.

Top Hospitals in Malaysia

* Penang Adventist Hospital.

Jalan Burma, Malaysia

First accredited by the JCI on November 2007. Established in 1924, this not-for-profit hospital is fully owned and controlled by a Malaysian company and has grown ever since as a tertiary healthcare institution using up to date medical equipment and procedures.

* Prince Court Medical Centre.

Kuala Lumpur, Malaysia

First accredited by the JCI on December 2008. Privately owned by Petronas, the hospital boasts of a 300-bed state-of-the art medical centre offering various healthcare services including cardiology, plastic surgery and wellness treatments.

* Twin Towers Medical Centre.

Kuala Lumpur, Malaysia

Located in the hearth of Kuala Lumpur as the in-house medical facility in the Petronas Twin Tower complex, this medical centre is the largest outpatient polyclinic in Malaysia's premiere commercial centre, catering to both local and international patients.

* Institute Jantung Negara National Heart Institute.

Also known as IJN, it is the leading heart institution in Malaysia offering advanced cardiovascular and thoracic health services to both adult and pediatric patients, working in conjunction with leading international medical organizations and using the latest techniques in heart care.

* International Specialist Eye Centre (ISEC).

Kuala Lumpur, Malaysia

First accredited by the JCI on February 2009. An ambulatory

surgical centre or ASC, ISEC is Malaysia's premiere centre for ophthalmology and eye care.

Treatments done in Malaysia and Comparative Costs

Hospitals and healthcare facilities in Malaysia offer a wide array of procedures and services for medical travellers, which include but are not limited to the following:

* Cosmetic and Reconstructive surgery
* Endocrinology
* Ear, Nose and Throat (ENT)
* General and Cosmetic Dentistry
* Gastroenterology
* General Surgery
* Dialysis and Nephrology
* Health Screening and Special Diagnostic Services
* Health Screening Packages
* Health rejuvenation packages
* Immunization and Vaccination Services
* Internal Medicine
* Obstetrics and Gynecology
* Ophthalmology
* Orthopedics
* Pediatrics
* Urology.

The following are cost comparisons between Medical procedures in Malaysia and equivalent procedures in the UK and the United States:

UK Hospitals	*Malaysia*	*Average*	*Savings*
Face Lift (rhytidectomy)	$11,000-$12,000	$2,500-$3,500	70%-77%
Breast Augmentation (Mammoplasty)	$7,000-$8,000	$3,000-$4,000	50%-57%
Breast Reduction	$8,000-$9,000	$3,000-$4,000	55%-63%
Breast Lift	$2,000-$3,000	$900-$1,000	55%-67%
Tummy Tuck	$6,000-$7,000	$2,000-$2,500	64%-67%
Liposuction (lipoplasty)	$5,000-$6,000	$2,000-$3.000	50%-60%
Nose Surgery (Rhinoplasty)	$5,500-$6,500	$2,000-$2,500	61%-64%

General and Cosmetic Dentistry			
Porcelain Bonded Crowns	$950-$1,000	$150-$200	80%-84%
Root Canal (per canal)	$300-$400	$200-$250	33%-38%
US Hospitals	Malaysia	Average	Savings
Medical Procedures			
Angioplasty	$55,000-$57,000	$7,500-$8,500	80%-86%
Heart Bypass	$120,000-$130,000	$11,500-$12,500	90%-91%
Heart-valve Replacement	$150,000-$160,000	$14,500-$15,500	90%-91%
Hip Replacement	$41,000-$43,000	$9,500-$10,500	75%-77%
Hysterectomy	$18,000-$20,000	$3,500-$4,500	77%-81%
Knee Replacement	$38,000-$40,000	$7,500-$8,500	78%-80%
Plastic and Reconstructive Surgery			
Face Lift (rhytidectomy)	$7,000-$9,000	$2,500-$3,500	61%-64%
Breast Augmentation (Mammoplasty)	$5,000-$8,000	$3,000-$4,000	40%-50%
Breast Reduction	$4,000-$6,000	$3,000-$4,000	25%-33%
Complete Liposuction (lipoplasty)	$4,000-$6,500	$2,000-$3.000	50%-53%
Nose Surgery (Rhinoplasty)	$5,500-$6,500	$2,000-$2,500	61%-63%
General and Cosmetic Dentistry			
Root Canal	$600-$1,000	$200-$250	67%-75%
Porcelain Crown	$600-$1,000	$150-$200	75%-80%

Malpractice and Liabilities Laws in Malaysia

Statistics from 2004 have indicated that at least 50 percent of private medical practitioners in Malaysia had no medical indemnity cover cover, although the Ministry of Health in Malaysia have declared an increasing trend in the amount of compensation paid by the Malaysian government for liability cases since the year 2000. At present, the Malaysian government follows the Tort system for the control and regulation of litigation cases due to medical malpractice of negligence, wherein compensation is paid only for proven negligent cases.

Pros

* State of the art medical, healthcare and diagnostic facilities.

* Competitive prices of medical procedures and treatments.
* English-speaking, highly trained and qualified medical specialists and staff.
* Strict adherence to internationally recognized quality medical standards.
* Affordable accommodations and favourable tourism destinations suitable for post-surgery recovery.

Cons

* Terrorist activities and kidnapping of tourists is still a primary concern particularly in certain areas in the country, which are geared for western visitors and tourists.

Travelling to Malaysia

There are six international airports in Malaysia catering to more than 35 international carriers from anywhere around the world, making it very accessible from neighbouring Asian countries as well as from outside the continent.

Average estimated travel time in hours

From/To	*Malaysia*
New York City	20
Los Angeles	19
London	12
Singapore	1
Jakarta	2
Dubai	7
Riyadh	7
Bangladesh	3
Pakistan	5
Tokyo	6.5
Sydney	8

Entry and Exit Requirements to Malaysia

There are various visa requirements to Malaysia depending on the country of origin. Length of stay is typically 1 to 3 months; however extensions may be available upon request to the Malaysian High Commission. The following is a brief summary of visa requirements from prominent nations where most medical tourists are coming from (October 2009):

* No Visa Requirements
* UK and British Commonwealth/protected countries
* United States of America
* Switzerland
* Netherlands
* No Visa Requirements depending on maximum length of stay:
* 3 months maximum.

Albania, Algeria, Argentina, Austria, Bahrain, Belgium, Brazil, Bosnia Herzegovina, Chile, Croatia, Cuba, Czech Republic, Denmark, Egypt, Finland, France, Germany, Hungary, Iceland, Italy, Japan, Jordan, Kyrgyzstan, Kuwait, Lebanon, Luxembourg, Norway, Oman, Peru, Poland, Qatar, Romania, Saudi Arabia, South Korea, Spain, Sweden, Slovakia, Tunisia, Turkey, U.A.E., Uruguay, and Yemen.

1 month maximum:

* Asean Countries, Hong Kong, Macau, British National Overseas and North Korea.

14 days maximum:

* Afghanistan, Iran, Iraq, Libya, Syria, Macau (travel permit) and Portugal Alien Passport.

Needs Malaysian Visa for a stay exceeding one month:

* Thailand, Laos, Vietnam, Myanmar, Indonesia, Cambodia and the Philippines.
* Needs Malaysian Visa for Entry .
* Bangladesh, Bhutan, China, India, Nepal, Nigeria, Pakistan, Sri Lanka, Angola, Burkina Faso, Burundi, Cameroon, Cape Verde, Central African Republic, Chad, Comoros, Congo Republic, Cote D'Ivoire, Djibouti, Equatorial Guinea, Eritrea, Ethiopia, Guinea Republic, Guinea-Bissau, Liberia, Madagascar, Mali, Mauritania, Mozambique, Rwanda, Senegal, Western Sahara, Taiwan.
* Special Approval Required.

* Citizens of Israel and Yugoslavia.
* Statistics for Medical Tourism in Malaysia.

The amount of medical tourists to Malaysia in 2007 has tripled since 2003, with figures already reaching more than 282,000 for the first nine months of 2008 alone, which is 16 percent higher than in 2007. The 2007 figures indicate Indonesia at the top of the list accounting for 72 percent of foreign patients to Malaysia, followed by 10 percent from Singapore and another 5 percent from Japan.

HealthCare Patients Visiting Malaysia according to the Association of Private Hospitals of Malaysia (APHM):

2003	*2004*	*2005*	*2006*	*2007*
102,946	174,189	232,161	296,687	341,288

Malaysia Medical Tourism Patients according to Country of Origin (Year: 2007)

Indonesia	*Singapore*	*Japan*	*India*	*Europe*	*Others*
72%	10%	5%	4%	3%	6%

Medical Tourism in Panama

Search Panama for or browse Panama hospitals and clinics. Earning the title as the "Hong Kong" or "Dubai" of the Americas due to its significantly lower cost of living and fully "Americanized" culture, Panama is slowly becoming one of the top medical tourism destinations, attracting US and Canadian health travellers due to its proximity and excellent healthcare services, US trained and certified medical staff and attractive natural beauty.

Healthcare System in Panama

Panama's long association with the United States have left a distinctly American footprint into its culture, giving it more than a hundred years advantage over other countries in providing healthcare to American patients using US standards of quality and service. This can be seen in the similarities in facilities and medical procedures and practices, as well as the abundance of US trained and board certified doctors and medical staff. There is currently one hospital in Panama that is fully certified by the Joint Commissions International. All of the other top hospitals however, most of which are privately owned, are fully certified by local medical accreditation bodies set by the Panamanian government as well as other non-government accreditation bodies. On top of that, most of these hospitals have affiliations and are duly recognized by international medical organizations such as the Johns Hopkins International, Baptist Health International of Miami, Cleveland Clinic, Tulane Health Science Centre, Miami Children's Hospital, University of Nebraska Medical Centre, the Harvard Medical Faculty, the Kendall Medical Centre and the Beth Israel Deaconess Medical Centre among others.

Top Hospitals in Panama

Major hospitals in Panama have affiliations with prominent international medical institutions, enabling them to maintain a high quality level not only in their facilities but also in procedures, methodology and technology as well. More prominent among these Panamanian hospitals include:

Hospital Punta Pacifica : This is the only Central American medical facility that is affiliated with the Johns Hopkins Medical International and maintains the same high-end standards in facilities, services and staff. It is also the only digitally connected hospital in the region and is the only hospital accredited by the Joint Commissions International.

Hospital Nacional : Starting out as a 10-bed facility, the Hospital Nacional has grown over the years into an 80-bed private healthcare facility with over a hundred specialists and ultra-modern facilities.

Clinica Hospital San Fernando : A private hospital affiliated with the Tulane University, Miami Children's Hospital and the Baptist Health International Miami, the Hospital San Fernando is one of Panama's largest hospitals with 24-hour medical services, facilities that are fully equipped with state-of-the-art medical equipments.

Centre Medico Paitilla : Located in Panama City, this 160-bed medical facility is affiliated with the Cleveland Clinic Foundation and has been in existence since 1975. It is also a certified training facility for the American Heart Association and was one of only two hospitals that provided healthcare services to US military personnel.

Popular Treatments done in Panama and Comparative Costs: Hospitals and healthcare facilities in Panama offer a wide array of procedures and services for medical travellers, which include but are not limited to the following:

Cosmetic/Plastic Surgery: Face, Breast, Body Contouring: Dental Services (surgeries, teeth whitening, dental implants, etc.).

* Fertility Treatments
* Bariatric/Obesity Surgeries
* Cancer treatment and Oncology
* Eye/Ophthalmology (LASIK, Cataract Surgeries, Vitreo Retinal Surgery, etc.)
* Stem Cell Therapy.

The following are cost comparisons between Medical procedures in Panama and equivalent procedures in the United States:

US Hospitals	***Panama***	***Average***	***Savings***
Medical Procedures			
Angioplasty with stent	$19,000-$21,000	$10,000-$15,000	25%-47%
Pace Maker	$4,000-$6,000	$1,500-$2,300	50%-60%
Laparoscopic Hernia	$6,000-$8,000	$ 3,500-$4,500	40%-50%
Laparoscopic Gastric Bypass	$24,000-$26,000	$14,000-$16,000	35%-40%
Hip Prosthesis	$19,000-$21,000	$11,000-$13,000	35%-40%
Artroscopy	$9,000-$11,000	$4,000-$6,000	45%-55%
Knee Replacement	$19,000-$21,000	$11,000-$13,000	35%-40%
Herniated Disc	$19,000-$21,000	$6,000-$7,000	65%-70%
Carpal Tunnel Release	$6,000-$8,000	$2,500-$3,500	55%-60%
Plastic and Reconstructive Surgery			
Neck Lift	$10,000-$12,000	$2,000-$3,000	75%-80%
Face Lift (rhytidectomy)	$10,000-$12,000	$2,000-$3,000	75%-80%
Breast Augmentation/ Reduction (Mammoplasty)	$5,500-$8,000	$3,100-$4,500	40%-45%
Breast Lift	$5,000-$6,000	$3,000-$4,000	35%-40%
Liposuction (Lipoplasty)	$4,000-$6,500	$2,500-$4,400	30%-35%
Nose Surgery (Rhinoplasty)	$4,000-$6,000	$1,500-$2,500	55%-65%
Buttocks Augmentation	$5,000-$6,000	$3,500-$4,500	25%-30%
Chemical Peel	$900-$1,100	$450-$550	45%-55%

Obstetrics and Gynecology			
Intrauterine Insemination	$1,000-$2,000	$800-$900	20%-55%
In Vitro Fertilization	$9,000-$18,000	$4,000-$6,000	55%-70%
In Vitro Fertilization with donated egg	$16,000-$20,000	$7,000-$9,000	50%-55%
Eye/Ophthalmology			
Cataract surgery	$5,500-$6,500	$2,000-$3,000	50%-60%
Refractive surgery (Eximer Laser)	$4,500-$5,500	$1,500-$2,500	55%-60%
Glaucoma surgery	$5,500-$6,500	$1,500-$2,500	60%-75%
Refractive surgery with intraocular lens implant	$5,500-$6,500	$2,000-$3,000	50%-60%
Eyelid Surgery (Blepharoplasty)	$4,000-$5,500	$1,500-$2,500	60%-65%
General and Cosmetic Dentistry			
Root Canal	$900-$1100	$250-$350	70%-75%
Porcelain Crown	$1,000-$2,000	$450-$550	55%-75%
Porcelain Veneers	$1,000-$2,000	$450-$550	55%-75%
Composite Veneers	$600-$750	$150-$250	45%-70%
Dental Implant	$2,000-$2,500	$900-$1100	55%-60%
Periodontal Surgery	$1,000-$2,000	$450-$550	55%-75%
Periodontal Plastic Surgery	$1,000-$2,000	$450-$550	55%-75%
Periodontal Regenerative Procedures	$1,200-$1,600	$500-$600	55%-65%

Malpractice and Liabilities Laws in Panama

The Panamanian system has not adopted the US legalities associated with medical practices, particularly in the area of malpractice. Although doctors are responsible for their activities and performance under the law in this country, they are not required to shoulder the damages incurred during a malpractice case.

The result is a lower malpractice insurance pre-requisite, which can be translated into lower procedural costs.

Pros

- * Hospitals in Panama provide high quality health care through a large staff of US-trained doctors, physicians and other medical specialists.
- * Techniques, medications, treatments and facilities used are based on the same standards used in the USA.
- * Doctors and medical staff can communicate well in English.
- * Panama City is considered Central America's safest and most modern city. Even the tap water is safe to drink.
- * Panama is relatively close to US and Canada.
- * The currency is the US dollar, so prices can be compared easily.

Cons

- * There is only one JCI-accredited hospital in Panama although a few have already submitted and are currently undergoing the accreditation procedures.
- * Costs of medical procedures are higher compared to other medical tourism destinations, although these are still significantly more economical as compared to the US, Canada and the UK.

Travelling to Panama

Direct flights to Panama City are available from major cities in the US and Canada and this close proximity and shorter travel time makes Panama a destination of choice for medical travellers.

Average estimated travel time in hours

From/To	***Panama***
New York City	5
Los Angeles	7
Miami	2.75
Houston	4
Dallas	4.5
Washington	4.75
Atlanta	4
Toronto	5
Vancouver	8

Entry and Exit Requirements to Panama

USA and Canadian medical travellers with a valid passport that is at least 6 months beyond the traveller's intended last day of stay do not need to get a visa to enter Panama. A tourist card can be purchased upon arrival, allowing the recipient to stay for 90 days in the country. Other requirements include return tickets, sufficient funds to shoulder the stay, and confirmed accommodations and other targeted facilities. Panamanian immigration laws are very strict so it is advisable to carry your passport with you at all times to show your proof of entry and avoid any complications during your stay.

Statistics for medical tourism in Panama

Doctors have estimated that there are only hundreds of medical tourists from the United States visiting Panama per year, with some hospitals declaring that they have received at least 400 to 450 international patients within the last four years seeking various medical procedures.

These figures would continue to grow as Americans without health insurance continue to seek healthcare in nearby medical tourism destinations such as Panama. More and more baby boomers are contemplating retiring to this Latin American destination as well as seeking healthcare services and beauty treatments at lower costs.

Medical Tourism in Turkey

Offering high quality facilities for medical, thermal, spas and wellness services while incorporating five-star hotel accommodations, Turkey has become a choice destination for medical tourists coming from England, Holland, Ukraine, Russia, Romania, Bulgaria and other European countries, as well as Middle Eastern countries like Iran, Iraq, Bahrain, Syria, Kuwait and the United Arab Emirates.

Turkey Healthcare System

Turkey is currently seeking to join the European Union and is set to receive membership by 2014. In preparation for this, both government and private healthcare institutions are conducting strict implementation of quality, technical and medical standards which are constantly being monitored by independent watchdogs set by the Ministry of Health. The MOH, together with an Independent Turkish Medical Associations sets the local standards and guidelines followed by hospitals, healthcare facilities and medical practitioners. The Turkish Ministry of Health owns and operates approximately 55% of Turkey's more than 1200 hospitals, while the rest is owned by Universities, private companies and foreign entities. These hospitals have local and international accreditation including the JCI (Joint Commissions International), the JACHO (Joint Commission on Accreditation of Healthcare Organizations), ISO (International Organization for Standardization) and affiliations with western medical groups and facilities. Most of these hospitals have English-speaking doctors and medical staff and are certified by the Turkish Medical Association as well as being members of organizations according to their specializations, including the Turkish Dental Association, Turkish Gynecologist & Obstetric Association, Turkish Orthopedic and Traumatology Association, Turkish Plastic Reconstructive & Aesthetic Surgery Association, Turkish Society of Cardiovascular Surgery, and other specialized associations.

Top Hospitals in Turkey

Turkey boasts of more than 30 medical facilities that are accredited by the Joint Commission International, the largest accreditation any country has achieved. Most of these hospitals are also affiliated with top US medical providers like the Harvard Medical School and Johns Hopkins Medicine among others. These hospitals are equipped with the latest medical technologies with board-certified staff, more than 35% of which are trained in the US and other western countries.

The top hospitals in Turkey include:

Istanbul Memorial Hospital-Instanbul, Turkey

The first hospital in Turkey that was accredited by the JCI in March, 2002 and has already been re-accredited twice-once in 2005 and again in 2008.

Anadolu Medical Centre-Kocaeli, Turkey : First accreditation by the JCI on February 2007. The facility is affiliated with Johns Hopkins International and focuses on cardiac care, neurological sciences, oncology, women's health and other surgical specialities.

Acibadem Healthcare Group : Affilitiated with Harvard Medical International, the Acibadem Healthcare Group is composed of five JCI-accredited hospitals located in different locations in Turkey including the Acibadem Bakirkoy Hospital, Acibadem Bursa Hospital, Acibadem

Kocaeli Hospital, Acibadem Kadikoy Hospital, and the Acibadem Kozyatagi Hospital.

Medical Park Healthcare Group : The Medical Park Healthcare Group is composed of four JCI-accredited hospitals located in various areas in Turkey which includes the Medical Park Healthcare Group-Antalya Hospital, Medical Park Healthcare Group-Bahcelievler Hospital, Medical Park Healthcare Group-Bursa Hospital, and the Medical Park Healthcare Group-Goztepe Hospital.

Florence Nightingale Hospital Group : The Florence Nightingale Hospital Group is composed of three JCI-accredited hospitals located in various areas in Turkey which includes the Sisli Florence Nightingale Hospital, Gayrettepe Florence Nightingale Hospital, and the Kadikoy Florence Nightingale Hospital.

Dunya Eye Hospital : First accreditation by the JCI on July 2006. It is one of the top eye hospitals in Turkey and is one of the best in the world in terms of success rates for its more than 1000 cataract operations per month.

Common Treatments done in Turkey and Comparative Costs: For generations, Turkey has been known for its excellent thermal spa resorts, some of which has been in existence since the time of the Romans. In modern times, the hospitals and healthcare facilities in Turkey offer a wide array of procedures and services for medical travellers, which include but are not limited to the following:

* Plastic Surgery
* Fertility and Sterility
* General and Aesthetic Dentistry
* Psoriasis Treatment
* Physiotherapy
* Spa and Thermal resorts
* Beauty Centres
* Eye Health
* Obesity and Bariatric Surgery
* Renal Dialysis
* Oxygen Therapy.

The following are cost comparisons between Medical procedures in Turkey and equivalent procedures in the United Kingdom:

UK Hospitals	*Turkey*	*Average*	*Savings*
Medical Procedures			
Coronary Angioplasty	$13,000-$15,000	$5,000-$6,000	60%-65%
Hip Replacement	$13,500-$14,500	$6,500-$7,500	45%-50$
Prostrate Removal (Prostatectomy)	$7,000-$8,000	$5,500-$6,500	15%-20%
Knee Replacement	$16,000-$17,000	$7,000-$8,000	50%-60%
Hemorrhoids Removal	$3,000-$4,000	$1,500-$2,500	45%-55%
Plastic and Reconstructive Surgery			
Face Lift (rhytidectomy)	$11,000-$12,000	$3,000-$4,000	65%-75%
Breast Augmentation (Mammoplasty)	$7,000-$8,000	$3,000-$4,000	50%-60%
Breast Reduction	$8,000-$9,000	$3,500-$4,500	50%-60%
Liposuction (lipoplasty)	$5,000-$6,000	$2,000-$3,000	55%-65%
Nose Surgery (Rhinoplasty)	$5,500-$6,500	$3,000-$4,000	40%-45%
Tummy Tuck (Abdominoplasty)	$8,000-$9,000	$3,000-$4,000	55%-60%
Eye/Ophthalmology			
LASIK Eye Surgery	$1,500-$2,500	$1,000-$1,500	20%-25%
Cataract Removal	$4,000-$5,000	$1,000-$2,000	55%-65%
General and Cosmetic Dentistry			
Root Canal (per canal)	$300-$400	$100-$150	55%-65%
Tooth Whitening	$900-$1200	$400-$500	50%-60%
Dental Implants	$3,000-$4,000	$900-$1500	70%-75%
Gold Crowns	$800-$850	$200-$250	70%-75%

Malpractice and Liabilities Laws in Turkey

In a report by Abigail Cotterill from the ADMD Law Firm on Medical Malpractice in Turkey, she described the there are relatively low malpractice suits in Turkey, even when healthcare providers do not normally carry malpractice insurance and the government paying for damages on suits against state facilities. In this regard, the Forensic Medicine Association was established in Turkey focusing on legal cases involving malpractice. Reforms have also been established to implement compulsory insurance for medical practitioners in both state and private-owned health facilities.

Pros

* With the highest number of JCI-accredited health facilities, medical tourists are assured of high quality infrastructure and services by these hospitals and their medical staff.
* Prices in Turkey are very competitive compared to Western European countries like the UK, Ireland, Austria and Italy.
* Turkey has long been a gateway between the East and the West and has been known for its brand of Turkish hospitality.

Cons

* There is a certain level of deficiency in English language levels for personnel dealing with medical tourists.
* There is a lack of knowledge of some hospitals on the required documentations issued to foreign medical travellers.
* Lack of medical tourism companies acting as link between medical tourists and Turkey's medical institutions.
* Petty theft, particularly pick-pockets, are a primary threat to tourists plying the crowded streets in Turkey's major cities.

Travelling to Turkey

Turkey has an easy access from all airlines coming from Europe with a total of more than 300 flights coming from various countries arriving to Turkey's five major airports on a daily basis.

Average estimated travel time in hours

From/To	*Turkey*
UK (London)	4
UK (Manchester)	5
Germany	3
Netherlands	4
Austria	3
Switzerland	3
Russia	7
UAE (Dubai)	4
Bulgaria	2
Romania	2

Entry and Exit Requirements to Turkey

In general, a valid passport and a corresponding visa are required for all travellers making their entry to Turkey. Depending on the country of destination as listed in Turkey's Ministry of Foreign Affairs, entry visas can be obtained upon arrival at Turkey or should be obtained from the Turkish Consulates located in the country of origin. The following are visa requirements for specific countries listed below. Other countries can obtain information from the Turkish MFA website:

* Austria: a 3-month multiple entry visa can be obtained at the Turkish borders for ordinary passport holders. Official passport holders are exempt up to 90 days.
* Australia: a 3-month multiple entry visa can be obtained at the Turkish borders for both ordinary and official passport holders.
* Bulgaria: Diplomatic and service passport holders are given 30 days entry without any visa requirements. Ordinary passport holders are exempt from visa up to 90 days.
* Germany: both ordinary and official passport holders are exempt from visa up to 90 days.
* Netherlands: a 3-month multiple entry visa can be obtained at the Turkish borders for both ordinary passport holders. Official passport holders are exempt up to 90 days.
* Romania: a 1-month single entry visa can be obtained at the Turkish borders for ordinary passport holders. Official passport holders are exempt up to 90 days.
* Russian Federation: a 2-month multiple entry visa can be obtained at the Turkish borders for ordinary passport holders. Official passport holders are exempt up to 90 days.
* Switzerland: both ordinary and official passport holders are exempt from visa up to 90 days.
* United Arab Emirates: a sticker type entry visa can be obtained at the Turkish borders for ordinary passport holders. Official passport holders are exempt up to 90 days.
* United Kingdom: a 3-month multiple entry visa can be obtained at the Turkish borders for both ordinary and official passport holders. "British National Overseas (BNO)" and the "British Protected Persons (BPP)" Official passport holders should

apply for visa at the Turkish consulate prior to arrival in Turkey.

* United States: a 3-month multiple entry visa can be obtained at the Turkish borders for both ordinary and official passport holders.

Statistics for Medical Tourism in Turkey

Located in a strategic area that borders Asia and Europe, Turkey is fast becoming a popular destination for medical travellers tallying more than 200,000 medical tourists from Europe and the Middle East in 2008, a 40% increase from 2007. On top of that, there were approximately 500,000 tourists who visited Turkey's more than 1000 thermal resorts and wellness spas. In a 2007 study on medical tourism, the British rated Turkey as one of the top three destinations for medical travellers coming from the United Kingdom, with India and Hungary sharing the top spot.

Medical Tourism in Mexico

In recent years, Mexico has been a popular destination for US citizens seeking health care. Its proximity to the United States and the relatively low travel costs have been drawing Americans and Canadians, and Mexican-Americans who return home to their family doctor dentist and save money. Initially gaining fame for dentistry and cosmetic surgery, orthopedic procedures now add to Mexico's attractions. With state-of-the-art facilities that can compare with American hospitals, Mexico has become one of the premier destinations for US medical tourists.

Healthcare system in Mexico

According to the World Health Organization Mexican healthcare system is ranked 61 in the world. The private hospitals in Mexico are usually similar in quality and care to those in the United States. There are medical packages which offer accommodations and aftercare away from the urban areas and closer to the vibrant beaches. Mexico's best hospitals and clinics are based in Mexico City, Guadalajara and Monterrey.

Many private clinics catering to Americans are located across the US border, in cities like Tijuana, Mexicali and Laredo.

Waiting times in Mexico are not a problem and are generally unheard of. There is also an option to save on prescription medicine for a quicker and smoother aftercare. Mexican costs of medicines are almost half those of the USA and Canada. International patients in Mexico are offered their own private room and face-to-face personal interaction with their doctor or surgeon. Hospitals and clinics are equipped with up-to-date technology, well-trained doctors and on-hand medical staff to cater to all types of medical tourists.

The following Mexican hospitals are accredited by the JCI:

The American British Cowdray Medical Centre IAP – Observatorio Campus, Mexico City

Hospital ABC is a non-profit private hospital regulated under the "Ley de Institution de Asistencia Privadas." Established in 1941, it is governed by a Board of volunteers, all prominent Mexicans and expatriates. Among the facilities are 200 in-patient beds and state-of-the-art medical technology. It offers a full range of diagnostic, medical and surgical services.

The American British Cowdray Medical centre IAP – Santa Fe Campus, Mexico City;

* Christus Muguerza Alta Especialidad, Monterrey, Mexico.

Christus Muguerza hospital network encompasses 3 hospitals in Monterrey and other Mexican cities. It recently opened a modern health centre that accounts for short stay surgeries.

* Clinica Cumbres Chihuahua, Chihuahua, Mexico.
* Hospital CIMA Hermosillo, Hermosillo, Sonora, Mexico.
* Hospital CIMA Monterrey, Monterrey, San Pedro Garza Garcia N.L. Mexico.
* Hospital San Jose Tec de Monterrey, Monterrey, Nuevo Leon, Mexico.

A world class hospital accredited for its high quality and best-in-class patient care. Since 1969, it has focused on the well-being of care, and the best medical professionals and procedures in a cost-effective way. It is sponsored by the internationally recognized Tecnologico de Monterrey and is located only 150 miles from the US border.

* Hospital Y Clinica OCA, S.A. de C.V., Monterrey, Nuevo Leon, Mexico.

The largest private hospital in the city.

Treatments done in Mexico and comparative costs

Wikipedia lists Mexico among the popular destinations for cosmetic surgery, dental services and surgery and general plastic surgery. Mexican hospitals have become popular lately for bariatric surgery for weight loss, which is an elective procedure that is not covered by some US insurers. The following are the popular treatments sought by medical tourists in Mexico:

* Eye surgery
* Cosmetic surgery
* Dentistry
* Hip surgery
* Knee surgery
* Bariatric surgery
* Medical spa treatment.

The following are comparative costs of general, cosmetic and surgical procedures between US hospitals with those of Mexico.

General Procedures	*USA Hospitals,*	*MexicoAverage*	*Savings*
Heart			
Angioplasty	$22,500	$11,500	50%
Angiography	$4,800	$1,200	70%
Valve replacement	$ 46,000	$16,000	60%
Bypass surgery	$44,000	$24,000	50%
Open Heart surgery	$64,000	$24,000	66%
Orthopedic			
Knee	$25,000	$10,500	65%
Hip Replacement	$28,000	$12,500	65%
Shoulder Replacement	$24,500	$9,500	75%
Birmingham Resurfacing	$24,000	$12,500	60%
Other Procedures			
Gastric Bypass Surgery	$30,000	$11,500	70%
Gastric Band Surgery	$24,000	$9,500	60%
Hysterectomy	$14,500	$5,500	75%
Fertility Treatments	$8,500	$2,650	55%

Cosmetic Procedures	***USA Clinic***	***Cancun, Mexico***	***Average Savings***
Face Lift	$18,000	$4,250	68%
Breast Augmentation	$7,800	$3,800	55%
Tummy Tuck	$8,800	$4,50	50%
Liposuction (per area)	$3,200	$1,150	60%
Rhinoplasty (nose)	$8,000	$3,200	65%
Brow Lift	$7,500	$2,850	70%
Brazilian Buttock	$10,500	$4,950	65%
Neck Lift	$10,000	$4,400	70%
Blepharoplasty (eyelids)	$5,400	$2,950	55%

Dental Procedures	***USA Clinic***	***Monterrey, Mexico***	***Average Savings***
Implants-6 teeth	$18,500	$3,600	75%
Porcelain crown (6 teeth)	$5,200	$1,600	70%
Bleaching discolored teeth	$250	$50	80%
Dental Vaneers (6 teeth)	$6,000	$1,800	75%
Total Dentures	$4,800	$1,600	70%

Another survey provides the following comparative costs as of 2009:

Medical Procedure	***USA***	***Mexico***
Angioplasty	Up to $57,000	$17,100
Heart Bypass	Up to $144,000	$21,100
Heart Valve Replacement	Up to $170,000	$31,000
Knee Replacement	Up to $50,000	$11,500
Hip Resurfacing	Up to $30,000+	$13,400
Hip Replacement	Up to $43,000	$13,800
Special Fusion	Up to $100,000	$8,000
Face Lift	Up to $15,000	$8,000
Breast Implants	Up to $10,000	$9,000
Rhinoplasty	Up to $8,000	$5,000
Lap Band/Bariatric	Up to $30,000	$9,200
Hysterectomy	Up to $15,000	$7,500
Dental Implant	$2,000-10,000	$1,000

Malpractice and liabilities laws in Mexico

Medical liability is not as strictly enforced by laws in foreign countries as in the United States. Accordingly, it is not surprising to note that malpractice compensation is not as generous.

Foreign doctors are not as secure in malpractice insurance like their American counterparts. An American medical tourist cannot have recourse to the American court system. An American court might not hold an intermediary liable since medical tourism promoters or agents are not health care providers and so cannot "commit malpractice".

Some medical insurers in the US have designed insurance packages for those wishing to get medical health care in Mexico. A California law in 1999 which allowed California insurers to reimburse providers in Mexico has paved the way to changes in the insurance industry or the medical tour package providers. Since Mexican medical care costs less, premiums are less than 2/3 of the cost of their US alternative plans.

Pros

* Distance: The proximity of Mexico to United States and Canada make it a clear choice for American and Canadian residents for their health care needs. Travel expenses are low and make it easy for patients to travel back and forth.
* According to the World Health Organization Mexican hospitals are similar in quality and care to those in the United States. There are medical packages which offer accommodations and aftercare away from the urban areas and closer to the vibrant beaches.
* High rate of fluency in both English and Spanish.
* Increasing number of insurers providing coverage for travellers, as out-of-pocket costs are much lower.
* The prices in Mexico can be lower by 50% to as much as 75% of US average costs.
* Like most Latin American countries, Mexico has an overall friendly and family-oriented culture.
* Waiting times in Mexico are not a problem and are generally unheard of.

* Mexican costs of medicines are almost half those of America and Canada.
* Climate – the wonderful climate deems it conducive to recovery.
* Lessened cultural differences with the US after more than a decade of low trade barriers under the NAFTA.

Cons

* Lack of standardized quality measurement and quality ranking systems.
* difficulty in seeking legal remedy in the event of malpractice.
* Travelling to Mexico.

*Mexico's advantage is its location; flights from US and Canada are short and relatively cheap.

* Californian citizens can even drive to Mexico.
* Flight times from US and Canada to Mexico.

Average estimated travel time in hours

From/To	***Mexico City***	***Guandalajara***	***Monterrey***
New York City	4.5	4.5	3.5
Chicago	3.5	3.5	2.5
Washington, DC	4	4	3
San Francisco	4	4	3
Los Angeles	3.5	3	2.5
Toronto	4	5	5
Montreal	5	5	5
Vancouver	5	5	5

Airfares

Airfares to Mexico peak in late March to early April and mid-June through August.

Holidays are also expensive. Midweek (Mondays – Thursdays) morning roundtrip flights run US$40-60 less than weekend flights but these are generally more crowded and less likely to permit frequent flier upgrades. Open return (no fixed return date) and open-jaw (different arrival and departure cities) tickets are more expensive than roundtrip flights.

Car Travel times from southern US to Mexico

From/To	Tijuana	Mexicali	Monterrey
Los Angeles, CA	2 hrs	4 hrs	
San Francisco, CA	10 hrs	10 hrs	
San Diego, CA	20-30 minutes	2 hrs	
Dallas, TX			10 hrs
Houston, TX			12-13 hrs

Statistics for medical tourism in Mexico

Americans, particularly those living near the Mexican border, now routinely cross to Mexico for medical care. It is believed that half of these medical tourists are US residents of Mexican heritage and merely "go home" for treatment

The number of medical tourists coming in to Mexico ranges from 150,000 to 500,000 annually. It is hard to keep track of the number people coming in to Mexico seeking medical care because there are no official records of such visits.

Bibliography

Andrew, N; Flanagan, S & Ruddy, J: *Tourism Destination Planning*, Dublin, Dublin Institute of Technology, 2002.

Apostolopous, Y and Leivadi, S: *Sociology of Tourism, The: Theoretical And Empirical Investigations*, London, Retailed, 1996.

Ashworth, G J and Dietvorst, A G J: *Tourism and Spatial Transformations: Implications For Policy and Plan*, Wallingford, CAB International, 1995.

Ashworth, Greg and Larkham, P J: *Building a New Heritage: Tourism, Culture & Identity in the New Europe*, London, Routledge,1994.

Baum, Tom: *We're all Going on a Summer Holiday: Images of Tourism Past and Person*, Buckingham, University of Buckingham, 1995.

Beeho, A & Prentice, R: *Conceptualising The Experiences of Heritage Tourists*, 1997.

Beeton, Sue:: *Film-Induced Tourism*, Clevedon, Channel View, 2005.

Belie et al.: *Tourism and the Inner City: An Evaluation of / Impact of Grant Assist*, London, HMSO, 1990.

Benefice, Brian G, and Cooper, Chris: *Geography of Travel and Tourism*, The, London, Heinemann, 1987.

Bolshevism, Germy: *Coping with Tourists: European Reactions to Mass Tourism*, Oxford, Berghahn Books, 1995.

Boniface, Priscilla and Fowler, Peter: *Heritage and Tourism: In the Global Village*, London, Retailed, 1993.

Bosselman, Fred P: *In The Wake of the Tourist: Managing Special Places in Eight Countries*, Washington, DC, Conservation Foundation, The, 1978.

Briguglio, L and Vella, Leslie: *Competitiveness of the Maltese Islands in Mediterranean in Tourism*, Chichester, John Wiley, 1995.

Brown, Dona: *Inventing New England: Regional Tourism in the Nineteenth Century*, Washington DC, Smithsonian Institution, 1995.

Brunt, Paul: *Market Research in Travel and Tourism*, Oxford, Butterworth Heinemann, 1997.

Burkart, A and Medlik, S: *Management of Tourism*, The, London, Heinemann, 1975.

Chambers, Erve: *Native Tours: The Anthropology of Travel and Tourism*, Prospect Heights, Waveland Press, 2000.

Chandler, Harry and Carter, John: *Chandler's Travels: A Tour of the Life of Harry Chandler*, London, Quiller Press, 1985.

Clark, Colin: *Tourist Services and Guidance: Heritage and Information*, Strasbourg, Council of Europe Press, 1989.

Coccosis, Harry and Nijkamp, Peter: *Sustainable Tourism Development*, Aldershot, Avebury, 1995.

Cohen, Erik: *Towards a Sociology of International Tourism*, 1972.

Dann, Graham M S: *Language of Tourism*, The, Wallingford, CAB International, 1996.

Davidson, R and Maitland, R: *Tourism Destinations, London*, Hodder and Stoughton, 1997.

Davidson, Rob: *Travel and Tourism in Europe*, Harlow, Addison Wesley Longman, 1998.

Ecotec: *Calderdale: Tourism Impact Study*, Calderdale, ECOTEC/Calderdale Council, 1990.

Edensor, Tim: *Tourists at the Taj*, London, Retailed, 1998.

Edgell, David L: *International Tourism Policy, New York*, Van Nostrand and Reinhold, 1990.

Elliott, James: *Tourism: Politics and Public Sector Management*, London, Retailed, 1997.

Fairgrieve, James: *Geography in School*, London, University of London Press, 1926.

Foster, Douglas: *Travel and Tourism Management*, London, Macmillan Educational, 1985.

Frechtling, Douglas C: *Practical Tourism Forecasting*, Oxford, Butterworth Heinemann, 1996.

Gamble, P. R: *The Educational challenge for Hospitality and Tourism Studies*, Tourism Management, 13, 1992.

Ghimire, Krishna: *The Native Tourist*: Mass Tourism within Developing Regions, London, Earthscan, 2001.

Goeldner, C. R: *The Evaluation of Tourism as an Industry and a Discipline, Paper Presented to*, International Conference for Tourism Educators, Guildford, University of Surrey, 1988.

Gunn, Clare and Var, Turgut: *Tourism Planning*, London, Retailed, 2002.

Hall, C Michael *Tourism Planning: Policies, Processes and relationships*, Harlow, Prentice Hall, 2000.

Hall, Colin and Jenkins, John: *Tourism and Public Policy*, London, Retailed, 1995.

Hall, Colin Michael: *Tourism and Politics*: Policy, Power, & Place, Chichester, Wiley, 1994.

Harrison, Lyndon: *Tourism Means Jobs*, Chester, Lyndon Harrison, 1996.

Harron, S and Weiler, B: *Ethnic Tourism*, Belhaven/Wiley, 1992.

Inkpen, G: *Information Technology for Travel and Tourism*, Harlow, Addison Wesley Longman, 1998.

Inskeep, Edward *National and Regal Tourism Planing*: Methodologies & Case Studies, London, Routledge/WTO, 1994.

Irwin, William *The New Niagara*: *Tourism, Technology, And the Landscape of Niagara Fal*, University Park, PA, University of Pennsylvania, 1996.

Jack, G and Phipps, A: *Tourism and Intercultural Exchange*: *Why Tourism Matters*, Clevedon, Channel View, 2005.

Jakle, John: *Tourist, The: Travel in Twentieth Century North America*, University of North Nebraska, 1985.

Jennings, Gayle: *Tourism Research*, Chichester, Wiley, 2001.

Judd, D R: *Promoting Tourism* in US Cities, 1995.

Karski, A: *Urban Tourism* - A Key to Urban Regeneration?, 1990.

Kotler, Philip et al: *Marketing Places*: *Attracting Investment, Industry & Tourism etc*, New York, free press, 1993.

Labarge, Margaret Wade: *Medieval Travellers*: *The Rich and Restless*, London, Hamish Hamilton, 1982.

Laws, Eric: *Tourist Destination Management: Issues, Analysis & Policies*, London, Routledge, 1995.

Leed, Eric J: *Mind of the Traveller, The: From Gilgamesh to Global Tourism*, New York, 1991.

MacCannell, Dean: *Tourist, The: A New Theory of the Leisure Class*, London, Macmillan, 1976.

Machin, Alan: *Retracing the Steps: Tourism as Education, Janus*, Fin, ATLAS / FUNTS, 2001.

Opperman, Martin and Chon, Kye-Sung: *Tourism in Developing Countries, London*, International Thomson Business Press, 1997.

Patullo, Polly: *Last Resorts*: *The Cost of Tourism in the Caribbean*, London, Cassell, 1996.

Pearce, Douglas: *Tourism Today*: *A Geographical Analysis*, Harlow, Longman, 1995.

Pearce, P L: *Social Psychology Of Tourist Behaviour*, The, Oxford, Pergamon, 1982.

Peters, M: *International Tourism*, London, Hutchinson, 1969.

Ringer, Greg: *Destinations: Cultural Landscapes of Tourism*, London, Routledge, 1998.

Ritchie, Brent: *Managing Educational Tourism*, Clevedon, Channel View, 2003.

Robinson, H: *Geography of Tourism*, A, London, Macdonald and Evans, 1976.

Robinson, M, Evans, E & Chalazion, P: *Tourism and Cultural Change, Sunderland*, Business Education Publishers Ltd, 1996.

Rogers, H Anthea and Slinn, Judy A: *Tourism: Management of Facilities*, London, Pitman: M & E, 1993.

Schwaninger, M: *Trends in Leisure and Tourism for 2000 - 2010*, Prentice Hall, 1989.

Scottish Tourist Board: *Visitor Attractions: A Development Guide*, Edinburgh, Scottish Tourist Board, 1991.

Seaton, A V et al: *Tourism: The state of the Art*, Chichester, John Wiley, 1994.

Shaw, G and Williams, A: *Tourism and Tourism Spaces*, London, Sage, 2004.

Stevens, Terry: *Island Tourism*: Malta, , WTO, 1993.

Trench, R: *Travellers in Britain*, London, Aurum, 1990.

Tribe, John *Corporate Strategy for Tourism, London*, International Thomson Business Press, 1997.

Urry, John: *Tourist Gaze*, The, London, Sage, 1990.

Van den Berg et al: *Urban Tourism: Performance and Strategies in Eight European Cities*, Aldershot, Avebury, 1995.

Van Harssel, Jan: *Tourism: An Exploration*, New York, Prentice Hall, 1994.

Veal, A: *Leisure and Tourism*: Policy and Planning, Wallingford, CABI, 2001.

Wahab, S A: *Tourism Management*, Tourism International Press, 1975.

Walle, Alfred H: *Cultural Tourism*: A Strategic Focus, Boulder, Co, Westview Press, 1998.

Wilkinson, Paul: *Tourism Policy and Planning: As Studies from the Caribbean*, Elmsford New York, Cognizant Communications Corporation, 1997.

Yale, Pat: *From Tourist Attractions to Heritage Tourism*, Huntingdon, Elm, 1991.

Zarkia, Cornelia: *Philoxenia: Receiving Tourists*-but *not Guests-on a Greek Island*, Oxford, Berghahn Books, 1996.

Index

W

□□□